Posted in Wartime

For Julia Martina Knott

Posted in Wartime

Letters home from abroad

Richard Knott

Featuring the wartime correspondence of
Cecil Beaton, Noël Coward and Freya Stark

Pen & Sword
MILITARY

First published in Great Britain in 2017 by
Pen & Sword Military
an imprint of
Pen & Sword Books Ltd
47 Church Street
Barnsley
South Yorkshire
S70 2AS

ISBN 978 1 47383 396 8

Typeset in Ehrhardt by
Mac Style Ltd, Bridlington, East Yorkshire
Printed and bound in Malta by Gutenberg Press Ltd.

Pen & Sword Books Ltd incorporates the imprints of Pen & Sword
Archaeology, Atlas, Aviation, Battleground, Discovery, Family
History, History, Maritime, Military, Naval, Politics, Railways, Select,
Transport, True Crime, Fiction, Frontline Books, Leo Cooper,
Praetorian Press, Seaforth Publishing and Wharncliffe.

For a complete list of Pen & Sword titles please contact
PEN & SWORD BOOKS LIMITED
47 Church Street, Barnsley, South Yorkshire, S70 2AS, England
E-mail: enquiries@pen-and-sword.co.uk
Website: www.pen-and-sword.co.uk

Contents

Exile is an illness … an illness of the mind, an illness of the spirit and even sometimes a physical illness.

Lara Feigel, *The Love-Charm of Bombs*

After a bad war, I've read, the officers stammer and the ranks become mute.

Annette Kobak, *Joe's War*

Here I am in the Army and I think I'm going to have a fine time, war permitting.

Gunner John 'Syd' Croft, Royal Artillery

Chapter 1

Keep Me Posted

When this war started, I suddenly found myself totally unable to write letters. I don't know why. I suppose I had the feeling that they would never get to their destination. But now the post does seem to be working, if a bit spasmodically. I expect you'll get this in about ten days.[1]

P.G. Wodehouse to William Townend, Le Touquet,
Pas-de-Calais, 3 October 1939

I do so hope it won't be like being in cargo ships where I didn't get a letter from one voyage's end to another. Your letters are about all I have to look forward to.

Tommy Davies to his wife Dorrie, at sea on board *Almanzora*, 23 April 1942

'You will write, won't you?' How many times in the last precious moments of a wartime lover's farewell did one or other of the soon-to-be-parted ask such a question, or breathe a promise that he or she would write? Such promises were all the more fervent, perhaps, when the prospect was of a posting far from home: you would not expect exile to be endured in a glum silence. And yet … there is no evidence that my father wrote anything in his four wartime years away in the Middle East, at least, nothing that merited keeping. Added to which was the fact that he would never talk about the war at all. Those two connected mysteries are central to this book.

The mystery of my father Jack had a way of shifting like quicksand as I wrote. For example, I had always believed that he was a bespoke tailor before the war, living in the English Midlands, an ordinary man plying an unremarkable trade in one of England's less green and pleasant towns. More than six years after he died, the publication of the 1939 Register revealed him to be a 'Forge Labourer. Shell Factory.' It was, dare I say it, a bombshell.

That revelation did not, however, alter the basic question: how different, I wondered, would his overseas service have been from others like him; and, more tellingly perhaps, how much of a contrast would the experience of the more celebrated have been in similarly distant situations? At much the same time as I was contemplating that comparison, I was loaned substantial bundles of letters written by two men whose war involved long journeys and prolonged absences from home. Their evidence begged the question that would not go away: why would some write at such length while my father seemingly remained so silent? Those letters and my father's reluctance to communicate comprise a major strand in this book. Woven into that story are the wartime experiences of three celebrities for whom the war also meant periods of exile: the photographer and designer Cecil Beaton; the playwright Noël Coward; and the traveller and writer Freya Stark.

Wartime exile is a key theme in this book; it is what connects the six principal characters, both the celebrated and the unknown. 'Posted in Wartime' has a double meaning, of course: the first of which refers to the role and nature of written correspondence during the war – the impact, for example, of censorship and stretched lines of communication, the slow and unreliable postal service on which those sent abroad relied for news and reassurance. Even, presumably, my tight-lipped father. The second meaning concerns the despatching of individuals to far corners of the world, sent hither and thither to fight, police, drive transports, administrate, liaise, or entertain. That process was often the result of some anonymous civil servant's whim or staff officer's hunch, which duly consigned someone to a rattling, cold Liberator or DC3, or a transcontinental train; or, more likely, some rusty troopship beating its way from one fly-blown port to another. There was no choice in the matter: the teacher and author Charles Hannam, for example, who had arrived in Britain on one of the last Kindertransport trains, decided late in the war to defer a place at Cambridge to sign on 'to join the fight against Hitler'; he was posted instead to Burma and then India 'to police the transition to independence'.[2]

And why the choice of Beaton, Coward and Stark? Why those three representatives of the more celebrated and fortunate? I was increasingly drawn to the fact that all three undertook wartime journeys whose trajectories crisscrossed and intertwined with those of my three 'unknown soldiers'. These comprised Tommy Davies, an officer in the Merchant Navy; an army doctor, Donald Macdonald; and my father Jack, an RAF policeman. All six, like so many others, were being moved like chess pieces around the board; never in a position to feel they had finally arrived, with no sense of permanence.

* * *

At some point in the war my father and his brother-in-law George Moreton bumped into each other in Alexandria – Jack would periodically complain thereafter that he had never recovered the pound note my uncle borrowed on that sun-baked Egyptian street. It was a typical wartime encounter, one of many where the logistics of a global conflict turned certain places into transport hubs, busy crossing points, where you stood every chance of meeting a relation, or an old friend, in what might once have been thought the most unlikely of circumstances. It might be in Cairo; on a pilot training camp in South Africa, Florida or Canada; in Brussels or Paris in the heady days of liberation in 1944; or just maybe the RAF base at Habbaniya, Iraq. Noël Coward, Cecil Beaton, Freya Stark and my father all passed through the dusty hell of Habbaniya at some point or other. So far as Freya's route to Iraq was concerned, it could not have been more different from Jack's. Hitler's war picked them both up and deposited them there, she with some measure of choice; poor Jack with none at all. The tailor and the writer were polar opposites. No letter writer he, while her correspondence over a lifetime of exploration and books stretches to eight volumes. He: aspirant working class, locked into a trade that he could do in his sleep, brain dormant, left school at fourteen; she, fluent in at least seven languages, middle class and cosmopolitan, and acutely restless.

Last night London looked like a dead city – all the houses dark, a drizzle descending, and the streets very empty as everyone stayed as stationary as possible so as to make the evacuation easier. I bought: (1) a gas mask, (2) a little bag for all one's toilet things to take with me to the basement, (3) a winter suit, and (4) French face powder which I may never see again for the next five years.[3]

Freya Stark to Herbert Young, London, 2 September 1939

Born in 1893, the intrepid Freya Stark began her series of remarkable explorations of Arabia in 1927, and by 1935, 'London was at her feet,'[4] bewitched by her evident qualities as a traveller. By the outbreak of the war she had written four acclaimed accounts of her journeying. Her travels had begun as a young woman when she arrived in the Lebanon intent on learning Arabic and armed only with 'a copy of Dante's *Inferno*, very little money, a revolver and a fur coat'.[5] A diminutive, 'rather ugly' woman with a taste for 'hypnotic hats',[6] she was eccentric, prone to laughter, and blessed with an insatiable curiosity. She wore her hair in such a way as to disguise a scar caused by a factory accident when she was twelve: her hair had been caught in a machine with the result that 'half her scalp was ripped

Freya Stark 'with London at her feet'. She has written 'Affectionate Xmas wishes from Freya, 1938' in the right-hand corner. (*Royal Geographical Society*)

off, including her right ear; the right eyelid was pulled away; and all the tissue around her temple exposed.'[7] Writing after the war, Vita Sackville-West wrote admiringly of her: 'I suspect you of being a born pirate, of being a born smuggler too, if life had cast you into a different century.'[8] Freya was hardworking, energetic and 'had a magic all of her own', a charm that allowed her to outmanoeuvre many. For example, when the Countess of Ranfurly moved in with her to her 'pretty bungalow' in Baghdad in 1942, Freya, apropos rent, 'just said, "Whatever you earn I'd like three quarters of it."'[9] Feted as she was, there were dissenting voices: Martha Gellhorn, for example, was wary of Freya's sense of her own importance, exemplified by her voluminous correspondence: 'I could not understand what held you, about her. How does she get her letters; keep carbon copies or ask for them back? I'd have no idea where my roughly five million letters were scattered over the globe.'[10] Gellhorn didn't like 'the sense that she stands off and sees herself as someone', a judgement that ignored Freya's evident charisma.

Never shy of expressing an opinion, she was, according to Harold Nicholson, with whom she dined in mid-January 1939, strongly anti-Chamberlain and convinced that 'we should intervene in Spain at once'.[11] In March she wrote to the Colonial Office from Aleppo in Syria: 'Things are getting to look so gloomy that I thought I would send you a line to ask whether there is anything I can do.'[12] By the early summer she had decided to set worries about the political situation in Europe to one side and 'carry on as if no war were anywhere about'. She was just back from Beirut, where a strike had potentially isolated her, but which she had circumvented by riding 'across the hills from Latakiah and down into the valley of the Orantes, one of the loveliest things in this world to do'.[13] Three days later, on 12 May, she wrote to Sir John Shuckburgh at the Foreign Office informing him of her decision to head for Greece, intending to visit the country before war came. In the event of the onset of war she had evidently been asked 'to go straight out to Egypt where I should probably be as useful as anywhere'.[14] An unknown civil servant's hand had expressed bureaucratic caution: 'these intrepid explorers are apt to be contemptuous of what they regard as "red tape regulations".' Notwithstanding, when the time came, Freya was absorbed into the Colonial Office's Ministry of Information, identified as a 'South Arab' expert, and provided with a salary of £600 a year. The day before war was declared she wrote in a letter: 'My ministry constitutes itself on Monday. I have met one of my colleagues and know two others already. I appear to be the only woman. I feel very frightened and inadequate about it.'[15] Anxious she may have been, but the difference between the clarity of her path into the early stages of the war and the uncertainty of my father's is, well, stark.

* * *

> Sir,
> I have to inform you that it has been decided to appoint you to be 1st Officer of the *Atlantis* during the pleasure of the Board of Directors.
>   You will please join the above-mentioned vessel in Southampton on Monday, the 30th of May, reporting during the forenoon to the Company's Southampton Marine Superintendent.

Head of Marine Department, Royal Mail Lines,
to First Officer Thomas Davies, 18 May 1939

Thomas 'Tommy' Davies was forty-one when he was appointed First Officer aboard the Royal Mail Lines' ship *Atlantis*. Born on 13 January 1898 near Folkestone in Kent, Davies had been at sea since leaving school. He was neat and dapper, invariably the shortest in any group photograph of his fellow officers. Spare and thin as a boy, he was increasingly prone to putting on weight; partial to a glass or two of gin, or the restorative bottle of Bass; and a committed chain smoker, a habit prompted by his service in two world wars and which provoked a persistent chestiness and a preoccupation with his uncertain health. It is symptomatic that his extensive wartime letters include a faded newspaper clipping advising on the best way of dealing with a bout of flu: 'When you feel the influenza coming on get a chemist (unless you have a very weak heart or are under six years of age) to make up my prescription. Go to bed.' He had an infectious laugh, an open, pleasant face, with a gentle smile, and dark hair brushed back from his forehead. After serving in the Dover Patrol during the Great War, he was demobbed on 24 November 1919, three months after he had met his wife Dorrie for the first time; they married in Southsea and lived in Southampton for the next five years. The Davies's home during the 1939–45 war, however, was in

Mansfield – almost as far from the sea as you could get. During the 1920s and 1930s, Davies had slowly worked his way up from junior 4th to chief officer, serving on some twenty different ships. Married for twenty years by the time the war broke out, Tom's letters to Dorrie invariably included heartfelt, earnest assurances of love and trust, written perhaps in the glow of his cabin's dusty light bulb before turning in, cigarette smoke swirling in the harsh light, or just prior to going on duty, when he would contemplate the sea swell and the cloud-streaked moon, and imagine himself at home. For his part he was greatly comforted by his wife's constancy, writing in an undated letter, 'How poor fellows get on who are at sea and have flighty wives, I don't know.'

Captain Tommy Davies in tropical whites. (*Angela Awbery White*)

In August 1939, Tommy Davies was on board the liner *Atlantis* bound for the Baltic. That summer, war seemed within touching distance and among crew and passengers there was mounting concern that the gleaming white liner might become trapped for the duration in the port of Danzig should the situation suddenly deteriorate. The uncertainty was increased when German police boarded the ship and confiscated a number of passengers' cameras. Instead of moving on to Hamburg, *Atlantis* sailed back to Southampton, arriving there on 25 August. Red crosses and a broad green stripe were duly painted on the hull, transforming her into Hospital Ship 33 that sailed for the Mediterranean almost immediately, arriving in Malta on 6 September and sailing thereafter between Alexandria, Gibraltar and Malta until November 1939, when she returned to Southampton for repairs. Tom then transferred briefly to *Almanzora*, a Royal Mail Lines' liner that had been stripped of its elegant finery to become a troopship, an action that prompted 'great despair among the adults to see all the beautiful fittings being ripped out'. It was a ship that Tommy knew well, having first served on her in 1933. The Davies family acquired two rugs from the Princess Royal's suite, and Tom's four-year-old daughter Angela played hopscotch along the deck planks while the ship was being transformed from the luxurious to the austere.[16] There was no place any longer for the mock Tudor and Jacobean furniture in first class, nor its winter garden. Instead it was fitted out to accommodate, in cramped misery, thousands of reluctant airmen and soldiers destined to be shipped off to war zones far away.

* * *

Dear Sir,
I am directed by the Minister of Information to inform you that your name has been entered on a list of authors whose services are likely to be valuable to the Ministry of Information in time of war.[17]

Ministry of Information, London, to Noël Coward, 5 September 1939

He is playing the piano and crooning, eyes on the middle distance, while a huddle of smiling children presses in on him. One small boy looks awestruck, or envious perhaps of this middle-aged man's savoir faire. The entertainer is tall, spruce, hair slicked back flat on his head, exposing the irresistible march of baldness. A pronounced frown is etched into his forehead and his nose is prominent, his eyes tired. He is togged up in a crisp white shirt, carefully knotted tie and well-cut, double-breasted suit. This is what theatrical success looks like, children. It is June 1939 and the venue is the Actors' Orphanage, Chertsey in Surrey; the man at the piano is Noël Coward. The children in the orphanage welcomed his visits: 'He came into our playroom with a box of Mars bars, one for each of us. We couldn't believe it – it would have taken a whole month's pocket money to buy one. He spoke to us and sat down at our very old honky-tonk piano and played – it sounded terrific.' Coward was frequently 'accompanied by very glamorous ladies'.[18] The same age as the century – born 16 December 1899 – Coward was, like these orphans, entangled in the theatre from an early age, making his first professional appearance in 1911. By 1939, he was regarded as one of the country's great theatrical figures, whether writing, acting, directing, composing or singing. There were those who were wary of him – Harold Nicholson described him as 'a bounder', for example, but recognised his 'real talent and energy'.[19] A year younger than Royal Mail Lines' Tommy Davies, he shared with him a

Noël Coward entertains at the Actors' Orphanage, June 1939. (*Getty*)

passion for the sea, making the first of many voyages on board a Royal Navy ship in 1930. He grew to cherish the 'traditions, the routine and discipline of the wardroom; the relentless Englishness of naval officers'.[20]

Like Freya Stark, he was appalled by appeasement; indeed, when Prime Minister Chamberlain returned from meeting Hitler in Munich in 1938 proclaiming that peace had been preserved, Noël was scathing about 'that bloody conceited old sod', believing that Chamberlain and his cronies were risking the peace of the world. 'We have nothing to worry about,' he wrote, 'but the destruction of civilisation.'[21]

None of this is apparent in the suave, polished performer in this Surrey garden. But that same month he flew from Heston Airport to Warsaw to begin a series of visits to various European capitals – Warsaw, Danzig (a couple of months before Tom Davies and *Atlantis*), Moscow, Leningrad, Helsinki, Stockholm, Oslo and Copenhagen. He claimed that he merely wanted to see for himself what was going on in Europe. There was, however, an unspoken subplot; he had been recruited as one of a number of agents charged with reporting back to the Foreign Office on the mood beyond the Channel. As Coward progressed through Europe, usually by train, the imminence of war seemed increasingly palpable. He carried with him a letter of introduction from the Foreign Secretary, and on his way to Oslo was entrusted with the diplomatic bag while 'carrying a courier's passport covered with imposing red seals.'[22] The writer Lawrence Durrell, who was then based in Danzig, 'later reported that German agents, already suspecting that Noël was a spy, became thoroughly convinced by his fleeting visit.'[23] Arriving in Moscow on the Warsaw train, Coward was 'unpacked to the last sock' by unsmiling customs men and was kept under constant surveillance. The first of his 'minders' in Moscow was a 'lady guide whose manner was sullenly affable', wearing (unwisely, Noël thought) 'a short cotton dress which was none too clean and exposed, to an alarming degree, her short, hairy legs'.[24] Later, having been followed for some time by a nondescript man in a green hat, he rushed up to him, shook his hand with great energy and said, 'I haven't seen you for ages and how are Anna and the children?' Understandably, he could not wait to escape from Russia and did so, he thought, only by the skin of his teeth. Finland, by contrast, seemed peaceful – if living nervously under twin threats from Stalin and Hitler. Eventually he slipped away to the south of France – to the Carlton Hotel, Cannes – to take one final look at it before it was too late.

It was clear that war was inevitable and Coward began to contemplate what he might do. His Great War service had been decidedly underwhelming, a catalogue of minor disasters, and he had hated the routine and regimentation. He had ended up in hospital, having distinguished himself by falling on his head. Concussed for three days and in a coma, he saw no military action. Now it seemed logical for him to contemplate some kind of naval service, but instead he found himself drawn into a world of secrecy and propaganda.

Back in England, Noël had two plays – *This Happy Breed* and *Present Laughter* – due to open in Manchester in the second week of September. However, at 11.00 am on 1 September 1939, the cast of both plays gathered on the stage of London's Phoenix Theatre, where they said their goodbyes and pretended to an optimism they did not feel for the future.

∗ ∗ ∗

And so everything we had dreaded had happened and it was very undramatic. And nothing had happened yet that was different and yet life had altered. One had no appetite for the sort of things that had been fun.[25]

Cecil Beaton's diary, September 1939

It is close to ten o'clock on a July day in 1939. The photographer is ushered into the palace, gawping at the family portraits as he is conducted through the dark red carpeted corridors, past obsequious footmen and unexpected signs of domesticity: crumbs on a breakfast table, and housemaids with dusters. He is 'quite grey and darts like a bird ... very observant, misses nothing.'[26] He is there to photograph the Queen, a commission to make the heart beat faster. She is the latest in a long line of the celebrated and photogenic he has captured, from Wallis Simpson to Edith Sitwell and Marlene Dietrich. Much later, he floats away, one hundred negatives under his arm and a flower-fragrant handkerchief belonging to the Queen in a trouser pocket, greedily snaffled when she tucked it down a chair during the photo shoot. Cecil Beaton is a happy man.

Later that summer, like Noël Coward, Cecil headed for France, keen to have one last Continental fling before the world closed in. He stayed with

Self-portrait: Cecil Beaton, 1938.
(*The Cecil Beaton Studio Archives
at Sotheby's*)

the American writer Gertrude Stein in the French countryside near Lyons, some six hours south of Paris. Despite the comforts of France, Beaton's unease about the evident drift towards war could not be dispelled, despite Miss Stein's optimism. So unheedful of the current crisis was she that, when Cecil disappeared one evening, lost in the French lanes as the light faded, she was more worried about his welfare than the state of the world: 'War?' she boomed. 'Who cares about the war? We've lost Cecil Beaton.'

Cecil was thirty-five when the war broke out. Born in Hampstead, London on 14 January 1904, his father was a prosperous timber merchant. Bullied at prep school by Evelyn Waugh, Cecil was later educated at Harrow and St John's College, Cambridge. He left in 1925 without taking a degree, already bewitched by the camera's possibilities and having begun to make his name as the man to turn to for fashion photography, or capturing in film the butterfly world of high society. Prior to that he worked in an office in London's Holborn, where he felt 'like a caged skylark'; he knew then he wanted a studio 'with a strict business side competently and energetically run by an ingenious manager, where we'd do designs and take photographs and do any other work we felt like doing.'[27] He went to the States, worked for *Vogue* magazine and won a lucrative contract with Condé Nast Publications, where he was regarded as an international star. On a crossing of the Atlantic in April 1930, he met Noël Coward for the first time, having longed to do so, although he hated him too, 'out of pique', he thought, envious of the older man's success, 'so much like the career I might have wished for myself.' To his horror, he was ridiculed by Coward, who mocked the way his arms waved around, his undulating walk and his over-exaggerated, flamboyant clothes. 'I had wanted enormously to be liked by Noël Coward,' he wrote, 'and now he thought nothing of me.'[28] There were other clouds on the horizon: an unsatisfactory love life and accusations of anti-Semitism in America, which led to a humiliating return to England. By the late 1930s he was highly celebrated as a fashion photographer, his subjects including 'five duchesses … one countess and three viscountesses'.[29]

Like Noël Coward, he was troubled at the outset of the war by what his contribution to it should be, certain as he was that he was unsuited to the army – 'too incompetent to enlist as a private', he wrote, recognising that he was quite 'unfitted to pass muster in any military capacity'.[30] Even before the hostilities had been declared, he had offered to drive evacuee children from London to the relative safety of the West Country; he also contemplated working on camouflage, but was turned down. On the morning of 3 September, he was about to step into the bath when Lord Berners' deaf butler shouted, 'The war has started.' Cecil listened to Chamberlain's sombre speech, delivered in his 'pewter-grey voice', in the parlour at Ashcombe, his house in Wiltshire, while his mother was in tears. With a state of war now existing between Britain and Germany, Cecil resigned himself to a mundane role as a telephone operator in an Air Raid Precautions (ARP) post in Wilton, Wiltshire, his first shift beginning on 17 September.

* * *

'Roselea' is the attractive name of this chic little villa by the sea. Ever since I was a baby the family has spent at least a few weeks of each year in Largo and I have come to look on this as a second home. This letter is being written in bed in the little front room, which used to belong to my Grandpa. (I'm sure his spirit haunts it still, but it is a kind of jovial ghost, which smokes reflectively and tells stories to little boys who are very fond of trains.)

Donald Macdonald to May Mott, Roselea,
Largo, Fife, Scotland, 10 September 1946

This is Glasgow 1939. The scene is a large, gothic examination hall with high ceilings and portraits of esteemed alumni staring down from the walls on the silent ranks of candidates. Pens scratch and a ponderous invigilator progresses through the lines with a funereal step. At one desk is medical student Donald Macdonald, erstwhile Sergeant Major of Dunoon Grammar School's Cadet Corps (1936) and would-be writer. He is sitting his Second Professional Examination and he is grappling with a memory hazier on the details of doctoring than he would like it to be. Somehow, Chamberlain's Munich peace the previous year had broken the ice inside him and opened up the magical possibilities of the stage. He could sing like Bing Crosby in a world where war had been banished! 'It was perhaps natural that, after such a reprieve, I should "break out" by taking part in the (travelling) University

Donald Macdonald –
posted in wartime.
(*Donald Macdonald*)

revue *College Pudding of 1939* and even taking up with a GIRL!'[31] In that austere examination hall in Glasgow's university, the price was about to be paid. Donald duly failed, the result being a parental inquest and a substantial family disagreement: both his parents ('rather undemonstrative in the matter of cuddles') were unhappy at their son's failure and there were harsh words spoken, with his father attributing it to his son's singing and pointing the finger of blame at his wife: 'Your Daddy blames me for encouraging you,' Donald's mother cried – she herself having been a thwarted soprano.

Donald Macdonald was born in Dumbarton in March 1919 and given the same name as his father. Donald Senior was a native Gaelic speaker who had been brought up in a croft on the remote island of Lewis, only learning English as a foreign language. 'He was a Highlander,' his son wrote many years later, 'even worse, a Hebridean, and so must cloak all emotion in jest.' Father and son had very different views on life and how it should be lived: Donald Junior wanted to be a writer throughout his life, but 'Daddy had always wanted me to study medicine,' and did not encourage artistic aspirations of any kind. 'What's this nonsense you're writing now?' he would ask, and perhaps follow it up with 'and have you done any grinding today?' The notion that studying was synonymous with 'grinding' was a depressing one, and even in old age Donald could write, 'Daddy still casts a long shadow, even though I have reached the age at which he died, ninety.' In those far-off days when his father was ascertaining whether his studies were being suitably grafted over, the younger Macdonald had just three ambitions: 'to sing like Bing Crosby; to write like H.L. Mencken and to speak like Alistair Cooke.' Although his father was a model of probity and by no means a tyrannical figure, the young Donald felt that 'at home I had been brainwashed into believing that my few accomplishments were liabilities.' The two Donald Macdonalds were very different: the elder one's favourite writer was the sombre Thomas Hardy, while the younger could never finish one of his novels, deterred by their worthiness.

Donald's failed examination year proved providential: he was allowed to continue with his studies and would only be called up if he failed the examination again. The day war was declared Donald was 'laboriously papering a wall in the big bedroom in Dunoon, while outside the scene was set perfectly, on a bleak day, with rain falling and the Clyde shrouded in mist.' The lights on Dunoon's esplanade had already been doused as if in expectation of the imminent arrival of a vengeful Luftwaffe over the river Clyde.

* * *

Dear Sir,

In accordance with the National Services (Armed Forces) Act, 1939 and 1940, you are called upon for service in the Royal Air Force and are required to present yourself on Wednesday, 22 May 1940 between 9.00 am and 12 noon, or as soon as possible after that date, to No. 2 Reception Centre, Cardington, Bedfordshire.

HM Government to Jack Knott, 1940

The cast of six characters is almost complete; it only remains for my father to step into the spotlight. When the war broke out, my father, Jack Knott, was twenty-five, married and with a young son, Peter, just twelve months old. So, what did you do in the war, Daddy? Well, I cannot see Jack readily volunteering for military service – he had responsibilities now, after all, and anyway, he would have struggled to make a decision about what best to do. Making snappy decisions was not a strength. As the autumn of 1939 passed, he would have been waiting for his call-up papers to drop through the letterbox. This is all supposition on my part, however, since he never willingly volunteered information about the war. It is fair to say he was what you might call 'a difficult man', and one of his 'difficult' characteristics was a compulsion to keep things close to his chest. He was not beyond a bit of artful dissembling too: for example, he had a deep scar on the back of his hand, which he once claimed had been caused by a German bullet. I shall never know if this was true.

There is an old, sepia-tinted photograph of Jack that puzzles me. It was taken in Northampton in 1934 and yet it could easily be Edwardian England: little traffic apart from two cars with running boards and narrow windscreens and bonnets. In the foreground is a young man striding purposefully, bowler-hatted and with a dark undertaker's overcoat flying open to reveal a sharp suit and well-buffed shoes. It is a suave Jack, clearly eager to get on

Jack Knott: the author's father? (*Author*)

with life, hurrying to work, or to some romantic assignation. He is twenty, but looks older, as if he has property to develop, money to make, or lives to save. He does not look the tailor's assistant that he was. I do not recognise his confidence or sense of purpose. Was it the war that took that away?

There was certainly no telling what kind of war he'd had, good or bad, although the silence suggested the latter. Those six years were shrouded in mystery: I knew nothing about what he did, or what he went through, or how long his posting abroad was – although I did know that he had been in Iraq for a time. Most important of all, I had no idea when he returned to the UK. Had he turned up, sun-burned and nervous, at the VE celebrations in the village? Given that I was born exactly nine months after VE Day, this was a question that bothered me greatly. Or did he return at some later date to find my mother carrying – even holding – the baby of a different and unknown father?

Chapter 2

On His Majesty's Service

Mr Noël Coward has asked me to thank you for your letter and to tell you that he has noted the instructions contained therein. He wishes me to say, however, that he fears he will be unable to comply with these as he is going abroad today for several months. Should you wish to get in touch with him, he suggests that you should apply to the Ministry of Information or to the British Embassy in Paris.[1]

Lorn Loraine to Mr A.D. Peters, Ministry of Information,
London, 5 September 1939

Just before the war began, Noël Coward took a mysterious phone call asking how he felt about Paris. The caller was Sir Campbell Stuart, a Canadian newspaper magnate who had become involved in the British propaganda effort and who wanted Noël to head up a Bureau of Propaganda in the French capital. Coward's initial reaction was lukewarm at best. He and the Conservative MP Robert Boothby drove to Chartwell to see Winston Churchill and seek the First Lord of the Admiralty's advice. After listening to Coward's trademark rendition of *Mad Dogs and Englishmen go out in the Midday Sun*, Churchill's advice was uncomfortable and forthright: 'Get into a warship and see some action!' Churchill boomed. 'Go and sing to them when the guns are firing – that's your job!' They had found him not in the best of moods and his forceful opinion infuriated Noël, who had thought himself better suited to the subtleties of naval intelligence, not entertaining the troops. He could not accept that servicemen under fire would be in the right frame of mind to enjoy a concert; behind his anger too was his wish 'to exorcise the ghost of his shadowy performance in the previous war'.[2]

In the event, after attending briefings at Bletchley Park on 3 September, where it was decided that Coward should be allocated to 'D' Section – 'the dirty tricks department'[3] – he set out for Paris, a passenger in a cramped RAF aircraft whose capacity was tested by its crew of two, and the paraphernalia the sombre-suited Coward had brought with him. It comprised: 'my bowler hat, my gas mask, my parachute, a contrivance for keeping me afloat in the chill waters of the channel', and an official briefcase crammed with papers, stamped 'Secret', 'Confidential' or 'Very Secret' and 'which could have been read aloud in the Reichstag without causing any sensation other than deadly boredom.'[4] The only piece of equipment he left behind in England was his umbrella. Once in Paris he set up an informal initial base at the Ritz. It was 7 September 1939.

While those early months in Paris may have included the pleasures of caviar, filet mignon and pink champagne at the Ritz, it was soon evident that the prevailing mood was one of tedium and that progress was minimal. Bob Boothby believed the bureau to be 'a ridiculous organisation' whose work consisted chiefly of 'endless and purposeless lunch, dinner and drink parties'.[5] There was a series of unsatisfactory discussions with the French, whose delegation included a bad-tempered colonel plainly distrustful of the perfidious English, as well as frustrating contacts with the Admiralty typified by the occasion Noël deployed his code name when telephoning ('This is Diplomat speaking'), which merely elicited a testy 'What the bloody hell are you talking about?' from an unknown official in London. What made matters worse was the pursuit of incomprehensible policies, the dropping of worthy propaganda leaflets over Germany being one such: 'If the policy of His Majesty's Government is to bore the Germans to death,' Noël observed, 'I didn't think we had enough time.' He was tempted to write 'Secret, Confidential and Dull' on thick files of documents. The most excitement came from the personal letters he received through the diplomatic bag. There was, Coward thought as the winter drew on, a 'Secret Service virus' that pervaded most things, but which achieved nothing at all.

To make matters worse, the English press started asking awkward questions as to what exactly Noël was doing in France. There were disapproving comments about him sauntering around the French capital togged up in naval uniform. The censors were obliged to kill a story in the *Daily Express* that claimed among other things that 'Mr Noël Coward, in impeccable civilian attire, sits all day behind a vast desk in a luxury office in the Place de La Madeleine, issuing orders to officers of the highest rank.'[6]

* * *

Tomorrow, either Germany has retired or we are fighting. I dined out with one of my new colleagues and came back in a drizzle through a London dark as an Arabian town: had to ring at a door and ask for my street! The city is gradually changing into khaki. The Air Force more than adequate and prepared. One thinks it may be a longer war than last.[7]

Freya Stark to her mother Flora, London, 3 September 1939

Freya Stark left London on 8 October 1939. It was a grey day of thin rain, which suited Freya's sense of melancholy – 'a horrid sadness', as she put it in a letter to her publisher Jock Murray. She wondered how long it would be before she saw England again, and even more unsettling, what sort of England would it be. She had embarked on a long, daunting journey, leaving from Folkestone on the afternoon tide for Boulogne; then crossing Europe by rail, and in the process, 'missing nearly every train in Europe and Asia', a problem since 'most of them only run three times a week.'[8] There was an anxious farewell to her mother Flora at their house in Asolo, near Venice, both of them wondering if they would ever meet again. It was the middle of November before she finally arrived at the Red Sea port of Aden. Strategically placed between the Middle East and the gateway to India, Aden was relatively pro-British, despite attempts by the Italians to promote their own interests. Freya was to work there on propaganda, under the direction of Stewart Perowne, a contemporary of Cecil Beaton's at Cambridge.

Aden was less of a concern to the British than Yemen to the north, where the Italian influence was growing and the atmosphere was volatile: in a letter to Lord Halifax, the British Foreign Secretary, Freya reported that Yemen was 'the only spot still unhealthy from our point of view. The rest of our Arabs are as good as gold, except for a murder now and then.'[9] Towards the end of January 1940, she wrote to Halifax again, asking if he would be willing to send some kind of greeting to the Imam. A few days later, on 2 February, Freya arrived in Yemen complete with the wherewithal to show British Navy and Air Force films, as well as a quantity of gold-embroidered shawls to offer as gifts for Sultans and their wives.

The Yemeni capital Sana'a had a disturbing atmosphere of cloak and dagger secrecy, intrigue and rumour. Bribery was endemic. Work for Freya was an exhausting cycle of gently subversive conversations amongst clustered groups of wives in the city's harems, and showing propaganda films. After one such show, the 'Crown Prince of the Yemen asked her, "Then it is not true that Italy rules the Mediterranean?" To which she replied, "Can it be said that you rule a house if someone else has the keys of the front and back doors?"'[10] Yemen was a world far from the conventions of the West: she was conducted cheerily around the city by a 'fat old lady' who turned out to be sixty-five, although Freya had guessed that she was some twenty years younger than that. In talking proudly about her age, the Yemeni suddenly 'pulled out her voluminous breasts and patted them to show that they were still "firm as a girl's".'[11]

* * *

> Snow fell on the day of our dress rehearsal, and for weeks thereafter we might have been in Alaska. While understudies were thrown on stage, the missing principal would be floundering in a snowdrift or, having slipped on the ice, being bound in a plaster cast.[12]

Cecil Beaton's diary, March 1940

The winter of 1939–40 proved to be one of the coldest people could remember, and as if that wasn't bad enough, life became ever more beset with inconvenience, even if the threatened Armageddon from the air had yet to materialise: petrol was rationed; signposts on the roads were removed; accidents plagued the blackout; and at Cecil Beaton's house at Ashcombe in Wiltshire, hot water had become a thing of the past. People sensed that the war was to be a protracted life and death struggle and simple pleasures should be treasured. At Christmas 1939, Cecil co-wrote, and appeared in, *Hello Cinderella*, a pantomime for nearby RAF servicemen. He played 'a glossy Ugly Sister in full drag, heavily sequinned and enveloped in a cloud of tulle'.[13] Like many others in this bleak time, Beaton recognised the comfort that could be derived from writing and receiving letters: 'In the absence of telephone and telegram, the art of letter writing is practised,' he wrote. 'The war has made correspondents of us all.'[14]

The difficulty of obtaining petrol caused Cecil to abandon his ARP job and he began working for the Ministry of Information (MOI) in London, taking photographs to illustrate 'England at War', as well as snapping key politicians – Anthony Eden, Ernest Bevin and Lord Halifax among others. Then, in the spring of 1940, he obtained a permit to visit the Maginot Line in France, only for the trip to be abandoned when the sudden, decisive German advance in early May carried all before it. To Cecil's initial disappointment, official approval for the visit arrived just a day too late, a delay that probably spared him from five years of captivity. Soon after, he was offered a lucrative contract in America (for Pond's Cream), and after much hesitation, he decided to take it, all too aware of his financial difficulties. His acceptance was made only after consulting Lord 'Bobbety' Cranborne, the Government's Paymaster General, who, while pointing out that the news was 'howwid', said that he should nonetheless 'pwoceed' to America. Beaton left Liverpool for America on board the SS *Samaria*. Once there he was shocked by the country's lack of readiness for war. He wrote to Lady Juliet Duff from Beverly Hills after the fall of Paris: 'This country cannot go to war. It is completely unprepared. It is tragic. There are six guns – hardly an army.'[15]

* * *

Darling B.,
I wonder if this will reach you – every post now one wonders. I have told Jock to keep in touch and, if you ever want money, he will let you have some. Do make all enquiries first – as to whether you want to stay; second, let me have an address for writing.[16]

Freya Stark to Flora Stark, Aden, 20 April 1940

Freya Stark was back in Aden by the beginning of April 1940, her spirits lifted by the fact that she would now be able to 'die with my hair curled, because this boat goes via Jibouti, where one can get a perm!'[17] Early the following month the Germans invaded the Low Countries and war was properly joined, all phoniness forgotten. The changed mood was reflected in Freya's letter of 28 May to Sir Sydney Cockerell: 'In a way there is a strange happiness in knowing that now we just fight or die.' She had made a will and felt that the decks were cleared.[18] Two weeks later, the Italians came into the war on the German side, and on 24 June, Freya's mother, Flora, was arrested and taken to Treviso prison. There she was body searched and put into an insect-plagued cell, 'with three small windows high up, heavily barred, one small shelf against the wall at one end and four truckle beds, in a space of 3 metres by 5.'[19] Meanwhile, Aden was being subjected to enemy air raids, the first of which Freya observed from a rooftop: 'A lovely moon hanging over the ancient crater, with jagged black outline like a great bowl around us: the lightless town inside, very hushed.' In the bright yellow beams of eight searchlights, an aircraft was pinned against the darkness, its wings and fuselage holding the light. Freya reflected on the 'rapture of loveliness so near to death'.[20]

A month later, she was aboard ship sailing for Egypt, part of the first convoy in the Red Sea since Italy declared war. 'We ourselves are dangerous,' she wrote, 'our cargo is ammunition,'[21] as well as some 70,000 tons of oil.

* * *

Tommy Davies was also at sea during the early summer of 1940, though in his case in the temperate climes of the English Channel, rather than the stifling heat of the Red Sea. He had taken up post as chief officer aboard the cargo ship MV *Brittany*, joining the ship in London early in the year. In the immediate aftermath of Dunkirk, her skipper, Captain Hooper, sailed for St Nazaire, intending to help in the rescue of more of the men stranded by the speed of the German advance. It proved to be a disquieting crossing: they passed the forlorn masts of the sunken *Lusitania* protruding from the water; a British destroyer approached them to warn that the Germans were occupying the port; and then an enemy aircraft scudded in and dropped a stick of bombs, which missed *Brittany* by less than 30 feet. Bomb splinters clattered on to the deck, followed by a wall of seawater stirred by the explosions. Remarkably, it proved a lucky escape, with no casualties reported. Tommy wondered how many more times before the war was over his own demise would be so close. Post-haste, *Brittany* headed for Le Havre, took on board more desperate and demoralised troops and turned thankfully for home. Within a matter of days, the French had capitulated.

Hooper then sailed for Africa. On 3 July 1940, the British attacked the French fleet at Mers-el-Kébir, on the coast of Algeria, killing 1,297 French servicemen in the raid, as well as sinking a battleship and damaging five other ships. One consequence of the attack was that large numbers of would-be British refugees needed to be rescued, in Casablanca and elsewhere; *Brittany* evacuated 1,500 men, women and children, half to Gibraltar, half to Liverpool.

Over time, when both Hooper and Davies had moved on from *Brittany*, they became close friends.[22] Tommy's daughter, Angela, still remembers the two cronies visiting a tailor's shop in Bristol 'after rather a bibulous lunch' and lying on the floor in beery contentment asking to be measured for suits. Perhaps the shop was my father's at 41 Old Market Street, Bristol, where he worked for many years after the war. Jack would have been thoroughly disapproving, no doubt wishing that he could snap his erstwhile military policeman's handcuffs on to those boozy sailors' wrists.

* * *

I think I should be only too delighted to register as a Government agent and I think it would do away with a lot of false rumour and wild surmise. I am most definitely not over here on personal business.[23]

Noël Coward to Sir Robert Vansittart, Fairmont Hotel,
San Francisco, 21 August 1940

By the Spring of 1940, Noël Coward had become disillusioned with his work in Paris, dissatisfied with the way 'an air of misty indecision enveloped our propaganda activities'.[24] It was with considerable relief that he took the train from the Gare de Lyon, heading for Genoa, and ultimately the United States, enduring a rough crossing aboard the SS *Washington*. It was the middle of April. In America he was charged with both judging, and helping shape, public opinion, significantly more important now that Britain was isolated. It seemed a worthwhile thing to be doing, but it galled him that his work must remain secret and he himself consequently at the mercy of some British newspapers that tended to treat him as a shallow, fly-by-night entertainer feathering his own nest. Noël's relations with the press were never straightforward; indeed, he was one of the names on a so-called 'white list', their existence to be ignored by the *Daily Express*, 'or not to be mentioned without consultation with the editor.'[25] That paper observed of Coward's war work in America: 'Mr Coward is not the man for the job. His flippant England – Cocktails, Countesses, Caviare [*sic*] – has gone.'[26] In the Spring of 1940, soon after arriving, he met with the American president, Franklin D. Roosevelt, reporting back to London that he was confident that the President had every intention of managing events 'towards the desired outcome'. Without such 'management', Roosevelt's sympathy for Britain's predicament would remain low-key, given the strength of isolationism in the States. Noël also met Mrs Roosevelt, commenting that he 'could imagine her driving through the nineteenth-century English countryside to take tea with Mrs Gaskell.'

Once France had surrendered, Noël was desperate to return home; 'Like the heroine of *Time Remembered*, Coward could not bear being so far from the action.'[27] But it was 8 June before he managed to get away, taking a flying boat to Lisbon in the company of the actress Madeleine Carroll. In his last weeks in the USA he took a train to Chicago; flew on to Los Angeles at night through a blinding rainstorm, before being greeted at the airport by the actor Cary Grant; then travelling on to San Francisco, Salt Lake City, Omaha, Cincinnati and Cleveland. He had a further meeting at the White House with an 'utterly exhausted' Roosevelt and later wrote to the President, declaring how much he admired his 'wonderful humour and sanity at a moment when the world is battering at you'.[28]

Noël's plan on arriving in the Portuguese capital was to take the Sud Express train in order to check on matters at the Paris office, but he was persuaded out of this, wisely as it turned out, since the Germans were just hours from entering the city. 'I should have arrived in Paris on the same day as Hitler,' Coward said in a subsequent radio broadcast, 'which I am sure would have been socially embarrassing for us both.'[29] Instead, Coward left Lisbon on the morning of 14 June, stopping en route at Bordeaux, flying in what he believed to be 'the last civilian aircraft to touch down in France for five years'.[30] It had been a close-run thing, evading the relentless German advance, but the beauty of the English countryside on his return, 'bathed in golden, late afternoon sunlight', was all the more glorious for seeming so fleeting.

Once home, he suffered his 'usual homecoming depression, his mother country was frustrating and life was difficult,'[31] and on 21 July Coward sailed to America again, this time on the *Britannic*, part of a convoy outward bound from Liverpool. It was an uneasy voyage, with passengers and crew in a constant state of apprehension, exemplified by the fact that many of the passengers chose to live in their lifebelts. In a New York that was 'hotter than hell', he met Bill Stephenson, Head of British Security Coordination, and was duly recruited as one of Stephenson's boys, along with Ian Fleming, Roald Dahl and Cary Grant; indeed, the latter became Noël's 'control'. They had met initially at the St Ermin's Hotel in London, where Coward was asked to meet a 'contact' in the foyer and was then taken up to the fourth floor in a lift that 'was only labelled to go up three floors.'[32] He was conducted into the premises of the Special Operations Executive. Coward recognised that 'celebrity was its own disguise' and he could safely rely on his 'reputation as a bit of an idiot … a merry playboy. It was very disarming.'[33] In due course, the FBI opened a file on him, evidently monitoring his every move as he went on a multi-city tour beginning in August 1940. That autumn he had 'a most unpleasant interview' with ex-President Hoover … Noël felt the American was 'contemptuous' and spoke 'slightingly'.[34] The press too – those 'mingy little journalistic twirps [*sic*]' – remained suspicious, and stories about what some pressmen saw as his unpatriotic behaviour proliferated. For his part, Coward vowed to exact revenge in time. It didn't help that he felt a long way from home. 'Sometimes,' he wrote on 6 September 1940, 'being so far away is almost more than I can bear.'[35]

He was to travel even further. On 16 October 1940, he left for Australia from San Pedro, California, a passenger on board the SS *Monterey*, a trip that gave him time to prepare the series of seven fifteen-minute broadcasts to the Australian public that he had been asked to make. His longing for home did not stifle his waspish sense of humour: in one of his letters he asserted that he was typing it in order that the censor would be able to read it more easily. On reaching Yokohama, the Japanese authorities refused to let the English passengers disembark, but Coward was not to be so easily denied, presenting himself in the unlikely guise of a tough American sailor and going ashore surrounded by a gaggle of crew members. It was disconcerting to find that Yokohama was full of Germans.

They docked again at Shanghai and Noël stayed at the Cathay Hotel, where he had written his play *Private Lives*. It was 16 November 1940 before the ship arrived in Sydney, and Noël immediately warmed to Australia – 'the thing that is nicest about it here is the Englishness.' On 3 December he wrote to Duff Cooper, the Minister of Information: 'I am fareing [*sic*] very well, and it seems that I am doing a good job. Please believe that I'm doing the level best I can, and intend to go on doing so until the damned war is won. I am feeling happier than I have felt for months.'[36] He was, however, faced with considerable antagonism from the press: one 'asked whether he was a bugger', while another journalist told him, 'You are nothing but a bloody queen.'[37] This phase of war work – a treadmill of broadcasts, concerts and visits – he found exhausting, leaving him drained and longing even more for the comforts of home. But the journeying was not yet over: he travelled on to New Zealand, arriving in Auckland on 15 January 1941 and staying nearly three weeks. When he did finally return to England, it was to discover that his home, Goldenhurst, near Ashford in Kent, had been requisitioned by the Army. Nothing else for it: he joined the thousands who had been obliged by the war to move – the evacuees and the bombed-out. He decamped to the Savoy Hotel.

* * *

Cecil Beaton also left America for England in mid-summer 1940, preferring to face an uncertain future in his own country than watch how events turned out from the other side of the Atlantic. His work for the Ministry of Information focused on the effects of the German bombing. Typical was the photograph of a hospitalised three-year-old girl, her head cut open by a bomb splinter, clutching a doll, her large eyes accusing the world. Beaton travelled the country capturing the endless permutations of bomb damage – fire-blackened bricks, collapsed walls, ruptured pipes, fluttering curtains with no windows behind them. He was bombed out of his London house, 8 Pelham Place in Kensington, a 'tiny but super-attractive snuff-box of a house' with 'red flock walls and varnished aspidistras in tall pots, and tight, little smart leather chairs', which the Luftwaffe had rendered uninhabitable.[38] He moved into the Dorchester Hotel for 'wine, music and company'. On those

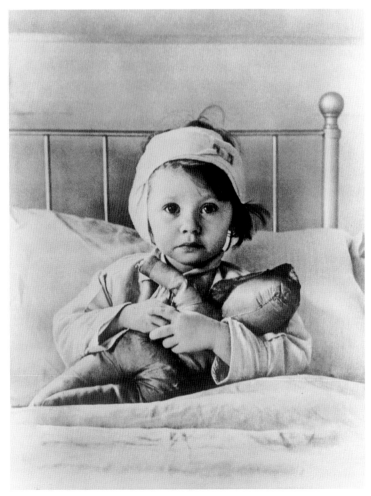

Cecil Beaton's photograph of three-year-old Eileen Dunne, in Great Ormond Street Hospital for Sick Children. She had been injured during an air raid on London in September 1940. (*Imperial War Museum, MH 26395*)

occasions when he had stayed at Ashcombe, travelling up to London from the Wiltshire countryside, he was obliged to hide vegetables in his swish Vuitton suitcase since permits were now needed to take them into the capital. On Christmas Day 1940, he wrote from Ashcombe to Lady Juliet Duff: 'I find myself bursting into tears a lot … [the result of] doing too much and being too long at fever pitch in London.'[39] The comforts of the Dorchester could not compensate for the pervading gloom of wartime Britain.

Chapter 3

First Posting

Jack looked out of the carriage window at Bedfordshire in the rain. It was Wednesday, 22 May 1940, the day he was due to enlist at the RAF Reception Centre, Cardington. Not so far away, the Germans had reached the Channel coast and Boulogne was about to fall; Panzer commanders, binoculars at the ready, stared out across the water and wondered how much further from home their advance would take them. Jack, meanwhile, was contemplating his own prospects, in all probability as far away from an aeroplane as possible, or so he hoped. The choice was narrowed down to 'steward, cook, batman, store man, driver or RAF Police NCO'.[1] What was it he said or did that had him earmarked as a policeman? Did he look the part? Or was it just a matter of chance?

At all events, he was soon to lose what little control he had of his life, embarking on a series of postings across the country: Topcliffe in Yorkshire; Cheadle in Cheshire, where Luftwaffe radio messages were monitored and passed to the code breakers at Bletchley Park; then on to RAF Dagnall in Bedfordshire. How he would have hated service life! The hut with thirty men, beds either side of a linoleum corridor, rough blankets and cold water, coke stoves, the communal eating, the drills and marching, weapons training, the savage haircuts ('Am I hurting you airman? I should be – your hair's so bleedin' long!!'), unreasonable curfews, and equally unreasonable early morning calls ('Put 'em away and get out of bed!'), the inspections, buffing of boots, spit and polish – the whole long-established, well-rehearsed rigmarole of making the individual subservient to the service.[2]

* * *

I think I was disappointed, if I'm honest, that his war was spent as a policeman: somehow the romance of that blue uniform conjures the 'Few' or the night-after-night operations over Germany by Bomber Command; not simply being a copper. I took no pride in what Jack may have done, and for his part, he never uttered one word, proud or otherwise about his police service. When I first set out to unravel his secret war history, it was mostly concerned with ascertaining the date when he returned. It was only over time that I realised the particular kind of challenge that long periods of wartime exile meant to men like Jack, the disruption to people's lives. There was so much he never told me, so much I never asked. What was he obliged to face, and what did the RAF do to him? Did he volunteer, or was he conscripted? When did he go overseas? How long was he away? (Crucial one, that one!) What did he do? Did he get leave? Did he write to my mother? How often? Was he frightened of losing her? And could I prove that he was my father, or merely the man who brought me up?

The Knott Family
before the war. (*Author*)

I have two photographs of him in front of me: the first is dated 1934. He is twenty-one. His face is unlined, his hair swept back from a high forehead, and his moustache trimmed neatly. He is smartly dressed with a sharp knot in his tie, a double-breasted suit, and cuffs revealing enough shirtsleeve to draw attention to his snazzy cufflinks. He looks like a young Clark Gable. The second photograph was taken perhaps seven years later. It is a family group – my parents with their firstborn son, Peter. My mother, Greta, looks levelly at the box camera, while my brother stares into the distance, his father's hand against his knee. Jack is smoking anxiously, his face lined and careworn.

Setting out on a search for someone's life story, you wonder just where to begin. What evidence exists? Is there anyone from his war years who would remember him? How many are still alive? Once, in his suburban garden, while I attacked the weeds and he leant on the rake, Jack had mentioned two names – men with whom he had shared the same billet. In that frustrating way of his, he immediately changed the subject, opting for the safety of complaining about prices in the Co-op, or muttering about whether it was worth having another MOT for his aged and rusty car. Later, when I was alone, I wrote the two names down. I suppose that was the moment when the search began.

But where do you begin when the evidence is so thin? All I had at that stage were the names of my father's two old comrades. Thankfully, one of them had a surname sufficiently unusual to search online and that took me to a far corner of East Yorkshire. Goole is a small town of the kind you don't visit without a reason. It has docks – spidery cranes over a tidal river – and a lingering Dutch influence in some of the buildings, the legacy of those pioneers who drained the local floodplain. My father-in-law had 'bombed' it, he told me, on a wartime training exercise, since Goole, with its serpentine river bends, is instantly recognisable from the air, and good practice for the real thing over Germany. It proved, however, to be a dead end so far as evidence was concerned. One of Jack's wartime friends had once lived in the empty shop that I tracked down in a bleak, treeless street, but it was far too late. I should have brought Jack here twenty years before.

With no witnesses available, I drove to Topcliffe near the North York Moors, Jack's first posting, making the trip in the same month as he had, albeit some seven decades later. I tried to see it through his eyes and realised that it would have felt quite alien, though a world far more remote was waiting. The sense of space would have unsettled him, although he liked landscape, particularly high hills and rugged coastline. I was driving through wintry weather, lingering overnight frost and whirling, tumbling leaves. The trees were wind-twisted and the landscape held little but moorland, stone walls, and occasionally, thick-set, stolid Yorkshire farmhouses. I drove to Thirsk railway station, judging that he came by train: it would not have stayed in his memory – mainline tracks, a road bridge, dowdy platforms. I imagined him, kitbag on his shoulder, stepping out into a cold winter's night from the railway carriage, steam swirling in the darkness; the sound of voices further along the platform barking orders, and the clatter of military boots against stone.

A few aircraft – single-engined trainers – rose and fell, practising circuits and bumps. One closed in on me, aiming down the line of the road, its landing lights on. The pilot banked and looked down, before turning away towards the moors. I considered myself conclusively strafed. I drove past the barracks, stopped the car and contemplated the cluster of red brick buildings. High hills, big skies and a cold northern light: Jack would have felt this was a foreign country. I felt huge regret too: why had I never brought him back here? That might have opened him up to the past. One thing was certain – unexpected too. I realised I missed him, irrespective of whether he was my father or not.

Chapter 4

Aliens in an Incalculable Land

> My dearest Jock,
> Things here are what you might call in a rather volcanic state – and one has the unpleasant feeling of being aliens in an incalculable land. One brother in each camp is the policy of most families. The present government is generally considered in German pay …
>   Meanwhile, I must say I wish I were fighting instead of doing propaganda, which feels like uninterrupted contact with pitch.[1]

Freya Stark to John Grey Murray, Baghdad, 14 April 1941

Jack's wartime fate was sealed more or less in the year he was born. Shortly before the start of the Great War, the British elected to switch from coal to oil to fuel its battleships. From that moment, supplies of oil were vital and the strategic importance of the Middle East confirmed.[2] The fear of 'oil starvation' prompted the British Government to buy 51 per cent of the Anglo-Persian Oil Company and thereafter Britain was locked into an unhealthy reliance on Iraq and Iran, as well as the wider region; hence the importance of Freya Stark's wartime work in Aden, Cairo, and later, Baghdad.[3] Oil also changed my father's life forever, since he and tens of thousands of men like him were needed to protect those distant oilfields and pipelines. Between the wars, oil was invariably squabbled over, both amongst politicians and oilmen themselves: 'Oilmen are like cats,' one observer noted, 'you can never tell from the sound of them whether they are fighting or making love.'[4] Politicians could be just as feral. Once the Second World War began, and particularly once the Italians had entered the conflict, it was clear that maintaining the flow of oil was a critical factor in achieving a final victory.

Iraq was a young country: Jack was only six years older than the country he was sent to protect, while for Freya, Iraq was 'unique in being a kingdom imagined, fashioned and established by an alien race'.[5] The British had seized Baghdad from the Turks in 1917, and at the 1921 Cairo Conference it was decided that the RAF should garrison Iraq. Churchill had been Colonial Secretary at the time; nearly two decades later, he wrote to General Wavell (on 4 May 1940) insisting on Iraq's strategic importance: 'A commitment in Iraq was inevitable. We had to establish a base at Basra, and control that port to safeguard Persian oil in case of need.'[6] Interestingly, Churchill had received £5,000 from 'Shell and Burmah Oil ... to lobby for their purchase of the Government's controlling stake in the Anglo-Persian Oil Company.'[7] At all events, Iraq had long been a trouble spot, with British planes regularly patrolling the skies, and dropping bombs to quell local unrest. Such action had implications for the way Iraqis viewed the Royal Air Force. Indeed there was a legacy of mutual distrust that went beyond the fear of British bombers: in 1929, Freya met an Iraqi woman who 'rather pathetically' said, 'We should so much like to be allowed to love the English, if they did not always make us feel they were snubbing us.'[8]

On 8 April 1941, Freya Stark noted that the head of a girls' school in Baghdad had asked for the examinations to be held two months early, in the hope that they would be completed before the Germans arrived. The heat in the city was unforgiving: 122 degrees in the shade and only dropping to 101 degrees at night. Moreover, the country was a hotbed of rumour and uncertainty, with the German influence evident and growing. Soon after, oilmen at Iraqi oilfields found themselves placed under arrest. Wellington Dix, the Yorkshireman in charge of the refinery at Kanaqin, woke to find the barrel of a gun pressed against his throat. Confined to the main room of the town's principal coffee shop, it was all 'frightfully British', Dix wrote later, with Iraqi soldiers offering him tea and cigarettes. The politeness, however, was cosmetic, typified by the Iraqi who murmured, 'I am looking forward to the privilege of personally cutting your throat, sir.'[9]

At the end of April, a group of Iraqi rebels appeared on a scarp some 200 feet above the RAF base at Habbaniya, north-west of Baghdad. Troops could be seen moving on the hill; trenches were being dug and machine-gun emplacements set up nearby.[10] Early one morning, an Iraqi officer appeared at the camp's main gate demanding that all flying and armoured car movements should cease. Failure to comply would mean shelling from the rebel position in the hills. British resources were limited: some sixty-four aeroplanes – obsolete and painfully slow trainers – and fewer than forty pilots, but orders from London were unequivocal: Habbaniya must be defended to the last man. A further cable from Churchill followed: 'If you have to strike, strike hard.' Over the ensuing five days, the RAF flew 647 operations and dropped 3,000 bombs, flying in antiquated aircraft, long past their combat years. The rebel leader, Rashid Ali, was left isolated, the anticipated German assistance never appeared, and so Habbaniya remained in British hands, waiting to welcome my father's reluctant arrival a year or so later.

* * *

At dawn on Sunday, 4 May 1941, a Wellington bomber flew slowly over Baghdad. Freya Stark thought it a beautiful sight, the aircraft 'slowly sailing along at about 1,000 feet, up the river from south to north, very dark against the green sky and the sleeping houses.'[11] Throughout that month, the British Embassy was besieged, surrounded by Iraqi police, and cut off from any communication with the RAF base at Habbaniya. Freya heard gunfire – it drowned the sound of doves cooing – and watched the skies anxiously. She saw her first Messerschmitt of the war, predatory and ominous; it was on the tails of two RAF aircraft in the thin white cloud. Buckets of sand were distributed around the embassy, in anticipation of bombs, and the Iraqis threatened to cut British throats in the compound if the RAF bombed the city.

The British Embassy stood on the west bank of the river Tigris within 2 acres of carefully tended lawn and garden. Palm trees provided welcome and necessary shade. Since the rebellion, the imposing western gate was barricaded, with lines of cars and barbed wire between the gate and the sweeping gravel drive. The river was flooded, full of melted snow from the mountains to the north. As the situation deteriorated, the order was given to start burning the official archives, the compromising memoranda, top-secret correspondence and sensitive briefing papers. Bundles of files were brought into the open and fed to the flames, the blackening paper stirred by sweating men with long rakes.

The last person to enter the sanctuary of the embassy compound before the gates were barricaded had been Freya Stark. She had, with the greatest difficulty, re-entered Iraq from Persia, arriving on the sleeper train, which rolled into Baghdad at dawn. The streets were unnaturally quiet and the policemen at the station looked grim when she said she intended to go to the embassy. She was advised not to go there by three or four police who spoke in an ominous, threatening tone. Hearing the postern gate to the embassy shut behind her, Freya walked past the bonfires, the sandbags and barbed wire, and wondered what lay ahead.

* * *

> I think the simplest thing would be to get conveniently incapacitated, come home and ignore the war.[12]

Keith Douglas to Jean Turner, undated (1941?)

While the Baghdad embassy was under siege, both Cecil Beaton and Noël Coward were in England. On returning from New Zealand early in 1941, Coward had expected to be involved in clandestine operations, courtesy of Bill Stephenson, work that would make a real contribution to the war effort. He had been briefed in New York and Washington and was hugely disappointed when, without explanation, the plan was abandoned. He was in Bermuda when 'a greater power than we could contradict had thwarted our intents' – an unholy alliance of Beaverbrook and the Prime Minister, he believed. 'God, what enemies I must have,' he confided in his diary.[13] His return to England was a dispiriting affair: the press hounded him, relentlessly seeking to raise doubts about the motives behind his overseas travels. On one occasion he was snubbed by the Foreign Secretary, Anthony Eden, in the Carlton Grill: 'A foolish mistake on his part,' Noël wrote, 'although perfectly consistent with his career.' Then, on 16 April, Coward's house was damaged in an air raid, its skylights blown in. It necessitated abandoning the house for a while, although the shock was eased somewhat when, in the immediate aftermath of the attack, Coward overheard two women chatting as they picked their way through the littered debris of bricks and twisted pipework in the street outside: 'You know, dear, the trouble with all this

is you could rick your ankle.'[14] Despite everything, Coward could see the
funny side of it all.[15] Nonetheless, it was a grim time: his house in Kent,
Goldenhurst, sequestered by the Army; his London home uninhabitable,
and financial worries worsening. He was relieved to leave London in early
summer, staying in Portmeirion in North Wales, where, in less than a week,
he wrote *Blithe Spirit*. The play had its first night in Manchester on 16 June
and opened in London two weeks later. It was to run for 1,997 performances.

While Coward was temporarily drawn back into something more
resembling his old life, Cecil Beaton was still struggling to find a wartime
role that would keep his guilt at bay, but wasn't ordinary soldiering of the
kind that my father was obliged to pursue. Through much of 1941 Cecil
was travelling the country, an exhausting round of visits to hospitals and
rehabilitation centres – in Torquay; visiting Wrens in Portsmouth; spending
time with the Navy in Harwich and the Army on tank duty on Salisbury
Plain. He consoled himself with the fact that at least he was no longer taking
the kind of photographs that involved 'posing people round apple blossom'
– he was disenchanted with such work; instead he was employed by the
Ministry of Information, taking photographs of the war, an occupation that
provided him with 'opportunities to storm what were previously to me the
unknown citadels of the Royal Air Force'.[16] He poured his energies into a
book, *Winged Squadrons*, which drew on his RAF experiences and combined
some of his photographs with text derived from his diary. It was 'a fictional
composition, written for propaganda'. He saw it as a chance to ease his pangs
of guilt about what he saw as his uncertain contribution to the war effort.

Cecil became increasingly fascinated with the war in the air and the lives
of the men obliged to fly in it. He visited a string of RAF stations – some two
dozen – Tangmere, Lossiemouth and Mildenhall among others. At Biggin
Hill he was taken up in a Spitfire to photograph from the air. The period at
RAF Mildenhall was particularly gloomy; it was a bomber station in Suffolk,
and his time there left him stricken with guilt because of what the crews
were facing on a nightly basis. It all provided the raw material for *Winged
Squadrons*, which he worked on throughout 1941. He was acutely conscious
of the dangers the airmen faced. His camera devoured this new, unsettling
world: airmen relaxing before flying on operations, reading a book in front
of a fire; a rear gunner staring out from his perspex canopy; the gaunt faces

The pilot and co-pilot of a Wellington bomber photographed by Cecil Beaton, probably at RAF Mildenhall in 1941. (*Imperial War Museum, D4737*)

at the post-operation debrief at dawn; aircrew dwarfed by the brooding aircraft in the darkness; an airman's boot poised on the ladder leading up to the bomber's belly; the packing of parachutes; men weighed down with kit; the dingy huts with corrugated iron roofs; ground crew leaning over sleek, fat bombs. At the de Havilland Aerodrome and Training School he was asked when his photographs would eventually appear, and when he replied that they were expected in about six weeks' time, he was told, 'Oh, most of us will be dead by then!'[17] He spent time with a bomber crew at RAF

Mildenhall, renaming the nineteen-year-old pilot 'Robert Tring' to preserve his anonymity. He spent a long night waiting for him to return with his crew from a raid on the Ruhr in Germany. He was the last to return safely. One 'gaunt, ghostlike youth' who landed before Tring muttered to Cecil: 'I thought those photographs you took of us, Beaton, were going to be our memorial.'[18]

By the middle of 1941, Noël Coward was also involved in a kind of propaganda exercise, in his case, the making of a film, *In Which We Serve*, which told the story of a Royal Navy destroyer during the battle for Crete. He spent time with the Navy at Scapa Flow in Scotland in mid-August 1941, and increasingly was convinced that he had been right not to return to America. He felt sorry for those actors who had remained in Hollywood and not returned to the UK: they were missing, he thought, an 'indescribable' experience.

Coward and Beaton met up by chance in January 1942, shortly before filming started. Cecil arrived at Denham railway station, near the film studios, at the end of a gloomy, wintry day. 'Wet feet – cold feet all day long – in the snow and railway carriages going to and from a Ministry of Information job.' It was bitterly cold and dark and no one was there to meet him. He blundered through the snow 'waving a lantern in an endeavour to find a telephone box, like Lear on the heath.' Later he thawed out in front of a roaring fire, clutching a cocktail and melting the long-established ice between Noël and himself. Coward congratulated him on doing a great job, earning respect and 'sticking to your guns', comparing it unfavourably with his own wartime efforts: where once he would have reflected that his action in giving up two plays when war broke out was commendable, he now realised that he had gone on to do a job that anyone could have done. He and Cecil ended the night as 'staunch buddies' and Beaton, for one, nursed a hangover next morning as the London train clattered through the frozen Buckinghamshire countryside.[19]

Medical student Donald Macdonald, meanwhile, was yet to be drawn into the war, or indeed go beyond the borders of Scotland. Some mornings he would walk into lectures through Glasgow streets littered with broken glass and rubble, the result of the Clydebank Blitz. He was a less than enthusiastic student, such motivation as he had arising partly from the fact that continued study kept both enlistment and his dour and demanding father at bay. It was five and a half years of 'horrid grind' nonetheless, with the study of anatomy, for example, offering, 'no philosophical divagation but [only] a precise knowledge of things like nerve pathways and the intricate structure of the renal glomerulus'. He became, in his own words, 'a very earnest, reclusive young man for the next few years', buried in a 'scholastic hermitage' where he would occasionally reflect on his continuing virginity.

How different were people's lives despite the war's omnipresence: Noël resuming a semblance of a pre-war existence; Cecil's camera focusing on airmen's lives; Donald carrying heavy text books through the university's cloisters; Jack counting the days till his next leave and a brief escape into the world beyond RAF Leighton Buzzard's perimeter wire; and Tom Davies at sea, bound once again for Buenos Aires and Montevideo.

* * *

Meanwhile, they are tampering with telephones – the palace ones are cut and neither the RAF nor embassy get contacted except with difficulty – and yesterday it thundered and lightened, so wireless was interrupted.[20]

Freya Stark to Hon. Mrs Hore-Ruthven, Baghdad, 6 April 1941

The siege of the Baghdad embassy continued through May 1941. Occasionally, Wellington bombers flew over the city, a threat or a reassurance depending whether you were inside the embassy grounds or outside. Once, a flight of three Wellingtons in tight formation bombed the area near the railway station; when a group of Iraqi policemen aimed rifles at the disappearing aircraft, Freya pointed out that it was ridiculous to think they could hit targets so far away. They lowered their rifles, with 'shattering docility'.[21] She never doubted that the siege would be lifted, since 'our neighbourhood to Oil will prevent us from being forgotten,'[22] and indeed, not long after the RAF base at Habbaniya had been secured, a contingent of troops reached the outskirts of the city, having made its way across the desert from Haifa.

In time, British officers arrived at the embassy's perimeter gate, dust sent spiralling by their sand-caked transport. They made their way into the building, past the fountain playing in the hall, conscious of the uncanny resemblance to an English country house. They climbed an old-fashioned staircase and walked along a corridor, all dark wood, shadows and gilded picture frames, before entering the Ambassador's room. Sir Kinahan Cornwallis was reclining in bed and sporting a blue cummerbund round his waist. He sat up, asked for half an hour to allow him time to dress, and offered them tea in the canteen. Later, wearing a white topee and drill suit, he was driven around the city, every inch the stern figurehead, 'a man rude to look upon, but apparently forged from one of those incredible metals with a melting point of thousands of degrees. So he could remain for months hotter than other men's white-heat, and yet look cold and hard.'[23] His face a mask of imperial froideur, he looked out at 'all the colourful pageantry of an eastern city – tarbushes, keffiyehs, turbans, robes of every colour; donkeys, mules; and many more soldiers'.[24] The faces of the Iraqis who spat in the road as the car passed, however, were unforgiving.

The embassy siege might have been lifted but the mood in Baghdad more generally remained volatile, not least for its Jewish population. There had been Foreign Office concern about their safety before the war and that anxiety was to prove prophetic: throats were cut; buildings set alight; windows shattered; and scores ruthlessly settled.[25] Some 700 Jews were murdered and there was criticism of the British for not doing more to stem the bloodshed; indeed, there were those who believed that Cornwallis had deliberately chosen 'to hold back the troops'.[26] Baghdad's narrow streets at night felt deeply threatening: 'Did I tell you,' Freya wrote in a letter, 'that the blackout here had to be stopped because everyone knifed everyone else in the dark?'[27] Moreover, danger was not just confined to the hours after sunset. Assassination became so commonplace that a British embassy official, expecting a lunch guest and receiving the grim news on the telephone of their murder, merely remarked, 'I suppose we needn't wait lunch any longer.'

* * *

Iraq is still like a volcano with a rather thin crust – the explosion however more likely from outside than in.[28]

Freya Stark to Captain Oliver Lyttelton, Baghdad, 28 July 1941

Freya's work in Baghdad was modelled on a method she had successfully adopted in Egypt; the formulation of propaganda by groups – 'brotherhoods' – of local people. In Cairo, the numbers of the pro-British Brotherhood of Freedom were continuing to rise, a fact that had gratified Freya when she visited the city in June 1941 and lifted her spirits as she drove back across the desert from the Egyptian capital to Baghdad, in a tiny Standard 8, following the oil pipeline from camp to camp, sitting forward on the edge of her seat so she could see over the car's sand-streaked bonnet. She believed herself to be the first Englishwoman to pass that way since the fighting. She stayed a night at Habbaniya before finally driving on to Baghdad. There the heat was unpleasant enough to encourage her to sleep at night on the roof, where in the early hours the air was cool. Later that year, her health began to suffer, sufficiently at one point for her to stay in a sanatorium on Mount Carmel; while, on another occasion, she succumbed to a bout of sandfly fever, something she regarded as both depressing and difficult to recover from.

Compared to some, my father Jack was an intrepid traveller, thinking nothing of driving through the night to Portugal or Austria in the post-war years. But his love of the road was of a different order to Freya Stark's, who always assumed that any journey was possible, and a God-given right. Perhaps that difference reflected their disparate backgrounds: hers – exotic, cosmopolitan, comfortable; Jack's – urban, grey, short-lived, and narrow; Freya brought up in an artist's sprawling house near Dartmoor, its grounds thick with rhododendrons; and my orphaned father from his Black Country two-up, two-down, with its weedy yard and outside privy. She regarded the wider world as hers to explore; he, though, would have chosen to see the war out in gloomy boredom in some obscure RAF station in the English Home Counties. That was all to change in 1942 when Jack was posted to the Middle East.

Did their paths ever cross? It's certainly possible. Was he perhaps part of her police protection on one of the occasions when she passed through Habbaniya? One thing is certain: Freya understood exactly why she was in Arabia, writing in her diary towards the end of March 1942 that 'Hitler must make for oil or die.'[29] Jack was not a man to keep a diary, or care about the bigger picture. He was there simply because his luck had run out and some miserable bugger behind a comfortable desk had decided that Jack Knott's war would not be complete without taking in some years in the desert sun, and before that, a long sea voyage around the Cape of Good Hope.

Chapter 5

Sea, Sea and More Sea

> Well, my love, I am touching wood when I say this, but we have been lucky in more ways than one on the voyage. We have got so far without any excitement – one or two alarms though, nothing more, and the weather ever since we left home has been remarkably good. It blew a little for a day or two just after leaving, but nothing to be concerned about, and since leaving the last port it has been really delightful at sea, with very pleasant warm days and cool nights.

Tommy Davies to Dorrie, at sea, on board *Almanzora*, 23 April 1942

Ten days or so out from England, the weather had turned hot enough for the officers aboard *Almanzora*, Tommy Davies among them, to dispense with cold weather gear and instead go into 'scanty panties'. Tom's ship was part of WS (Winston Special) 17, one of many wartime convoys shipping troops to the east, in this case India. Cecil Beaton was part of the same convoy, having been 'loaned by the Ministry of Information, for a period of three months, to the Air Ministry'. It was the end of March 1942 when convoy WS17 left Glasgow, although the time and place of departure were deemed 'most secret' and Beaton's luggage, in common with others, had a coded destination label. He shared a cabin with Gordon Young, a *Daily Express* reporter heading for Cairo; a Cable & Wireless technician; and a Battle of Britain ace with a Distinguished Flying Cross. The voyage was to prove challenging since 'the lavatories stank, the water taps only worked for an hour a day, the heat was stifling and the food inedible.'[1] Initially, Cecil was absorbed in the intricacies of life aboard the ship; he drew, and as time passed, he observed how the colour of both the sky and the ocean changed. 'The Bay of Sierra Leone,' he noted for example, 'was bathed in a mauve steam.'[2]

On reaching Freetown, Tommy Davies was able to post a letter home before continuing south. Beaton and Gordon Young, looking out at the waters of Sierra Leone Bay, anticipated a measure of preferential treatment, a transfer on to a flight to Cairo. The signs, however, were not good: they found themselves transferred, but only to another ship, the *Altmark* 'of 3,000 tons with an alarming list and a good deal of unfavourable vanguard publicity'. Cecil was warned that his troubles were only just beginning; that without influential politicians to help him, and being on a different ship, he was now on his own: 'You're among men now.'[3] *Altmark* had seen better days and was infested with cockroaches, flies, ants and bugs, and

Dorrie Davies and baby Angela, March 1935.
(*Angela Awbery White*)

the captain was 'an embittered, cinder-faced man, with the parched skin of a lizard, and hangdog eyes'. The ship was blisteringly hot, overcrowded and stinking (of sweat and diesel); there was no toilet paper in the primitive lavatories; the air had a funereal stuffiness to it; waiters dribbled beads of sweat into the soup; the glasses went unwashed; and attempts to get something to drink involved long chaotic queuing in unbearable temperatures: 'What's the use of sweating a quart in order to drink a pint?'[4] It was with immense relief that, after days of incarceration in this grim hulk, Beaton and Young eventually managed to secure an escape by air. They would soon be in Egypt.

Almanzora meanwhile was already well to the south and on 23 April Tommy reported that they were 'nearing port and soon I shall be able to mail this letter to you.' It had become increasingly hot, 'with everything shut up, [and] the rooms and decks ... like ovens.' He also warned Dorrie that he 'must not say anything about our comings and goings – even if we knew anything about them – which I certainly don't!' In fact, part of the convoy was involved with Operation Ironclad, whose purpose was to attack and hold the Vichy French base at Diego Suarez at the northern tip of Madagascar and thereby prevent a possible Japanese landing. The 5th Infantry Division was a key part of the convoy. Another two weeks or so and Tommy hoped 'soon to have my nose pointing the right way', homeward bound after 'a very trying voyage', but it would take until mid-July before *Almanzora* returned to home waters.

* * *

TRAVEL WARRANT

The Directors of the Railway Company or Steamship Company concerned are hereby requested to provide conveyance for one airman by the recognised direct route to Liverpool.

Airman number: 1162335
Surname: Knott
Initial: J.

 the

The next Winston Special – WS18 – sails at noon on Wednesday, 15 April 1942. My father is just one airman of many on board the Union Castle liner *Capetown Castle* in a convoy transporting some 40,000 soon-to-be exiles. Leaning on the ship's starboard rail, Jack looks inconsolable. In two days' time, he will be twenty-eight, but just now his mind is darkened by the memory of the unsatisfactory goodbye of a few days earlier, when the prospect of leaving his wife and son for an unknown destination, and for an undisclosed length of time, proved too much to bear. To make it worse, he has not been able to go ashore to phone or to post a letter, both strictly forbidden. With the ship now under way, he watches Liverpool slide past, its cranes leaning over the river, the tanks on the quayside destined for desert action, the smoke-blackened churches, railway bridges, and back-to-backs – then sand dunes, and finally, glistening mudflats as the river opens up to the sea. Faintly, he can see smoke

Jack in February 1942, two months before his posting. He is sitting on the right – and looking anxious. (*Author*)

still rising from the previous night's air raid. Beyond the river's reach, there are the beginnings of a sea swell, enough to make men look at each other and grimace at the prospect of the seasickness to come.[5]

The ship closed in around him, dark below decks and smelling of oil, steam and bodies. There were pools of slimy water everywhere. Jack's billet was at the stern of the boat, too far from daylight, and as he was to discover, such a position was liable to exaggerate the natural movement of this large (27,000 ton) ship. He shared the space with another forty men and he anxiously tried to find a spot where his near neighbours would leave him alone. He found what he hoped would be a quiet corner, close to some warm steam pipes, dropped his kitbag, and tried to find his way back to the main deck. Around him there was a barrage of shouting: orders, jokes and curses as these landsmen tripped over coiled ropes, buckets of sand, and the labyrinth of pipes that cluttered the ship's decks. Now they were out at sea, the world was grey: ocean, distant ships, the Royal Navy's escorting destroyers at the edge of the horizon, smokestacks just visible; even the clouds had gathered to hide the sun. The *Capetown Castle* headed west at 13 knots, rendezvousing the next day with a contingent of ships from the Clyde. The two destroyers eventually turned for home, while WS18 ploughed on, taking the less usual route through the Azores.

Conditions on the convoys were invariably unpleasant. Three months before, in early January 1942, an important and trusted former member of Churchill's staff in 10 Downing Street, John (Jock) Colville, had sailed in WS14. The overcrowding was desperate, he told the Prime Minister, 'nearly 300 men had to sling their hammocks in a hold which could have held 50 comfortably.'[6] It was a common complaint: the Royal Artillery's Gunner John 'Syd' Croft on WS3, for example, complained of the cramped conditions he had to endure, made worse by the 'fact that we were sleeping in uncomfortable hammocks which insisted on swinging with the movement of the ship.'[7] Officers, according to Colville, were more fortunate – 'using up a great deal of space and living the lives of first class passengers in a peacetime luxury liner.' On Croft's ship, 80 per cent of the men were seasick. Food for most was in short supply and so too were washing facilities; drinking water was rationed and tasted of lime. 'The heat in the cabin is incredible,' wrote the poet Keith Douglas in 1941 on his way to the Middle East. 'There are no portholes and the apparatus for pumping air is quite inadequate.'[8] Jock Colville noted that men were desperate to return home, but their impatience and complaints were largely disregarded. Conditions, he averred, closely resembled 'the living quarters in the *Victory*'.[9] He professed himself ready to 'take to drink' after seeing the ship's accommodation. It was, he wrote, 'horrifying: we live between decks, messing eighteen at the tables which might hold twelve comfortably.' In September 1941, the shocking conditions had been enough to provoke an 'incipient mutiny' at Halifax, Nova Scotia, when nearly 300 airmen had refused to board the troopship *Empress of Asia*. They had walked off the ship, and resisting all attempts to force them back aboard, watched the steamer leave for Liverpool. Some simply jumped overboard. They were all reduced in rank and forced to sail at a later date. The novelist Evelyn Waugh, who sailed to West Africa in May 1941, was amused by a scrawl on a troop deck wall, 'Never before in the history of human endeavour have so few been buggered about by so many.'[10]

On board, there was nothing to lift the spirits: airmen slept on hammocks strung above the mess tables, so close they almost touched. There was 'no difference between this and a refrigerator ship except that in the latter the corpses are hung vertically.'[11] Even the Secretary of State for Air admitted that 'it takes ten or fifteen minutes for them to get out of the cabin.'[12] Darkness and low ceilings fostered a sense of claustrophobia. On a previous sailing of the *Capetown Castle* an airman called Black had removed his boots and socks, climbed over the ship's rail, dived into the sea and began to swim in the direction of the land he had been forced to leave. There were desperate shouts of 'Man Overboard!' but the ship ploughed on, its captain resolute. Cockroaches flourished; men were spectacularly seasick; Colville himself suffered physically and mentally: from constipation, and from resentment at the preferential treatment meted out to officers. Like my father, he was 'Other Ranks'. The days went by in a series of drab rituals: breakfast at seven; lining up by the muster stations at ten; lunch at noon; a shave in the late afternoon; tea at six and lights out at nine-thirty. Colville read (Dickens and Scott) and played poker for low stakes. Not everyone was so cautious: 'Men lost the shirts off their backs,' my father once told me in a rare revelatory moment. Sweepstakes were run on the number of miles sailed in a day; there were games of deck tennis, bouts of boxing, tug-of-war competitions and lectures on the dangers of VD. In the more southerly latitudes, the sticky heat drove men on deck to sleep; out came the topis to ward off the sun, and lime juice and quinine.

For WS18, the weather was unexceptional and the days passed in military tedium: weapons training, PT and lectures. Aboard the *Empress of Canada*, 2nd Lieutenant Jack Hawkins devised a broadcast concert party – good practice this for his later flurry of war films. On the 28th, the convoy was spotted by pilots of some Sunderland flying boats patrolling out of Freetown, where the heat was relentless and dispiriting, the view from the ship a canvas of vivid green wooded hills and steamy mists. Africans in small boats offered up fruit to the crimson-faced white men high above them. For Syd Croft this was his 'first view of native life', although he was unable to 'disclose the name of the port'. The troops were offered 'bananas, oranges, limes, coconuts, an occasional monkey, and some imitation highly-coloured silks with the label "Made in Japan" foolishly left on'.

On Jack's ship there was a rapid death from meningitis, the soldier-victim there one day and gone the next, as if he never was. It was a first taste for many of how war could simply erase in a moment the man in the next hammock. The convoy continued to trend south, with little to see but vast expanses of ocean, any novelty provided by cold trade winds, flying fish, porpoises and, once, an albatross. 'It's a question,' wrote one soldier, 'of sea, more sea, and yet more sea.'[13] Approaching Cape Town, two ships hit mines and were lost, and then, a month or so after leaving England, after dire warnings about nests of spies in South Africa, the *Capetown Castle* docked at Durban. The men on board were warned not to take cameras ashore; to refuse drinks from the locals; to refrain from discussing politics; and not to talk to the 'natives'.

It was 17 May 1942, and Jack was well on his way to the desert and the deadest of dead ends.

* * *

After Durban, some ships of WS18 sailed for India, while 'the remaining 19,163 [men] were now destined for the Middle East comprising various workshop units and 18,000 in drafts [8,600 RAF, 7,500 Army and 1,900

Navy].'[14] Jack and *Capetown Castle* went their separate ways, five weeks after leaving Liverpool in each other's company. He would have been glad of the change of scene, even if the prevailing prospect remained one of blue-grey ocean and grey-blue sky; the same numbing monotony; the grudging restrictions on food and water. The need to eke out supplies through a voyage was a perennial issue: Evelyn Waugh, towards the end of his voyage in October 1940, told his wife: 'We have been in this ship so long that we have drunk all the wine and smoked all the cigars and eaten most of the food.'[15] For 'Other Ranks' Jack, conditions would have been far worse: after all, wine and cigars weren't for the likes of him. He was a bottle of Bass and a packet of fags. After so many indistinguishable days, Waugh, my dad and thousands of others would have been 'rather tired of one another's company'.

Landfall was Basra in southern Iraq. The port, 'a hateful place … festers along the banks of the Shatt-el-Arab River and the prevailing colour of this flat unlovely landscape is lifeless grey.'[16] It was some compensation that this was merely a stop on the way to somewhere else, but there was nothing to lift the spirits. Jack's shirt was drenched with sweat and his head gleamed with hair oil and reflected light. Typically, he had spurned his tropical sunhat – too heavy, and anyway, he felt foolish in it – with no thought of what that fierce sun might do to his scalp in later life. He looked out over a landscape devoid of hills and starved of colour; an unchecked sprawl of low buildings, robotic cranes and derricks, morose men on the dockside leaning against bales of this, boxes of that. There were stores of weapons and ammunition; vehicles, spare parts, barrels and sacks – all waiting to be moved on to somewhere even more remote and godforsaken.

It took time to get the ship tucked against the wharf and its ropes tied up. With the end of forward motion, there was now no hint of wind and the heat took Jack's breath away. The temperature was 110 degrees. Jack was not to know it yet, but it would get worse. Freya Stark noted that the summer temperatures – at 127 degrees in the shade – were hotter than usual, while the nights were hot too, and the sand flies voracious. 'Everyone looked thin and pale and most people were cross.'[17] Jack was someone who was never blessed with a placid temperament, and throughout his exile, he would have seethed for England. Angrily he threw his damp cigarette into the oil-streaked water and watched it disintegrate, then wiped the sweat from his eyes with a grubby handkerchief before preening his ginger moustache, this way and that, as if to soothe its whiskery ill-temper.

The gangplank swayed as the men, canvas bags over their shoulders, heavy-booted their way on to dry land, kicking up dust and sand. Dockside workers watched them with an air of disdain. Jack looked miserably back, so far from home now that he didn't care much where he was or where he might be sent next. Soon he was on the move again, embarking on a smaller troopship, which steamed slowly south through the Persian Gulf, the brooding shore of Africa to the west, the mountains of southern Persia to port, thirsty, brown slopes sweeping down to the sea, and beyond, higher, jagged peaks stretched far into the distant east. By now Jack was sure that this was not going to end well, that smiling British faces would be in short supply for the foreseeable future.

Chapter 6

Smile – You Are in Sharjah

The German radio announced that their armies would be in Alexandria on the 6th and in Cairo by the 9th. The front lines are so near that the journalists go up to the battle for the day.[1]

Cecil Beaton's diary, 28 June 1942, Cairo

I can imagine all too clearly the process by which my father was posted to the Middle East, the moment when some anonymous man at a desk in London scribbled a note on an office pad, or perhaps two humourless, middle-ranking civil servants colluded in a meandering telephone conversation that determined that <u>this</u> group of men must go <u>there</u>. Such decisions in wartime do not get taken with much thought for the well-being of ordinary service personnel. For those who were 'someone', however, it was very different: in Cecil Beaton's case, for example, the conversation about where the photographer might be sent took place between Randolph Churchill and the Minister of Information, Brendan Bracken, and it was the Prime Minister's son – of whom Noël Coward said, 'I am so very fond of Randolph: he is so unspoiled by failure!'[2] – who arranged that Cecil should travel to Cairo. The photographer duly left for Egypt at the end of March 1942, a fortnight or so before Jack was to follow the same sea lane southwards.

Cecil found it 'very strange being in a neutral country again. So much food and thousands at the races.'[3] If Beaton held any lingering doubts as to why he was in Cairo, officials there soon dispelled them: 'We want "might" in our propaganda,' he was told when he first arrived, the implication being that, rather than snapping a photogenic aircraft in splendid isolation on a sun-baked runway, he should photograph sixty or more drawn up in ominous, serried ranks.[4] There remained the issue of his official status: shouldn't he be in uniform? Without such protection, he was at risk of being shot out of hand as a spy, but despite his Harrow School and Cambridge University background, was the chap actually, you know, officer material? In the end, the solution was a typically British compromise: a regulation uniform, but with 'RAF Official Photographer' stitched on the shoulders.

Wishing he was fifteen years younger ('a bare bullock face looks best in uniform [and] there is altogether too much going on in my face'), Cecil arrived at Cairo's Air House for eight o'clock breakfast with the Air Officer Commanding, Middle East, Air Chief Marshal Arthur Tedder. 'Shall we nibble?' Tedder inquired, looking 'like a bilious schoolboy'.[5] They breakfasted in a building that reminded Cecil of the kind of houses to be found in Godalming, but there were few other reminders of England. The heat, for one thing, was debilitating, both in Cairo itself and in the desert. Beyond the barbed wire fence that marked the city's outer limit, there was the desert landscape – shorn of features and profoundly desolate and a stark contrast with Cairo's showy tumult. 'Cairo demands too little of a man,' Cecil noted, 'and the desert too much.' For all that, he did feel 'fifteen years younger than when I left England'. He thought 'life in the desert makes everyone healthy and happy'.[6] However, he was yet to feel that the conduct of the war was tangible; instead he observed as if at a distance the conflict's almost theatrical scaffolding, the 'spade work', the maintenance, the field telephones, the digging, transport, repairs, feeding, the brewing of tea. There was no escaping, though, the harsh conditions endured by the troops, for example, 'the irregularity of the mails (and) the shortage of reading matter'. He was convinced that 'Whitehall should change their men out here every few months.'[7] The desert's cold hostility was evident in the extensive debris scattered across the sand, the one-time property of the dead or wounded, the discarded paraphernalia, the empty bottles, scuffed footwear, spent ammunition, shell cases, and perhaps most poignant of all, the flimsy, wind-blown remnants of lost letters in the sand. Correspondence in German, English and Italian blew everywhere. Sandstorms flung grit and dust into angry, spiralling confusion. It was all just plain uncomfortable, seedy and dispiriting – those squalid and unnervingly public latrines! They were a recurring nightmare for the constipated, of whom Beaton was one.

Sometimes his hosts misjudged what might warm his photographer's heart: 'My God, you're lucky, Beaton!' he was told when he was able to watch a major operation in a field hospital in Tobruk. He snapped away dutifully, only too aware of the large flies in the operating theatre. Later, though, he would consider himself 'particularly content in Tobruk, camped out there in a wadi with yellow flowering cacti'.[8] A visit to the Long Range Desert group – 'the highwaymen of the desert' – where he watched the men 'avidly reading the mail that had arrived during their long absence',[9] was more to his taste. One man laughed as 'he read aloud to his friends a letter saying: "I cannot wait until after the war, when we can get married and live together for always."'[10] Back in Cairo in early June, he found himself longing for the beauty of English summertime, tired of the city's faded colour and its stale dust. The serenity of the desert had gone and he became preoccupied with practicalities other than food, transport and his bowels; getting his photos sent back to England, for example. Eventually, at the end of May, as Jack was sweltering on a troopship in the Gulf, Cecil succeeded in getting a consignment of his work 'as large as the pyramids' put into the diplomatic bag to be sent to England.

* * *

Many new men have come straight from the UK and consequently are feeling a certain amount of strain.[11]

RAF Sharjah, 21 June 1942, Operations Record Book

Situated some 30 miles north of Dubai, RAF Sharjah was 'a forbidding place, surrounded by a salty marsh with a sandbar as the only protection from the sea. Flying in, pilots were conscious of square miles of empty desert, the sole relief being lonely camel trains crossing the wilderness from Saudi Arabia. It was bare of vegetation, remote from anything save sand and flies and the heat struck as though someone had opened a furnace door.'[12] Jack arrived there in June 1942,[13] no doubt manifesting all the telltale signs of strain, characteristic of the new arrivals from home. His jaundiced eye would soon have taken in the cluster of tents, the searing light, the aircraft runway's patina of oily, hard-packed sand, and the humidity that afflicted clothes, cigarettes and matches. But a few days and nights brought home other misfortunes: the sandstorms, the heavy night mists that bedewed everything; the flared blotches of prickly heat; and the cases of heatstroke only partially mitigated by the disconcertingly early start to the working day. Food was rudimentary – the staple monotony of bully beef, supplemented by tinned stews, seagulls' or turtles' eggs, and barracuda shark. Vegetables were in short supply and tablets were often provided as an alternative, although senior officers recognised that they were 'not a perfect substitute for green vegetables'. There were also shortages of bread, more through low-level illegal activity than anything else ('due to greed of certain personnel'). Water was precious and a preoccupation, carried by donkeys in large tins strapped to their sides. The toilets comprised oil drums – 'desert lilies' – and primitive 6-foot trenches surmounted by two wooden bars across.[14]

Accommodation for RAF personnel when they arrived there in early 1942 was initially in the Sharjah fort itself; then tents were pitched by the landing ground. Stores and equipment were offloaded from ships by barge. There were outbreaks of smallpox, and malaria was a constant threat – hence the order to permit the wearing of slacks until breakfast time. Nights could be surprisingly cold and men wrapped themselves in blankets, as indeed they did watching an evening film – its flickering light projected on to the whitewashed end wall of the fort as they sat on the petrol tins that served as cinema seats.

Later, a permanent camp of *barusti* huts was set up to replace the tented accommodation; these had fibre matting walls and allowed air to flow through. It was isolated and desolate. Supplies came by boat from Basra every three months. There was deep sand everywhere and keeping the aircraft serviceable was a major headache. The men lived in tents whose sides were open to the weather and the only substantial buildings were the brick-built messes. Dead donkeys were left in the sand when they died and the vultures gathered, sitting on the rotting carcasses.[15]

Oh, how my father would have hated it here! And not just the heat and bugs and lousy food. He liked to be at the centre of things, the focus of attention, and Sharjah felt to him like the very edge of the world. In truth, not much happened in Sharjah; 'operations' were largely confined to patrols over many miles of empty sea – anti-submarine patrols, convoy escort duty and ship spotting over the Gulf of Oman. The station's Operations Record Book (ORB) was reduced to logging what was on at the cinema – when it wasn't broken – ('*Private Affair* earned fair praise'), or the positive behaviour of the locals ('Good crowd of natives at the Arabic cinema show enthusiasm for Churchill and the Union Jack when appearing.'). There was more concern about the shifting moods of the local population, and the need for a 'strong line' in all dealings with them, than over the conduct of the war. 'Palestinian Arab personnel' could be a problem, it was felt, 'owing to their clannishness'. On 4 July there was a 'lightning strike of water coolies'. In a telling reflection of attitudes, the ORB complained about 'uppity coolies',[16] at the same time as it noted their crucial importance, since they controlled the water supply. Entertainment was minimal, and such as there was, not always straightforward: the men were advised not to swim in the creek; to keep a weather eye open for sharks; to beware of underground currents and avoid swimming in the afternoons. With those caveats, the swimming was judged good, although some found the 'waters of the Persian Gulf too hot'.[17] Other than that, men sweated, moved petrol bowsers and serviced aircraft; typewriters and teleprinters clacked; phones rang; salutes were exchanged; maps were furled and unfurled; and supplies were replenished, or not.

Decades after the war, Sharjah remained unappetising to visitors: the Sharjah creek was unwholesome, and the arbitrary sprawl of high-rise buildings 'silhouetted against the hot, white sky' gave the impression that the planners had sought 'to recreate downtown Croydon in the middle of Death Valley'.[18] At one point, drivers passed 'a rusting sign peppered with bullet holes [that] said, 'Smile, You Are in Sharjah'. I cannot imagine Jack smiling much during the war, and certainly not in Sharjah. The expectation was that 'personnel were rotated there two weekly because of conditions',[19] but my father was there for a year. I imagine him, his mood declining through every one of those fifty-two hot, tedious weeks. I find it harder to picture what he wrote to my mother and I certainly cannot see him making much effort to cheer her up. Easier to see him essaying a morose breaststroke in the Gulf, a melancholy eye alert to the possibility of lurking sharks and fretting why he had not heard from home. Why did the mail from England take so long to come? So slow was it that postings away from the base moved faster than post: 'Quantity of sea mail arrived,' the ORB noted, but it 'took such time to reach Sharjah that many of the recipients had been posted.'

* * *

So this was escape! I suppose I am the first of the rats, but I prefer to think of myself as fortunate in having finished my contract perhaps just in the nick of time.[20]

Cecil Beaton's diary, 2 July 1942

While Jack was beginning his exile in Sharjah, Cecil was contemplating moving on from Cairo. He was well aware of his privileged position as a visitor to the region, and despite the discomfort and the expectations placed upon him, his time in the Middle East was temporary. At the beginning of June 1942, he left Cairo for Teheran, where his plans to photograph American bombers being transported to Russia were thwarted by a platoon of humourless Russian soldiers who first demanded the negatives, then stopped him filming altogether. From Iran, he flew to Iraq, landing at the RAF base at Habbaniya, where there was 'an excess of heat that is like a scourge'. After a dawn swim in the lake he flew on to Baghdad, where he was greeted by Stewart Perowne, whom he had known at Cambridge. A series of phone calls followed from the 'indefatigable' Miss Freya Stark: 'Would we come at four o'clock?' – then at five-thirty, four-thirty, six? When they finally met at her house, Freya appeared strangely attired in scarlet and white and with a bow in her hair, giving her a childlike quality. She tottered on to the lawn to meet a group of English neighbours gathered in a circle of deckchairs, 'spotty youths, old men in Panama hats, and chicken-like women in voiles'.[21]

As he travelled on, through Jerusalem and Amman, Cecil was increasingly troubled by the intensity of the sun, and by the time he had arrived in Beirut, he felt more despondent than he had been for years. It all served to make him empathise with the men who would be left behind after he had returned to England. 'Whenever I am asked when I am going home, and I reply: "Soon, perhaps", the eyes that once regarded me in a friendly way are suddenly filled with loathing.'[22] It troubled him that there were many in the Middle East who would not get home for years and whose *cri de cœur* envisaged sacrificing a 'right hand if I could get to England now!' In some dark moments Cecil considered the prospect of a sudden German advance leaving him trapped far from home, a possibility that the heightened sense of crisis in Cairo – the 'Flap' – did nothing to allay.

Eventually, engrossed in his well-thumbed copy of *War and Peace*, Beaton succeeded in securing a flight out for home, leaving Cairo all too aware that the Germans were just 90 miles away. It struck him that in England they were even closer, just 20 miles across the Channel. The flight crossed Africa and involved an anxious delay in the humid, mosquito-plagued air of Lagos, before reaching neutral Lisbon on 9 July. He rapidly succumbed to a bout of 'Lisbon tummy', a misfortune that prompted a plaintive note in his diary: 'Oh Lord, how many sorts of stomach must one suffer.'[23] By mid-July he was home, savouring England's blowsy summer and his luck in comparison with that of those left behind. 'This is the goal,' he wrote in his diary, 'their homecoming – that all the men in the desert dream of during the years they are existing in such unnatural surroundings.'[24]

Chapter 7

Turning Tide? Silver Lining?

> Sweetheart,
> They say that every cloud has a silver lining, and when I left you last night things seemed very cloudy. I felt so downcast and miserable at having to leave you. But now this is where the silver lining comes in. I am to travel to London Sunday night to be there Monday morning so as to answer a few enquiries. Fisher doesn't know at the moment what is in the wind, but he thinks I may go in command right away.

Tommy Davies to Dorrie, on board *Almanzora*, 23 July 1942

Was this the moment Tom Davies had been waiting for? Captain of his own ship after nearly three decades at sea and three years of war? After returning from Bombay in mid-July 1942 aboard *Almanzora*, he had had a brief, unsatisfactory leave before returning by train to his ship, travelling through the night ('next thing I knew was Hellifield and broad daylight at 5.00 am.') His gloom at leaving Dorrie was compounded by the uncertainty of what might lie in store. He woke at dawn with a taste like ashes in his mouth on a train that seemed to have lost the will to move, but when he went on board ship later that morning he found that he was to be relieved on the coming Sunday afternoon and then ordered to London for some unspecified reason before taking some more leave. 'What a lovely surprise too if I go in command after a week or two with you.' At last, his own ship! The only certainty for now, however, was that he was required to attend a navigation course in the capital.

He stayed at Cranston's Kenilworth Hotel in Great Russell Street, near the British Museum and Bloomsbury, 'a very stuffy old-maidish kind of place', but convenient for the train to Acton. It was cheap ('only 9/6 B&B') in an area he knew from his boyhood, and after leaving his bag and gas mask in the hotel, and decidedly thirsty in a rain-deprived, dusty city, he headed for a nearby pub. Later, sitting on his hotel bed, contentedly eating Dorrie's homemade rock cakes and drinking tea, he wrote another letter home.

Next morning he should have been in Acton for the beginning of the navigation course by 9.00 am sharp, but the hotel bed was too comfortable and he arrived ten minutes late 'in a hell of a lather'. He needn't have worried since shipboard urgency appeared to have been dispensed with, and after a long wait, he was eventually escorted to a lecture room with a number of small tables and an atmosphere thick with cigarette smoke. There was little sign of activity; indeed, time drifted until coffee and digestive biscuits were served an hour or so later. At 10.30, the lecturer suggested they begin work and they 'worked until 12.30 and then adjourned for lunch,' a leisurely meal of soup, roast beef and vegetables, date tart, cheese and coffee – and a bottle of beer, all courtesy of the Brown Compass Company. The tone of the morning lifted Tommy's mood and hopes: surely this was exactly the way captains designate should be treated?

But it was not to be: within a fortnight he was writing to Dorrie from Liverpool: 'Beloved. Here endeth my first day on board this new ship!' He was to serve on *Highland Monarch*, but not in the capacity he had hoped; instead he was bitterly disappointed about not getting his own command. He was inconsolable, all too aware that his ill luck was common knowledge: 'everybody seems to know that I have been disappointed'; Liverpool was as 'mucky as ever' and seemed to fit his mood, a sadness made worse by the news of a sister ship being sunk, with four crew drowned, and necessarily a further delay in potential captaincy. 'It makes my command come a bit later still.' When he wrote next, he begged his wife not to expect leave any time soon: 'Don't build up any hopes about seeing me again, because it might not happen. You know how uncertain life is.' He may have hesitated – Dorrie too, when she read it – about how his choice of words could have a more sombre meaning, a hint at some future catastrophe.

* * *

I have just seen Ludlow Hewitt in Habbaniya. A message came to ask me to dine and a lovely grey Air Force car was sent for me. I took a white dress full of frills, as they have no women there except a few nursing sisters, so I thought they would like something feminine to look at (and so they did) and drove in ghastly heat for one and three-quarter hours.[1]

Freya Stark to Flora Stark, Baghdad, 18 June 1942

RAF Habbaniya was 55 miles from Baghdad and 3,287 from London, close to the river Euphrates and a lake where flying boats en route to India settled, like great sea birds. Freya Stark arrived there by official car just as Jack was beginning to realise what RAF Sharjah might have in store for him. It would be another year before he reached Habbaniya. Freya's chauffeured drive was not an unalloyed pleasure: it was slow and the heat was appalling, worse even than sweltering Baghdad. The camp's size took her by surprise, as did its broad avenues and regimented lines of shady trees, and the infestation of sand flies tended to detract from its faux Englishness. She was ushered to the camp cinema, where 1,000 men were watching a film, at least until they saw this diminutive representative of the opposite sex. Had Jack been there he would have been ungrateful for this fleeting sight of English womanhood and resentful when she escaped the fly-blown desert a few days later by the long distance Nairn bus to Damascus. He was not to know that the bus journey had its own kind of misery, the journey from Baghdad taking twenty-seven hours with the air conditioning broken and the windows tightly sealed.

Later that summer, Freya took an extended leave in Cyprus, travelling via Jerusalem. Her stamina had been undermined by 'overwork [and] too much travelling', as well as anxiety about her mother's well-being. Freya, a colleague reported, 'suffered headaches and could be difficult.'[2] She stayed in Jerusalem at Government House, whose tranquil beauty was deeply pleasurable after the acute discomforts of Iraq. It was cool and remote, with a herb-filled terraced garden stretching down to a verdant, manicured lawn. The view was dominated by the rise and fall of nearby weathered hills, and in the middle distance, the white sprawl of Jerusalem shimmered in its heat. Compared to Habbaniya and Beirut, where she had stayed on her journey east and where her accommodation had no bathroom, the official residence bordered on luxury, something that, in her low state, she cherished. Moreover, here there were no insistent demands, no deadlines, while earnest thoughts of propaganda initiatives could be ignored; there were no long meetings, no struggles for the right words to dispel opposition or uncertainty. Instead she was now delightfully anonymous, all need to make decisions removed, and so she sat under the trees and alternately wrote, or just sat. For Freya Stark, at least, the wartime tide seemed to have turned; the pace of things slowed to a leisurely crawl.

Soon after, she travelled to Cyprus in a shabby, ramshackle Greek ship, the passage sufficiently uncertain for her to keep one hand on a lifebelt through the night. She arrived in the Cypriot town of Famagusta early in August 1942, and then moved on to another Government Official Residence, this time in Nicosia. The house was both remarkable and comfortable, its rooms 'so permeated by arts and crafts of the island that even the drawing-room curtains were cross-stitched with Crusader patterns.'[3] She shopped (for a beige-coloured fur coat made of goat skin); explored the island by a train full of priests, Cypriot peasants and their sheep, the engine and carriages rocking and swaying like a fairground scenic railway; and walked (to a castle high above the Mediterranean). The only shadow on the horizon was an unsettling telegram she had received from her masters, proposing that she make a lecture tour of the United States in the near future, a prospect she viewed with huge disquiet. It seemed to her that her work in the Middle East was more valuable than any benefits arising from seeking to propagandise the Americans. Nonetheless, she declared that, if necessary, she would do her duty and go. If she was obliged to do so, she wrote to her mother, 'the Ministry will have to buy me at least four beautiful gowns on arrival.'[4] She kept the thought at bay with, for example, a trip up into the hills, walking in glorious country, the upland thick with mature pine woods, and vineyards stretching down to the valley floor.

By the autumn of 1942, she was back in Iraq, her return coinciding with the German defeat at El Alamein. On a personal level, there was also the news of her mother's death, as painful to her as the war news was exhilarating. A week before victory at Alamein she had written to Jock Murray: 'News has come that Mama is dying. It was a week ago and I am hoping now that all may be over soon for her sake. It leaves me in a very lonely world.'[5] She deeply regretted that she had not seen her mother again after leaving Italy when the war had first intruded on their lives.

* * *

Mummy hurried into my room. She pulled the curtains earlier than usual. No nonsense about lying in bed – however late I'd been writing last night. This was worth waking up for: the most exciting event of the war – the turning point: 'Wonderful news! Rommel's army on the run – in full retreat.' The whole look of the war suddenly changed.[6]

Cecil Beaton's diary, Ashcombe, 5 November 1942

It was, the Prime Minister said, 'the end of the beginning', after the Germans had been defeated in North Africa. 1942 ended with hope, but there was also a recognition that there was a long way still to go before the return of peace. For individuals caught up in their own personal wars, hope and optimism were often shadowed by other factors: Freya Stark, for example, was in Baghdad, saddened by her mother's death and unsettled by the spectre of an American lecture tour; Jack was shiftless in Sharjah; Noël Coward was in England being commiserated with over his failure to earn a knighthood – '[Mountbatten] explained that he considered sabotage had been at work.'[7] Through that summer he had been working on *In Which We Serve*, a film portraying the Royal Navy and the reality of naval warfare, both for those in the firing line and their families left at home. HMS *Torrin* is sunk in combat off Crete, leaving the survivors desperately clinging to a life raft hoping to be rescued. As they hang on for dear life, the camera takes the viewer back through their individual, private lives. The storyline drew heavily on the loss of HMS *Kelly* off the Cretan coast: the ship's skipper, Lord Louis 'Dickie' Mountbatten, had recounted the events of that sinking to Coward, who had been both impressed and deeply moved by what he heard. Noël insisted that his 'Captain D' was not based on Mountbatten, but was 'quite ordinary, with an income of about £800 a year, a small country house near Plymouth, a reasonably nice-looking wife (Mrs, not Lady), two children and a cocker spaniel'.[8] But the parallel was clear; indeed, several of the speeches comprised Mountbatten's own words.

The film soon ran into difficulties: the *Daily Express* was critical of the basic idea and questioned its cost; an official in the Ministry of Information objected to the wisdom and appropriateness of making a film about the sinking of a British ship; some senior figures in the Admiralty called the film '*In Which We Sink*'. An opening shot of the *Daily Express's* headline that had appeared on 1 September 1939 – NO WAR THIS YEAR – floating in the battle-stained water enraged Beaverbrook to the extent that he subsequently vented his spleen on Mountbatten: 'You and Coward have gone out of your way to insult me and try to hold up the *Daily Express* to ridicule … You will live to regret the day that you took part in such a vile attack on me.'[9] Not everyone liked the film when it came out: Martha Gellhorn, for example, thought Coward 'has found a way to act in which you do not have to move a single muscle of the face nor vary the tone of your voice. It is really ludicrous.' For all that, she wrote, 'it all adds up to something.'[10] The *Daily Mirror* columnist Cassandra objected to its 'stilted mannerisms, [Coward's] clipped accent and his vast experience of the useless froth of society'.[11] Swearing in the film – 'sailors were heard to use the words "hell", "damn" and "bastard"' – resulted in it not being approved initially for release in the United States.[12] However, *In Which We Serve* was nominated in the 1943 Academy Awards for Best Picture and Best Original Screenplay and Coward was presented with an Academy Honorary Award for 'his outstanding production achievement'. It also won the New York Film Critics Circle Award for Best Film (beating *Casablanca*).

The film completed, Coward undertook a twenty-eight-week provincial tour, beginning in Blackpool. He regarded it as a pleasant enough acting job, which had the additional benefit of earning some money, but he was aware that it made little contribution, if any, to the war effort. For a few months he played a series of concerts in hospitals and munitions factories: it was challenging and exhausting work, so much so that he claimed he would rather 'sing to an audience of hostile aborigines than to a group of overtired, and obviously ravenous, factory girls.'[13]

Cecil Beaton had returned from the Middle East by midsummer 1942, and had begun writing an account of his time there, choosing to work in the comfort of the sitting room at Ashcombe rather than in London.[14] An exhibition of his war photographs was shown in Lisbon, and at one point he was summoned to Buckingham Palace to photograph Eleanor Roosevelt and each member of the Royal Family. He also spent a week in Bristol in October taking photographs of Noël Coward's play *This Happy Breed*. Cecil 'remained astonished that Coward, who appeared to him so second-rate, could have produced something so outstanding.'[15] The following winter seemed endless to Cecil: bitterly cold and gloomy; the war proceeding with little prospect of an early conclusion; and his beloved house designated as a base for an anti-aircraft searchlight and some radio-location apparatus. The persistent clatter of soldiers' hobnailed boots on the cobbles broke the peace of Beaton's country retreat.

For his part, Donald Macdonald was reflecting on which would come first: his enlistment, his medical degree, or the war's end; while Chief Officer Tom Davies was at sea on board *Highland Brigade*, still hankering after his captaincy – and still writing his loving letters home from the other side of the world, his family's private lives painfully far away.

Chapter 8

'I Wonder If This Will Reach You?'

No sign of any mail ship all these days: every morning at breakfast I sit and watch the night's arrivals. But something must come soon.[1]

Freya Stark to Flora Stark, Aden, 6 January 1940

A global war means exile for many, and with that, a rise in the importance of written communication to and from those exiled. How else can relationships be sustained and news of well-being or otherwise conveyed? 'Mail was the only means of communication' and yet, sadly, 'servicemen often made poor correspondents,' partly because 'by one estimate, one in five of them was functionally illiterate.'[2]

To make matters worse, one of the first casualties of war is the very mechanism that allows exiled servicemen and women to keep in touch with home: the wartime postal service was slow, unreliable and vulnerable to unforeseen events. Letters could take months to arrive: Freya Stark, for example, when she was in Aden, fretted about postal delays, only for that to deteriorate when she travelled into even more remote Yemen. On 20 April 1940, she wrote to her mother in Italy, 'I wonder if this will reach you – every post now one wonders.'[3] Occasionally she was able to send post by air with a friend, but with mail and troops both avoiding the Mediterranean and travelling via the Cape, sea mail took months and would often arrive in clutches, rather than singly. The Royal Artillery's John 'Syd' Croft wrote home on 26 January 1941: 'You can just imagine how glad I was to get my first mail today from England since leaving nearly four months ago' (so glad was he that he celebrated 'by having a decent "all-over" wash, change of clothes, brush-up and having our pictures taken').[4] Two months later, things had not improved: 'The postal arrangements are very disappointing out here and I think the least the Army could do for the men is to give them regular post.'[5] A letter posted in the UK in late May, for example, might not arrive until the end of August. Sometimes mail disappeared, lost forever as the result of enemy action perhaps, or simply happenstance. Evelyn Waugh, writing from Freetown to his wife on 13 September 1940, observed, 'There was an untoward incident at Liverpool when the marine in charge of the officers' incoming mail emptied it all down the rubbish shute.'[6]

Many of those sent abroad could recount stories of post being delayed for months: one soldier serving in North Africa received a letter from home on 14 December that had been posted on 20 October.[7] They could send telegrams, but only from major cities and at their own expense. Gunner Croft reported that letters were taking between six and eight weeks to reach Egypt and then could only be delivered to the men when they were not mobile but back at base.[8] Sometimes the extent of delays was significantly worse than that: 'Four days ago,' Croft wrote on 17 January 1941, 'we received our first mail from England in sixteen weeks.' He was 'unlucky' he noted – there was nothing for him. On another occasion he received a letter in March that had been posted the previous October. Then there was the single day (6 January 1942) when he received a batch of sixteen letters from home. Inevitably, delays hindered any meaningful interaction since the exiled soldier or airman in replying to a two-month-old letter knew that his response would suffer the same time lag before reaching its destination. A question asked in a letter from home in December might not receive an answer until March or April of the following year. 'What is the good of my asking these questions?' Evelyn Waugh wrote on 13 October 1940, 'I shall never get an answer until I get home. We always move before the mail.'[9] The novelist Graham Greene had the same experience: 'My last mail missed me here and is now pursuing me up and down the coast.'[10] It was a problem that Jack's colleagues at Sharjah, for example, would have recognised.

To compound the issue, there was no knowing whether any particular letter was in fact the last that had been written, before a son had been killed in action, or a parent, lover or wife had died in an air raid at home. Those waiting at home might be counselled not to worry and 'to remember, where a soldier is concerned, "no news is good news",' but it was easy to be misled about an exiled soldier's whereabouts: Syd Croft's mother, unaware that her son was in great danger in Greece in April 1941, wrote to him as if he were still in the Middle East: 'I do hope you are safe and well and am anxiously

Syd Croft in a captured Italian officer's uniform after the capture of Derna. (*Jeannette Croft*)

waiting for news of you.' The following year, his mother received a letter from the Army: 'We regret we have to notify you that W/Bombardier John Charles Croft was reported missing on 20 June' – this was after a lapse of some five weeks. However, she had already received two telegrams from Croft saying he was safe and well. It wasn't until 11 August that a further official letter arrived informing her that 'your son has been located'.[11] There were potential problems with the unreliability of telegrams too, as Evelyn Waugh reported in a letter of 2 June 1941, describing how Randolph

Churchill had been dining in Cairo when his host sent a cable to the Prime Minister, '"Your son is at my house. He has the light of battle in his eye." Unhappily, the cypher group got it wrong & it arrived "light of BOTTLE". All too true.'[12]

One consequence of postal uncertainty was not knowing whether a letter or letters had gone astray. 'Your letters have been awful,' Captain Pat Hore-Ruthven wrote to his wife Pam, one of Freya Stark's assistants in Cairo, 'Please, please put dates as they all arrive in different order and I just don't know what is going on at all. My mail did start to catch me up here at the time, but nothing for the past fortnight and I get so downy. This is a horrid letter but I am no longer any cop without you – it gets worse and worse.'[13] Occasionally, letters simply disappeared: 'We have heard,' Syd Croft reported, 'that mail sent during the last three weeks of November was lost and Air Mail letters sent between 13 and 17 February were destroyed.'[14] That same November (1941), Freya Stark reported that no post was arriving in Cairo: 'hoping for a huge batch, and there is nothing.' Whimsically, she envisaged the eventual finding of 'a huge reservoir' full of 'all the world's lost post bags'.[15] Some correspondents devised a stratagem for dealing with the problem: 'My lovely Bessie, What do you think about us starting to number our letters? It is a good check-up; a missing number is easily spotted.'[16]

For troops overseas there were a number of different ways of writing home, but inevitably there were limitations on all of them. Chris Barker, for example, told Bessie that 'we only get one green envelope and one LC [letter card] a week' and disconsolately pointed out that 'we only get one of this LC type monthly, and here I am spending two months' supply in three days.'[17] Gunner Croft described the system of postage home from the North African desert in a letter of 5 December 1940: 'It is possible for you to send me two telegrams a month (as next of kin) at a rate of a penny a word. I cannot reply except in exceptional circumstances. I can use the civilian telegraph system, if available, but this is costly … I shall write once a week and, where possible, send the letter by airmail. Our letters will now be censored at Base, not by unit officers.'[18]

In the early part of the war, post was sent by sea: mail from Southampton to Cairo was carried in the WS convoys, travelling at the speed of the slowest vessel. As a result, the usual journey time was eleven weeks. Eventually the decision was taken to take advantage of aircraft flying from West Africa to Egypt to carry bags of mail, but obtaining sufficient room in the aircraft holds was a problem and the minimum charge for each letter was deemed, by some newspapers, as scandalous. 'An ingenious solution was found in the airgraph.' This was a message form that was photographed and sent as microfilm, thereby saving space and weight.[19] The scheme had a significant impact: Syd Croft's mother reported that she had seen 'in the paper that 50,000 film letters from soldiers in the Middle East have now arrived' and was hoping one was from her son. On 13 September 1941, Croft wrote home, 'Your airgraph was the first I have seen and I think they are very good. By writing smaller, you can say far more and the reproduction is just as readable.' A few months later, he wondered whether because they were short, airgraphs 'encourage slackness in writing letters.'[20]

Like everybody else, Freya Stark wondered about censorship: on 28 January 1940, she asked her mother in a postscript whether her letters arrived having been opened. A couple of weeks later, she ended a letter by indicating that she had decided not to send it by post but would ask her publisher, Jock Murray, to forward it for her. Even though she was able to make use of the diplomatic bag in sending letters, she remained alert to security issues. 'One is afraid to say anything at all,' she wrote in July 1940, – hence 'these miserable letters' – and in the previous month, 'I must not tell you what ships are in harbour.'[21] She was horrified by the recklessness of her boss, Stewart Perowne, who had openly used the code word for 'Italian' in writing to her – 'you might at least have said chaffinch instead of sparrow!' she wrote on 3 March 1940. Her concern was partly because she thought his letter had been opened and subsequently sealed again, the consequence perhaps of Perowne sending the letter in an 'On His Majesty's Service' envelope. As late as 12 July 1945, a letter home from Tommy Davies had been 'OPENED BY EXAMINER'. Ignoring the rules of censorship could be counter-productive: a letter to a prisoner of war who had paid no heed to either British or German censors 'was reduced to: "Dear Buddy … Love Nana",'[22] while the writer Martin Armstrong wrote to the poet Lascelles Abercrombie on 10 February 1940 telling him that he had received a letter from the war correspondent Philip Jordan, which read: '"Philip Jordan wishes you a Merry xxxx and a Happy New xxxx", the cancelled words heavily blotted

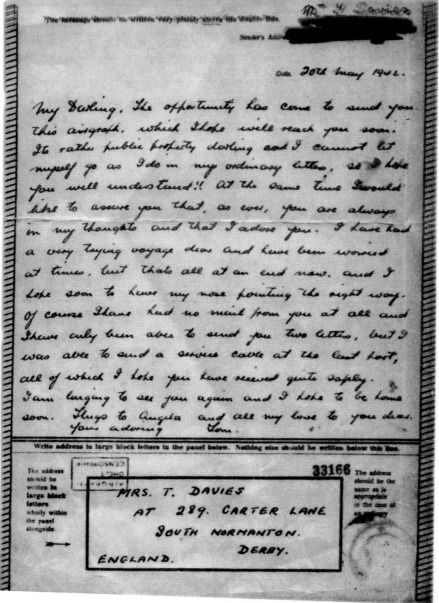

An airgraph to Dorrie from Tom. (*Angela Awbery White*)

out and an official stamp across the card, "Passed by Censor".'[23] No one, it seems was safe from the scissoring censor: Duff Cooper's son, John Julius Norwich, received a letter from his father, 'which arrived so cut up by the wartime censor that it looked like lace. I sent it back to my parents to show them. As Minister of Information, he was responsible for all censorship at the time.' His mother, Lady Diana Cooper, 'cried with laughter over Papa's censored letter,' which she thought looked like a Christmas decoration.[24] There were occasions when the censors were less than thorough: one soldier who had written home from a ship en route to the Middle East had evidently commented unfavourably about conditions on board, but they had been 'blue-pencilled by the censor. However, he wasn't very efficient and I could read through his scratchings out.'[25] There were times too when the censor showed a sense of humour, albeit of a dubious kind: 'Was there not a censor who, having scissored a hole in a soldier's letter, and realising that he had spoiled a salty story on the other side, carefully wrote in the pay-off along the margin?'[26]

There were ways and means of circumventing censorship: the poet Keith Douglas, who was another man posted to North Africa, was reminded 'of a soldier who is supposed to have written home – "I can't say where I am, but there are Pharaohs at the bottom of my garden."'[27] Tommy Davies was a diligent correspondent, loving and steadfast, churning out letters in his neat fountain-penned handwriting, but the rules of censorship severely cramped his style. His ship's location, the events of the voyage, the war itself – all were taboo. 'It seems difficult to find anything to write about these days dear,' he wrote to his wife Dorrie on 23 April 1942, 'as one must not say anything about our goings or comings – even if we knew anything about them – which I certainly don't!' Freya Stark was similarly hindered by the censors: 'I could tell a lot about Syria if it weren't for the censor,'[28] she wrote. Every so often restrictions on information were lifted: 'We are now allowed to write and tell you of our personal experiences up to 23 October,' Syd Croft wrote, in the aftermath of the Battle of Alamein, on 7 December 1942. But for the most part, the threat of the censor hung over every correspondent. LAC Bob Bleach, sailing on the *Capetown Castle* in April 1943, was threatened with a court martial after he had 'broken censorship regulations' – he had used a 'green' letter, which meant that he had undertaken not to include sensitive information. In the end, he was simply 'admonished', not brought before a court martial.[29] Censorship necessarily limited correspondence, so letter writers were often obliged to resort to the same broad agenda – love and trust, perhaps, or food, which was a constant topic. Letters from the desert war would often include reminders of specific needs: Syd Croft wanted 'pants and vests, socks, toothbrushes and paste, soap, blades, film, books, handkerchiefs', but had 'plenty of paper and envelopes captured from the Italians'.

Some couples before the particular convoy had sailed for the east devised a code to reveal the ship's eventual destination – a letter home might contain a reference to a remembered journey to 'Yorkshire' and cherished friends in 'Sheffield', knowing that the reader would interpret 'Yorkshire' as Africa, and that 'Sheffield' stood for Suez. Tommy Davies hinted at his location in a letter to Dorrie, referring to the place where he 'had prickly heat last time.'[30] 'Uncle Joe' might refer to Russia, while other codes might be more subtle: one prisoner of war, captured in North Africa, 'used a code when writing to his mother that relied on a sequence of letters.'[31] Evelyn Waugh, for example, told his wife in a letter of 14 January 1940, 'If I write about Wickham it means "abroad immediately", if about Winstanley, it means "training for a week or two, then probably abroad", if about Abercrombie, "all plans still perfectly vague".'[32] For their part, censors were required to scrutinise letters for secret codes and pass suspicious examples on: for example, a letter that showed an 'excessive number of dots throughout' was sent to be reviewed ('Please examine for possible code') on 8 October 1944.[33] Instructions to the Postal Censorship Staff were detailed and extensive: specified in May 1940, they comprised fifty-six paragraphs over nine pages. The process was complex and included: checking the envelope; opening it with a paper knife; looking for secret messages (perhaps under the seal affixed to the envelope); holding it up to the light to check for anything below the postage stamp; and sending anything in an unusual language to the Uncommon Languages Department.[34]

In some dusty, faraway posting, the letter from home was, for the most part, greatly valued. But it could bring heartache too: there were instances, for example, of 'busybody neighbours who tattled in poison pen letters to absent husbands.'[35] Letters from home were cherished, but any one of them could bring the worst possible news: 'One of my friends received bad news in the mail. In the recent raids on Bath, his brother and two relatives were killed and his home severely damaged, though fortunately his wife and young son escaped. It makes us feel terribly helpless out here when we hear of raids in England.'[36]

Above all, for many like Gunner Syd Croft, post was a lifeline: 'Your letters, more than anything, kept me going during those difficult times.'

* * *

> Sweetheart,
> It's now 8.30 and I have just returned from the phone, which may be the last little talk I shall have with you. I enjoyed so much every second of it and was sad and sorry when it was all over. How lovely it would be if I could only talk to you while I am at sea.

Tommy Davies to Dorrie, on board *Highland Brigade*,
Avonmouth, 12 December 1942

On 23 August 1942, Tom wrote once again to Dorrie; he was simmering with rage at the inadequacies of the telephone system: 'It is now 10.45 pm and I have just returned from the phone call box at the top of the dock, where I have been standing waiting patiently for a call to you since 8.30!' He was desperate to hear Dorrie's voice since he had bad news: 'I have to go to Avonmouth tomorrow, Saturday, by the 9.10 am train to join the *Highland Brigade* as Chief [Officer] and I believe she is due to sail Monday or Tuesday.' He had only just unpacked. Moreover, Tom would not be able to return home before the ship sailed, and worse still, he anticipated that her letters to him would arrive after he had set out for Bristol. 'I cannot say what ship I am joining as it is sure to be stopped by the censor,' he wrote, although in fact he had already told his wife that he was to join *Highland Brigade*. He joked about the ship's captain's weight, the corpulent Captain Watts, and his own – 'as you have often heard me say darling, "If all the world were fat men, we would have no more wars!"'

Highland Brigade sailed on 28 August 1942, as part of WS Convoy 22 (which carried a total of 51,000 troops), the ship leaving Avonmouth for the Clyde in the utmost secrecy. Tom Davies 'didn't even know we were going there when we left our original port.' He still hankered after 'the dear old *Almanzora*', but the new ship was pleasant enough: his quarters had a comfortable armchair and even a sprung settee. The weather was glorious – hot but with a cooling breeze. Tom was proud of the fact that he was cutting down on cigarettes – the war had made a chain smoker of him – and, at risk to his waistline, he had resorted to McIntosh's toffees and fruit drops for consolation. Although his duties included an early morning watch, he welcomed 'the cool of the bridge at 4.00 am after those hot nights and stuffy rooms with this blackout'. It was a happy ship: the skipper, 'Daddy' Watts, was a warm, avuncular figure who loved his food. His breakfast, Tom wrote to Dorrie, might consist of 'six rashers, three eggs, three sausages and about six half slices of toast and marmalade'. Then, at 11.00 am, he would refuel with bread, cheese and a bottle of beer. 'But at lunch and dinner he really lets himself go!'

The mail at sea was never less than uncertain and usually disappointingly tardy. To Tommy's surprise, though, convoy WS22 saw 'the first time since this war commenced that I have known letters to overtake us'. It was a welcome anomaly; mostly it was a question of posting and hoping for the best. There were sound reasons why mail could be delayed or lost: for example, during this voyage, Davies was worried by the loss of the Empire Flying Boat *Clare*, destroyed off Bathurst in mid-September; he thought his letter home, mailed from Freetown, would have gone down with the aircraft. Whenever he could, Davies would send a telegram from an unnamed port, in an attempt to allay Dorrie's worrying: 'Fondest love darling. My thoughts are with you. All well and safe,' for example, he cabled on 12 October 1942, probably from Durban.

Highland Brigade sailed for Freetown from Cape Town on 20 October, and reached Avonmouth on 18 November. Tom went on leave for a couple of weeks, after which he said another mournful goodbye to Dorrie, whom he watched waving him goodbye from the smoky platform and slowly disappearing into the fog as his train pulled out of Nottingham station. They were reunited briefly in Bristol, where they stayed at the Royal Hotel – 'such a frowsty old place and old-fashioned – and with single beds!' The weather in the West Country was grim, relentless rain necessitating the wearing of 'galoshes all the time'. A week before Christmas, *Highland Brigade* sailed again, on the midday tide (with convoy WS 25), initially for the Clyde.

Chapter 9

Taciturn Jack

Most of Iraq is desert country, not great sandy waste like the Sahara in Africa, but flinty, harsh, monotonous desert, treeless but covered with a thick scrub vegetation. The only water in this region comes from waterholes and these are jealously guarded.[1]

Guide for US Forces in Iraq, 1943

'You want to be careful with all this family history,' Jack mumbled. 'You never know what you might find out.' It was only much later that it occurred to me that that was precisely the point; the very purpose of research, to lay bare what had been hidden. What on earth could I uncover that mattered so much? Moreover, his dismissive resistance was guaranteed to have exactly the opposite effect from the one he wanted. Was there some family secret that he was set on erasing from sight? What if his taciturn defensiveness about the war was the result not of those miserable wartime postings, but because of something closer to home, a painful memory of what had happened in his absence? My brother was sure he could recall a uniformed man about the house, someone who was decidedly not our father. Was he Canadian? Or American? 'I was too young to realise any deep significance,' Peter said, 'and in any case, it may have been entirely innocent.' He remembered an idyllic day on the river, mother laughing and a stranger rowing with studied elegance. There was a photograph he had seen – since lost – of our mother, smiling and carefree, under a spreading tree in the garden, with a man in air force blue – a stranger to us both, but evidently not to her. He even remembered the man's name – Ron. I joked about changing my name to Ronson and we laughed, uneasily, wondering whether this was a bit too close to the truth – and what else we didn't know about our parents.

All this left me even more uncertain: not only was my father's war service in those expanses of desert an obscure shadow, so were the years at home in

Greta's day out, Broxbourne 1944. (*Author*)

the time immediately before I was born. Living witnesses were noticeable by their absence and I had contributed to the problem by leaving it all too late, never asking the right – well, any – questions until those who might have been able to answer had gone. At the National Archives in Kew I tracked down my father's service number and rank. I did not expect him to be officer material and I was right: he never made it past corporal. There was no other reference to him amongst all that paper. When I approached the RAF Personnel Records, held at Innsworth in Gloucestershire, I met with a firm rebuff. Unless the subject of the inquiry is dead, or has given permission, they could reveal nothing. Permission! There was no chance of that. I had reached a dead end, at least until Jack himself was gone.

* * *

Arriving in Iraq must have felt to Jack that he too had reached a dead end: a landscape of bleak railheads, fuel dumps, spiralling coils of barbed wire to deter the light-fingered, smoke drifting, dogs scavenging. And men bored to tears. 'We do all the things that soldiers have always done,' wrote Private James Boswell, Royal Army Medical Corps, radiographer and unofficial war artist, 'drink, gossip, gamble, fight, sleep as much as we can and carry on a guerrilla war against the ennui that descends on an idle army.' The life gave a whole new meaning to remoteness: 'Fifty miles out here,' Boswell thought, 'is as good as fifty years.'[2] Perhaps there were occasions when Jack regarded this blistered, empty wasteland with something close to contentment, that he was alive, despite the best laid plans of Hitler, and that one day all this would end and he could go home. And yes, this alien world would be something to tell his children and grandchildren about. But I cannot see him content and philosophical faced with the hellish brew of heat, tedium, and exile. And he certainly didn't talk about it.

… So this was Habbaniya! Jack screwed his eyes against the sun's glare before stepping down from the lorry. The dust swirled around his boots and he hoped that he and the other new arrivals would soon be chivvied into the shade. As well as being blessed with military ranks of shady trees, the camp seemed reassuringly calm, half asleep in the unforgiving sunshine. There was a heat haze over the Euphrates, a river 'as wide as the Clyde', according to one airman writing home.[3] Beyond the fence that enclosed the camp, the desert stretched away into the distance, all the way to the Holy Land, Jack surmised, unsettled by the implications of such a thought, the unknown miles and the shadow of the past. He would soon learn a more practical consequence of the desert surroundings, the way the sand shifted with the wind, blew into any unguarded nook without quarter, insinuating its grit into eyes, nose, ears, and hair; machines, food, and clothes.

The camp had been built during the 1930s, constructed for comfort, with 'no concessions to the unpleasant thought that anyone might ever go so far as to attack it'.[4] There was something of India or Aldershot about the place: long, straight roads named to evoke home (Regent Street, Piccadilly); and tidy planting of bougainvillaea and oleanders, stocks, sweet peas and roses. There was a tall water tower; aircraft hangars and a high fence, which kept the hyenas at bay during the hours of darkness. It was blisteringly hot, supremely isolated, scorpion-plagued and very unhealthy (it was hard to avoid prickly heat, a permanently volatile stomach, and a heat-soaked debility). For all that, there were worse postings. Indeed, for some, being sent to Habbaniya was something for which to give thanks: Leading Aircraftman S. Carson, writing one of the 210 letters he wrote to his parents in Glasgow over a two-year period, told them of his posting there: 'This is the happiest day I've had since I arrived from Blighty,' since it was regarded as 'being the finest RAF station in the world.'[5]

Not everyone felt the same way: 'I was in some stores in Blighty where there were cases marked for Habbaniya. I asked the store basher where it was and he said, "At the end of the earth: don't get posted there at any cost." So here I am at the world's backside.'[6] The writer Roald Dahl – like Noël Coward, involved with the British Security Coordination in America – was posted there in 1940. Warned beforehand that it was 'the most godforsaken hellhole in the entire world', he could not understand when he got there 'why anyone should want to build a vast RAF town in such an abominable, unhealthy, desolate place.'[7] There were compensations of a sort: it had its own yacht club, sports fields, golf course and polo pitch, as well as fifty-six tennis courts. The fox hunting man posted there could enjoy following hounds, plentiful jackal substituting for fox. The heat, and the location far from the front, encouraged a languid routine: up in the cool of dawn; cup of char; cycle across to the aircraft hangars; flying by six in the morning; breakfast in the mess at nine-thirty; more flying till noon; and then a siesta through the afternoon. 'At 6.00 pm change into Dinner Jacket, soft silk shirt, nip into the mess, bow to the senior officer and then quaff two or three whiskies and soda, before supper at 7.30.'[8] Such a comforting pattern was not for the likes of Jack, of course. He would not wear a dinner jacket until, in middle age, he and Greta began to frequent the South Gloucestershire Conservative Association dinner dances, when he would act the RAF officer he never was.

Standing in the camp that first day he saw immediately that it was poorly sited, too easily overawed by the escarpment that separated it from the lake. Defending it against any well-armed army established on the heights above would not be easy. By no stretch of the imagination was Jack any kind of military man, but his eye for landscape was acute; he never forgot a road once travelled, and he invariably trusted his memory or instinct for finding the right way. He liked maps, but rarely used them to follow a route. It is a characteristic he passed on to me and for which I am grateful. Having passed a critical eye over the surrounding landscape, he sighed, but kept his thoughts to himself – well, you would expect him to – and, together with the other new arrivals, was conducted around the camp by a stiff-backed sergeant who provided a running commentary. 'Five hundred acres ... based on camps in India ... oasis in the sand ... little piece of Blighty ... water from the Euphrates ... that's what keeps the trees and shrubs flowering ... laxative qualities of the lake's water, not that constipation is an issue here ...' Jack noted that there had been a sustained attempt to make the place less inhospitable, at least for officers: playing fields for rugger, soccer and hockey, a golf course, riding stables, an outstanding swimming pool, a first-class gymnasium, and tennis courts. At some point they were reminded that they were far safer in Habbaniya than in London, a fact that, in Jack's unspoken opinion, ignored that fact that London was temperate and unplagued by flies. Best of all, London's Liverpool Street station was less than an hour by train away from his family.

Instead of an early morning flight, leisurely breakfast, more circuits and bumps and an afternoon nap, the routine of the RAF Police was infinitely more prosaic: supervision of the Detention Barracks; looking after the mounted section (for the life of me, I cannot imagine Jack on a horse); patrolling the perimeter and key buildings; and manning the main gate (occasionally glancing wistfully at the sign that proclaimed the mileages to Baghdad and London). There was also a 'Special Investigations Branch' (SIB). Jack would have been deployed across the full range: 'All corporals were switched to various sections i.e. patrol section, transport, DB [Detention Barracks] when required, gate manning and SIB.'[9] The scope for airmen offending against the law was large: The Manual of Air Force Law (1943) runs to 984 pages and covers such eventualities as the predictable 'absent without leave' or drunkenness, to the more colourful 'riot, insurrection and unlawful assembly' and 'scandalous conduct of an officer'. 'Disgraceful conduct' covered stealing, embezzling, malingering, 'wilfully maiming/injuring himself with intent to render himself unfit for service', receiving stolen goods and so on. RAF Policemen were deployed to counter the threat of sabotage, subversion and espionage; to control out-of-bounds areas and the entry and exit from 'official' brothels;[10] to investigate the theft of alcohol and petrol; to combat smuggling; to investigate 'homosexual orgies' (allegedly a problem at RAF El Adem); to arrest thieves stealing from RAF bases, and so on. Jack would have been a busy man.

It was a strange all-male existence at Habbaniya – Jack didn't like that, since he much preferred the company of women. But women were a rarity in the camp, and when they appeared, they invariably made a powerful impression. Freya Stark, who visited Habbaniya in 1942, was struck by the reaction she got when arriving at the base: '"My God, it's a woman!" the captain in charge apparently said when he saw me coming.' A year later, as she was being driven home from Habbaniya, her RAF driver remarked how good it was to see her at the picture show the previous night. There were a few nursing sisters in uniform, but otherwise Freya was the only woman there and she had worn an evening dress. '"You can't think what it means to us," said the driver, "just to see a lady sitting at a table pouring tea."'[11]

Station life varied little: supply problems meant that cigarettes were rationed; a Blenheim crashed when its tyre blew on landing and an aircraft fitter was killed; beer allocations rose by half a bottle a man per week. There were four cases of tuberculosis, and five more men were killed in an early morning crash, this time of a Wellington bomber. The heat dominated and made men long for the sun to go down. The Soviet ambassador, Ivan Maisky, flew in a week or so after Jack arrived – would my dad have stood unflinching on the tarmac runway, eyes front, while the Red entourage disembarked and headed for the shade? With Maisky was a Soviet army officer, Major Yevseyev, who had made no concessions at all to Middle Eastern heat, wearing a 'regulation thick serge Red Army uniform and jackboots'. Their Liberator aircraft touched down at 12.35 pm on 7 July 1943, in a temperature of 110 degrees in the shade. The two Russians both suffered in the heat.[12] They were driven around the base and then taken to Air House, previously the BOAC rest house on the lake shore, where they were provided with a guard of RAF Police, and as much luxury as Habbaniya could muster. Later, a dust storm blew up. The wind and turbulence lasted for more than an hour and spoiled the official dinner – was Jack's NAAFI supper also sacrificed? Did he spend that night dragging on a Woodbine, listening to Russian snores from the guest bedrooms? Maisky and Yevseyev had turned down an invitation to the camp's open-air cinema that evening, choosing instead to listen to the news, both from London and Moscow, and then retire early to bed, only too anxious for the morning to bring escape. They made an early start, taking off for Russia before dawn, but only once the queasy Yevseyev had been plied with water and aspirins.

There is an irony in the fact that this remote outpost frequently found itself at the midpoint of wartime journeys of those with the freedom to travel, heavyweight politicians, perhaps, or top brass soldiers en route to some crucial conference on strategy. Jack's melancholy, disapproving eye would have seen two TUC members, for example, en route to Moscow. He would have been significantly less grudging about the arrival of Foreign Secretary Anthony Eden and Chief of Combined Operations, Louis Mountbatten; they were, after all, the kind of aristocrats whose sleek hair and well-cut suits Jack sought to emulate. Given half a chance, he would have tested the material on Eden's lapels with a tailor's inquisitive thumb and forefinger. Then there were the entertainers, the actors, comedians and singers, whose travels were devised to boost morale, and make 'Have a Banana' – Habbaniya – or somewhere else like it, seem that little bit closer to home for the men and women in exile. They included Jack Benny (my Jack would have thought him a bit too slick); Larry Adler (moderately entertaining); Winnie Shaw ('Boy what a girl she was!');[13] and Noël Coward (to be honest, not really Jack's sort of thing).

Chapter 10

Jack, Noël and Tom: the Show Goes On

My dear General,
I am sending you this letter by hand of Noël Coward, who will need no
introduction to you from me. He is visiting the Mediterranean battlefields and
is most anxious to see the troops under your command. He would be very glad
to do all he can to entertain them during his journeys.[1]

Brendan Bracken to General Montgomery, Ministry of Information,
Malet Street, London WC 1, 19 July 1943

Through the autumn of 1942 and the early part of 1943, Noël Coward was
touring the country 'playing in unget-at-able places to packed jammed
audiences who look upon it as a terrific event.' The 'unget-at-able places' were
the British towns at the end of the line, no thought yet of anywhere further
afield. Christmas 1942 he spent in Aberdeen, and then drove from there to
Inverness through a heavy snowstorm in an open army lorry, performing two
concerts en route. The company played Hull in a bitter winter – there was
no heating and fires could only be lit if a doctor's note could be provided.
He played Northampton in a theatre next door to a boot factory; a location
that he rightly surmised would be a challenge on matinee days. In Carlisle,
illness forced the deployment of a swathe of understudies. Food was short
(soggy salad and Spam); trains were usually unheated; transport was
invariably a problem in provincial towns: the trams were no longer running
when the curtain came down, taxis were rare and walking anywhere in the
blackout was hazardous; actors came down with colds and the treadmill of
travel and performance rendered them dog-tired. Occasionally the show
went on to the accompaniment of an air raid. It was a relentless tour, which
ended for Noël in a bout of jaundice, sufficiently debilitating to require a
lengthy convalescence in Tintagel, Cornwall. Meanwhile, in January 1943,
while Noël was criss-crossing the country, prisoners of war at Oflag VIIb

– with Coward's special permission – put on a production of his hitherto unperformed play *Post Mortem*.[2]

It had been a difficult and demanding few months: on top of illness, intense touring, losing two homes to either German bombs or Army requisitioning, there was the considerable shock of being taken to court for financial irregularities. In mid-October, two policemen from the Finance Defence Department arrived at his door, informing him that he must shortly appear in court to face charges, the potential punishment for which was a £22,000 fine. The case related to a contravention of the currency regulations affecting his American finances and his stay in the United States in the early years of the war. Coward was much aggrieved and strongly protested his innocence, arguing that he had drawn heavily on his own personal account when he was in New York working for the British Government. Nonetheless, he was eventually fined, albeit much less than might have been the case. He was relieved when the unsavoury business could be put behind him, and grateful that the press had treated him with a kindness he had come not to expect.

* * *

Beloved,
Here endeth my first day on board this new ship! My feelings are much the same as when I finished my first day on the *Almanzora* as Chief – with this difference – when I was there I was keen and interested but here I am doing things automatically because I know they have to be done.

Tommy Davies to Dorrie, Liverpool, 18 August 1942

Highland Brigade sailed at two o'clock on a December morning, with Christmas 1942 in the offing. She soon ran into foul weather, before the gradual shift from northern winter to equatorial heat. Freetown was reached on New Year's Eve, and after Takoradi, the ship set course for South America. On board it was stiflingly hot, the men living 'in a steel shell – with temperatures outside at 80 degrees – no ports open – no ventilation – all doors covered with double heavy canvas curtains'. It was little better in Buenos Aires, from where Tom wrote on 23 January: 'It's very hot just now and I am in a continual bath of perspiration,' his fist sticking to the flimsy air mail paper as he sweated over his disciplined, earnest script. He was resolute about corresponding, despite having heard nothing from Dorrie since leaving England, but he was convinced 'that the powers-that-be have no wish for the merchant navy to get their mail'. He was more optimistic about UK-bound mail, however: 'I believe,' he wrote, 'that there is a fair chance of an air mail getting home in reasonable time darling, so I am having three shillings' worth.' It clearly frustrated him that 'owing to censorship' there was 'so little one can say'. The trip was simply 'routine', and Tommy confined himself to heartfelt variations of 'I shall be anxious and keen to see you again, as ever dear, and I am longing to hold you in my arms again'. There was no mention of the 'extremely conspicuous white shapes in the form of a destroyer or corvette' painted as camouflage on the ship's side, which troubled *Highland Brigade's* captain so much; nor of where they had been, or presently were; or the prospect of the forthcoming voyage, via Montevideo and Rio, back to Liverpool.[3]

It was towards the end of March before *Highland Brigade* returned and Tom could hold Dorrie close and say all those things the censor would have deleted, as well as briefly sharing some semblance of a normal life together. After ten days' leave, though, he was obliged to return to Liverpool, any sense of well-being soon eroded by the grindingly slow train journey up from Derby, not to mention the state of the ship when he reached the docks: 'I found my ship all arse up with repairs and alterations.' Then, two days later, there was the sudden return of the on-off captaincy saga. 'After more than twenty-five years at sea,' Tommy was to get his command after all, it seemed, although he wished it 'hadn't been in so much of a ruddy hurry!' He had travelled down to London to learn that he was to go on 'unattached leave' before assuming the captaincy of his own ship. Within days, however, everything had changed and his longed-for promotion had been deferred. 'I hardly know how to commence this letter,' Tommy Davies wrote on April Fools' Day. 'Twice they've played the same bloody rotten game on me and each time I have been messed about in the same manner.' In calmer moments he could see the difficulties arising from the continuing losses of ships, the most recent of which were the *Nagara* and *Naviva*, both sunk earlier in the week – 'about 10,000 tons of meat gone west I guess!' Fewer ships meant fewer skippers, and so, instead of being master of his own vessel, Davies was 'to do relieving Captain's work on the other ships'; he would have to be content with being thirtieth on the list for promotion. The Royal Mail Lines fleet, courtesy of mines and U-boats, was down to just twenty-three ships.

The disappointment was painful. On 3 April, he declared that, from henceforth, he would keep quiet about any possible promotion 'until my name is on the articles as master and [the money] paid for my brass hat!'[4] Nothing seemed to be going right: the weather was funereal, with lashing rain and ferocious winds that brought down the telephone wires and hampered ship movements into dry dock. Three days later, Tommy found himself on board *Nela* as a substitute captain, a dismal posting for which there was no additional pay. 'It's dreadful here too. There is no accommodation and the captain [Ingram] doesn't want to go just yet, so I suppose I will have to camp out tonight on somebody's settee!' To cap it all, letters from home were delayed, held up by 'this wretched censoring business'. 'How the dickens,' he asked, 'do they expect to find anything out by reading the letters we <u>receive</u>?' All in all, he considered that being a replacement captain was little better than being 'a glorified fire-watcher'. As ever, he didn't let his ill humour extend to the concluding words of his letter: 'All my love dearest one, Your adoring Tom.'

* * *

In the course of my long life I've had only one moment of unbridled joy. The occasion for this was not, as you might expect, my wedding day, or the birth of our firstborn, Anne Marie, though either or both might qualify.

Dr Donald Macdonald to Richard Knott,
Largo, Fife, Scotland, 17 July 2010

While Tommy Davies was enjoying the sharing of the matrimonial bed in Derbyshire on leave in March 1943, Donald Macdonald was waiting for the result of his Final Examinations. He had not enjoyed his five and a half years of 'demmed horrid grind'; it seemed to him that a doctor simply needed to know 'where things are in a general way'. At all events, that spring day when, 'in the gloomy cloisters of Glasgow University', he saw his name on the pass list 'for the degrees of M.B. and Ch. B.', was a moment of joy that he would never forget.

After graduating, Donald did a year's apprenticeship at an emergency hospital in the rural setting of the Campsie Hills, north of Glasgow. 'It was there I met "Nana",' he told me sixty-seven years later, the 'vivacious' Joanna of the 'sparkling dark eyes'. She was 'quite a doll' and the two young doctors shared a sense of humour, played bridge (badly), listened to Dinah Shore on the radio, and read Damon Runyon, Cornelia Otis Skinner and Ogden Nash. They went to the local cinema to see *Gone With the Wind* and soon thought they were in love ('which we weren't'). His internship over, Donald was called up and headed south to the 'leafy glades of Hampshire', where he 'waxed poetic and a correspondence with Nana began and flourished.' He was an accomplished correspondent who never lost his flair for words. On embarkation leave at the end of 1944, he and Nana saw *The Dancing Years* at the Alhambra, Glasgow, 'and so the smoochy music of Ivor Novello – not to mention my fruity rendition of it – lubricated our idyll.' Donald ended his letter of reminiscence to me with a typically engaging swagger: 'And, by the way, yes, I can still sing – bloody well!' I imagine him crooning softly in Nana's ear on their last night together …

* * *

Dear Dickie,
Noël Coward handed me this morning the note you sent by his hand. I am glad you asked him to call on me. I found him most interesting and a very attractive personality.[5]

General Eisenhower to Lord Louis Mountbatten, 5 August 1943

In July 1943, Noël Coward sailed for Gibraltar on board HMS *Charybdis* – 'he seldom travelled in anything but a battleship.' Having decided against offering his services to the Entertainments National Service Association (ENSA) – he found the idea of actors entertaining in uniform 'somehow ludicrous'[6] – he was heading for the Middle East with the blessing and support of Brendan Bracken, the Minister for Information. On board he entertained the troops and was made an honorary member of the wardroom, and while in Gibraltar, visited wounded troops in hospital going 'with great solicitude to every bed'.[7] In early August he flew on from Gibraltar to Oran in a government Hudson to visit the Battle School there. To his surprise, the war seemed far away: he borrowed some trunks and went swimming; enjoyed drinks in the mess; and was then driven along the beach to a restaurant on the water's edge. 'There was potage, langouste with a wonderful mayonnaise and sauce *Anglaise, poulet, haricots verts*, a salad which brought wistful tears to the eyes, and a great deal of *vin rosé*.'[8]

He visited Algiers for a few days, before boarding the destroyer HMS *Haydon* for onward transmission to Malta. Despite a heavy sea running and having no piano, Coward put on a show for *Haydon's* crew. On Malta he visited hospitals and continued the series of concerts. It shocked him that many of the hospital patients he met hadn't been home for several years, while some, he knew, would never return. In Cairo he stayed at Shepheard's Hotel, but the city made him uneasy, suspicious of its all too pervasive hedonism, while Middle East Headquarters seemed both over-populated and inefficient. He went swimming with the Minister of State, Lord Moyne, and was disturbed by the twinkling lights of what passed for Cairo's blackout. It was a punishing trip, with a protracted series of concerts to the troops – sometimes three a day – as well as hospital visits, sympathetic smiles and kind words to the sick and wounded. In Tripoli, where the hospitals were crowded with the wounded from the Sicilian campaign, he performed again, 'dressed as a Desert Rat, but somehow had managed to give his disguise a Cartier finish.' The reaction was tumultuous, the show a triumph: the audience 'roared, stamped and shouted for encores.'[9]

From Cairo he flew to Beirut, and then on to Baghdad. The Iraqi capital looked well enough from the air, but a closer view could not disguise its flaws: Noël thought it lacking in charm, grubby and stiflingly hot. Arriving at RAF Habbaniya 'felt like stepping into a blast furnace; the glare was blinding and there was a scorching hot wind.' He was lucky, the station commander said, that he 'had happened to pick a cool day.'[10] Later, when Coward performed yet another concert, my father must have been sitting in the audience; I see the airman resolutely unmoved and the entertainer with a smile welded to his face, streaming with sweat, that clipped voice singing about an England that my father would only dimly have recognised. Perhaps, despite himself,

Noël Coward entertains – on board HMS *Victorious*. (*Imperial War Museum, A 25390*)

he would have been moved by it: something in Coward's music evoked a pre-war world seemingly gone forever, and a longing for home. That homesickness was something that Noël frequently encountered amongst the troops and he saw too how rumours about Dominion and American troops exiled in England, their own loneliness partly eased by sweet-talking the wives and sweethearts of British troops so far away, could eat away at trust.

RAF Shaibah, like Sharjah, where Jack had been until recently, consisted of sun-baked huts, aircraft hangars and sand stretching to the distant horizon. Like Baghdad, it had a certain eastern glamour from the air, but, once they had touched down, the base proved singularly unattractive. There was nowhere to escape the heat and Coward found himself longing for home. He did a radio broadcast from there, operating from an airless and tiny studio, a room so stifling that he professed himself hotter than he had ever been in his life and 'like Gypsy Rose Lee I slowly stripped so that by the end I was virtually naked.'

All told, it had proved a challenging trip: the uncomfortable, buttock-bruising aluminium seats of the flight in a DC3; the concerts plagued with breaking microphones, passing trains, low aircraft, or poker-faced brass hats

Coward, in pith helmet and tropical kit, on a visit to Persia and Iraq Force. (*Imperial War Museum, E 26000*)

occupying the front seats in serried ranks of dubious, stiff-backed neutrality while Coward performed for those 'Other Ranks' beyond them; the tortured drive to Basra; and the constant reminders of so many lonely, homesick servicemen. Coward returned to England in October, after a three-month taste of Middle Eastern exile, reflecting on the great numbers of men to whom he had spoken, everywhere from ships' decks to front-line hospitals,

Jack and Greta at Weston-super-Mare before the war. (*Author*)

all of whom were missing home. On the return flight, the aircraft flew up the Bristol Channel low enough for Noël to look down on grassy hills to left and right, so verdantly green after Egypt's prevailing ochre – a sharp reminder of an England that the men in the desert would not see for years to come. Had Jack known where Noël was, he would immediately have remembered the seafront at Weston-super-Mare: my parents, before the war, watching the sun set over Wales in a wash of red and orange over the Channel, the two of them on a promenade bench overlooking the sea – he, with his arm around her, cigarette between his fingers, in sunglasses, a loose jacket hiding the braces that held up his baggy flannels; shapeless brown sandals on his feet; she, upright and pert, smiling as if this life, this moment, would go on forever.

* * *

Oh dear! I would just love to be able to pack my bag and pop off home tomorrow.

Tommy Davies to Dorrie, on board *Nela* in Liverpool, 8 April 1943

Exile in Liverpool was preferable to months at sea: Dorrie and Tom were able to see each other occasionally, although the cycle of partings did not get any easier. Oh, how she missed him! One day in May Dorrie wrote, 'I long so much for you: oh, for a glimpse of you again'; while on another occasion, when Tommy had rung from the dock master's office, she had breathed 'Do you love me?' into the phone. Tom was mortified to realise that the office was 'full of dock gate men, all silent, and listening in to what I had to say.' He had tried to sweet-talk her, whispering endearments, but even when he turned his broad back on the smirking listeners, he could sense their amusement. There was no alternative but to console Dorrie later by post: 'Of course I love you – silly goose – I just worship the ground you walk on.' That early summer night in Liverpool was as 'cold as charity' and he woke at three in the morning with the bedclothes on the deck floor and wanting 'a piddle like nothing on this earth'. He rushed to the bathroom 'holding on to "John" for grim death.' Relieved and back in bed, he ached for Dorrie's sleepy warmth.

The weather remained wet and cold, with the barometer falling rapidly. Worse, there seemed no certainty about when Tom would sail, or indeed where the destination might be. In the event, towards the end of May, he found himself aboard the liner *Aquitania*, now reborn as a troop carrier. The ship was a revelation – 'so huge dear, and very different to anything else I have ever experienced.' It was full of 'new gadgets' and comprised eight decks, luxurious captain's quarters – a day room, 'bedroom, bathroom and bog' – and every cabin on the ship had its own private bath. The ship's swimming pool was a blend of azure blue and cream, and despite much of the ship being boarded up to prevent damage, there were enough glimpses of beautiful wood to hint at her pre-war opulence.

Then, out of the blue at the end of June, Davies was summoned to London for an interview since 'a little dicky bird breathed to me that we are taking over some American ships in the near future.' A subsequent letter from the Royal Mail Lines office in Leadenhall Street, London, confirmed the news: Thomas Davies was appointed to the command of 'Unknown Vessel at present known as "Royal Mail No. 1".' His new salary of £650 per annum would begin in five days' time. It was July before he left the country, sailing for a destination that he could not reveal in the mail, but proved to be New York. He crossed the Atlantic at much the same time as Noël Coward was sailing for Gibraltar. The ship was 'bone dry to passengers' so Tom was obliged to drink coca cola instead of his favourite gin. ('The last intoxicant I had,' Tom wrote, 'was a glass of beer on Nottingham station platform.') Moreover, he was obliged to share a cabin with a prodigious snorer and the days had a strictly adhered to pattern, with breakfast at eight-fifteen, boat drill at ten, and so on, through a set of fixed points of mounting tedium, until dinner, when he sat down to eat with the same threesome, 'a lady going to her husband, who is in the Colonial Service in the West Indies, a young RNVR officer and a civilian official going to the States'.

Each day of the voyage, Tom struggled to forget the disappointment of having been unable to ring home before *Aquitania* had sailed. She docked in America towards the end of July 1943, and Tom soon disembarked, setting out to report to the Royal Mail Lines' agents, Furness Withy & Co, New York City. He was not to see England again for a very long time, but his assurances to Dorrie back in land-locked Mansfield remained constant: 'I shall write you every week my darling and post every Monday by ordinary mail.'

* * *

I believe Lady Astor has had something to say on the behaviour of a minority of the MEF [Middle East Forces]. I can only say the majority of the fellows here live a decent life. Some of the weak-minded are led astray, but they are a minority. Her article has had unfortunate repercussions, with many of the fellows receiving letters from their girls breaking off engagements and long friendships.

Syd Croft to his parents, Cairo, 6 September 1941

I found no letters at all in Jack's house after he had died, not even from the recent past, let alone the war years. Nearly ninety-three, he had lived alone almost to the end, only to be hospitalised for his final few days. The last thing he said to me was: 'I don't like to seem pernickety – but I am.' He looked unrecognisable, so shrivelled and diminished.

In the weeks that followed I searched his house methodically, even the loft, feeling like a scene-of-crime officer. He proved to be a hoarder, more I suspect because he was increasingly unable to make decisions about what to throw away than with any purposeful intent. The drawers and cupboards were full: broken spectacles, unsent Christmas cards, old coins, tailors' chalks and scissors, string, even used envelopes – without their contents, of course. Although the hoped-for wartime correspondence between husband and wife was absent, there were some photographs curling and fading with age, many of them in a glossy, dark-brown album evidently bought in some Cairo market, its leather cover embossed with camels, pyramids and palm trees. I have no memory of him ever admitting to its existence, let alone talking me through the contents. Some snaps were of the base at Habbaniya – a church, the open-air cinema, the swimming pool – and the Nairn bus in which Freya Stark had sweltered as she travelled through the desert long ago. It looked like a large metal coffin.

The album also provided a rare relic of my father's handwriting, surprisingly fluent for a non-correspondent, neat captions inked in white on the black pages. There were some terse messages for my mother – 'Fondest love dear, Jack,' – and one of him in his swimming trunks on a desert beach, 'Nearly in the raw, what!' That poignant, exclamatory echo of officer-speak from this aspirational corporal! There was also a photograph of airmen lined up beneath a limp flag, the desert sand as flat as concrete, though scarred with tyre marks. Beneath, Jack had written: '25th Anniversary of RAF. 1.4.43. 244 Squadron, Sharjah, Arabia.' Miles and miles of desert sand, churned by footmarks, both airmen's boots and native sandals. One photo he had labelled 'Lady Astor's Lido of the Middle East'; it comprised Jack and an anonymous airman standing listlessly before some sturdy, formal shrubs and an unlikely, neat lawn. Were it not for the evident heat, both men clearly bullied by a merciless sun, you might think this was some formal garden in a Cheltenham summer. Jack's pith helmet is awry, while his expression is one of a man who has long since given up hope. For Greta's benefit – and sympathy – he has written, 'Temperature around 130 degrees, 130!!' How he would have cursed Lady Astor's smugness, the insensitivity of her parliamentary question about reported luxury at Habbaniya, describing it as the 'Lido of the East'. Airmen far from home longed to deposit her in some dried-up desert wadi without a compass or a drink: 'Had she ever felt the heat/ At a hundred and twenty degrees/ Had she ever been in bed/ Overrun with bugs and fleas?'[11]

Many of the locations in the photos were hard to place: seemingly the same desert and palm trees; flat lands; houses constructed from sacks, tin cans and rushes; a roof of corrugated sheeting; a ferry; Arabs diving for pearls; a dhow; a bazaar with two airmen surrounded by shanties, beggars, robes and heat; a white-robed Arab on his knees, his face touching the sand ('Evening Prayers', Jack had written); bullet holes in a wall; barbed wire fences; a 'Desert Lily'; two Sudanese women, their faces covered, with thin elegant hands, and behind them, a fence and an Arab man with wary eyes. There was a group of men in shorts and sweat-stained uniforms: Jack with the Sharjah Police Department – Parsons, Hammond, Cunningham, Holmes, Hewitt, and Hardy. But more often, all that the photograph did was raise another uncertainty: for example, what was the story behind 'Film found in crashed aircraft, locality not known'? Jack had kept three pictures from the roll of film – one showing a disintegrated bomber in the desert; the

'Lots of love dear' – Jack in Habbaniya, August 1943. (*Author*)

second, the same aircraft surrounded by Arabs with guns; and third, a four-engined bomber, with a star on its side, droning over the sea, breakers below it and men swimming, looking at it flying overhead.

There are scores of other photos: of Jack with a towel under his arm – the intrepid swimmer; a wire fence with beyond, ghostly and fading fast,

The Sheikh of Sharjah at home and the RAF abroad, 1942. (*Author*)

two ancient biplanes; a minaret in the far distance. There are photographs
of Damascus, and several of Aleppo, up towards the Turkish border. Jack's
handwriting is fading fast, but with a magnifying glass I can just make out
a sign on a sun-struck wall, which advertises – in English – the services
of Thomas Cook and Son and lauds the merits of their muleteers. Jack's
preference is for photographs of places rather than people, a characteristic
that became more evident as he aged. He rarely identifies a person or place,
and the fading ink gives the writing an air of time lost. An exception is one
of a mixed gathering of officers and Arabs, khaki next to flowing robes. At
the back is a man in a double-breasted white suit. He looks influential –
an envoy from London, or a man with a talent for business (oil perhaps?).
At the front is Sharjah's CO, Wing Commander Patrick, next to the Sheik
of Sharjah. Jack is nowhere to be seen; is he patrolling the perimeter wire
perhaps, or checking the coolies, or even asleep on his charp dreaming of
home? Strangely, there is a postcard of the German general, Rommel, with

'All the Ancients',
December 1944.
(*Author*)

predictably no writing on the back. Only a scribbled 'stamp' drawn by the infant me in red crayon. Finally, there is one of my father in uniform – taken by whom, I wonder? It shows him in front of the pyramids, a boot placed on a crumbling wall; underneath he has written: 'All the ancients. December 1944.' It dawned on me then that the photographs were surely posted home, with his letters that no one thought to keep.

Chapter 11

East and West

I have a fire in my bedroom, and a Rajput bearer who walks in and out while I grease my face, in the most intimate way. Yesterday to lunch came the Tikaranee of Kapurthala, most fascinating with a Parisian touch and a real sari, lips, nails, and rubies all matching. I have hopes that the car and return overland may come about.[1]

Freya Stark to Nigel Clive, C-in-C's House,
New Delhi, India, 13 February 1943

For most, being posted overseas – the Middle East, India, Burma – meant many days consumed by travel; slow and uncomfortable journeys shadowed by risk and uncertainty about what might lie ahead. The privileged – the Beatons, Cowards and Starks – avoided the doubt about where they were bound, but not necessarily the danger or discomfort. Freya Stark, for example, knew exactly where she was going and why when she boarded a flying boat in February 1943: India, to work on propaganda there for a three-month spell at the invitation of Field Marshal Wavell. She thought the aircraft resembled a marine animal from the Greek myths; certainly it was painfully slow by modern standards, but there was no denying that this was as close to luxury as wartime travel could get. Nonetheless, the journey was not without its problems. At one point, she and five other passengers were faced with being required to disembark and be abandoned for an indefinite period in Basra, but eventually, after insisting that a telephone call should be made to Wavell's PA, Freya was reinstated and fifteen gallons of petrol ditched to compensate (she thought it misjudged her weight). India enchanted her, both the Kiplingesque hotel at Gwalior and then her subsequent stay in Delhi with the Wavells. It was authentic India but with the comforts of the English country house: extensive lawns, herbaceous borders, trees full of parrots and peacocks, and an ox-drawn lawn mower.

Her travel arrangements back to Iraq were unconventional, idiosyncratic and dangerous. She had bought a car, a dove grey Plymouth, with a 24 horsepower engine and blue leather upholstery, and after a short trip to Simla, she drove some 4,000 miles in nineteen days over the gravel and stones of what passed for the trans-Iranian road, only too aware that the value of the car's tyres alone made her worth robbing. En route, she saw long winding streams of Russian aid, flowing like a metallic river north towards the wastes of the Persian border. When the car's petrol tank punctured, it was secured with a mix of date paste. Eventually, on reaching Teheran, she sold the car at a considerable profit. In a letter to Sir Sydney Cockerell written on 6 March, she had asserted that 'the object of life, if I were asked, I should say is to conquer fear'[2] and the long road back to Baghdad seemed designed to prove the point. She was back in Iraq by April and returned to London in the summer of 1943, resigned to the inevitability of her American lecture tour.

* * *

I sometimes used to think when I had all those nice long leaves at home with you recently that I would eventually have to pay for it (I hope I don't – unduly – anyhow). But as the monkey said when he made love to the rocking horse, 'There's no pleasure without pain!!!'

I am awaiting a ship which has not yet been allotted to me. She may be here or at one of several other American ports on this coast, but so far as I know, I am likely to be here for another week or two yet, and then even may have to go somewhere else. All I hope is that I don't have to face another train journey like the one across the States!!

Captain Tom Davies to Dorrie, Olympic Hotel,
San Francisco, 9 August 1943

Both Tommy Davies and Freya Stark travelled to the United States on the *Aquitania*, though in voyages separated by some three months, Davies sailing on 21 July 1943 and Freya the following October. Tommy arrived in New York on 28 July, and at 7 in the evening, took the San Francisco train – California via Chicago and Utah! – stirred by the prospect of crossing the vast continent from east to west. Every rhythmic clatter of the rails took him further from Dorrie; he sat, head resting against the glass of the carriage window, and watched the immense landscape of America reel past. The compensation for his separation from his wife and daughter was the prospect of his own ship, presently raucous with shipbuilders' noise in some West Coast harbour.

The journey was not how he had imagined it. To begin with there was the uncomfortable fact that his newfound sea captain rank counted for nothing in America: 'Captains, officers and men were bundled in all helter-skelter, any old how, so that it was quite impossible to maintain any form of dignity.' Dinner on board often meant a seat 'alongside a greaser or a fireman at the dining table'. Moreover, the train itself was old, with no air conditioning, while the windows were necessarily closed throughout to keep out the smoke, dust and dirt. Nonetheless, somehow the 'appalling mess of dirt and ashes' proved inescapable and left him 'as black as a coal heaver'. The view beyond the grimy window failed to lift his spirits; this from a man who was used to long days staring at an empty ocean stretching to a distant horizon. There were seemingly endless miles of flat plains and big skies, and only the slow traverse of the sun indicated that time had not stopped. Chicago came and went, but the window still revealed a 'flat plateau land with little but Indian corn growing'. Occasionally a solitary, wind-twisted tree or isolated copse broke the monotony. Other than crops swaying in the breeze, there was little sign of human activity; perhaps a clapboard homestead at the end of a dusty track, or a black Ford roadster on a lonely road. They stopped briefly at Ogden, near Salt Lake City, 'a Wild West town with a street full of boozers', then passed over the Great Salt Lake, 70 miles long and 30 miles broad, 'just one blinding expanse of white salt' as far as the eye could see. The train slowed, cautiously crossing a wooden trestle bridge while Tom gazed out across the vast stretch of water and beyond, to the distant mountains. Safely past the Great Salt Lake, the train speeded up, passing through sandy desert and scrub in a heat-hazed afternoon, and on into the night, a mournful whistle blowing at each level crossing. By morning, they were in California, the desert replaced by fertile, green hills, the valley floors thick with fruit trees.

Once at San Francisco's Olympic Hotel, he 'wallowed' in a long, luxurious bath, which left a 'high watermark of muck so thick that you could dig it off with a trowel'. His stay was comfortable enough, the splendour of the accommodation, he informed Dorrie, typified by the fact that each room had its own radio set. His room was three floors up and looked out on the main street. Food was cheap and plentiful – a portion fit for one person could feed three back in England – and all that fruit! There were 'peaches, pears, apples, oranges, BANANAS, lovely Victoria plums, greengages, apricots'. His letters, with their detailed descriptions of meals, speak volumes about the hardships back home. At one point he professed himself 'ashamed' to eat a steak, though it didn't stop him demolishing it with relish. Resenting the long wait for his ship, he was at a loss to know how best to pass the time, and so the sea captain turned tourist, visiting the Golden Gate Park and taking the street car to Ocean Beach. His impatience was worsened by worries that his letters to Dorrie weren't arriving (air mail, he complained, was frequently held up). How he wished that he could have waited at home rather than in a city where he was anonymous, knowing no one! Letter by letter, he poured his heart out to Dorrie, so 'staunch and true and loyal'.

The launch of the Liberty Ship *Samthar*, Portland, Oregon, 1943. (*Angela Awbery White*)

It was the end of August before he joined his ship, not in San Francisco but in Portland, Oregon, more than 600 miles north up the American West Coast. Originally called the *Charles A. Broadwater*, the Liberty ship was renamed *Samthar* and had been built as part of the 'largest shipbuilding programme the world has ever seen'. 'Liberties' were designed for a short life, perhaps five years; would be 'slow and seaworthy'; and were 'the best that can be devised for an emergency product to be quickly, cheaply and simply built'. Some 2,710 were built to meet emergency wartime transport needs. There were doubts voiced about their construction: 'owing to the unwieldy proportion of trainees and to inadequate supervision and inspection, many Liberty ships built in the West Coast yards had had plates badly joined.'[3] The *Charles A. Broadwater* was built by the Oregon Shipbuilding Corporation and launched on 29 August 1943.[4] Tom arrived in Portland only just in time and the photographs of the launch show him dressed, not in Merchant Marine

Captain Thomas Davies at the launch of *Samthar*. (*Angela Awbery White*)

uniform, but in a nondescript raincoat. By 9 September, *Samthar*, as she had become, had sailed for 'destinations unknown', India, it transpired. It would be another three months before Dorrie and daughter Angela received any news: a nine-word Cable & Wireless telegram – FONDEST LOVE DARLING WRITE SAME ADDRESS GOD BLESS YOU. For a long time afterwards there were no letters at all and they began to fear the worst.

* * *

> I am on the point of departure and have got everything essential done, including my will ... and had a great fight with the Treasury, who wanted to cut £300 off my salary ... I must say, however, the Foreign Office are more of gentlemen, for Sir Maurice Petersen asked me to call and talk about my mission, and told me that the M. of I. had a hideous reputation.[5]

Freya Stark to Christopher Scaife, London, 10 October 1943

On 7 October 1943, Freya Stark had been at a party in London 'dressed like an Eskimo in a white fur coat.'[6] A few days later, she took the sleeper train north from King's Cross, and on the 12th, sailed from the Clyde for America on the *Aquitania*. There were 5,000 troops on board; the air was thick and unpleasant; and every inch of the ship was packed with people, predominantly men. The majority of the women were with babies, crammed into the bow area of the ship. Freya took a wry amusement from the captain's great care for the children on board, whose fate she thought would be 'to grow up for another war'.[7] The prevailing colours on board were khaki and the blue haze of cigarette smoke, and the Atlantic 'howled by in its usual gruesome and useless hurry, putty green flecked with white.'[8] The liner had lost its pre-war gloss, stripped back to its basics, its catacombs below decks a bedlam of hammocks. Freya's single cabin housed three other women, and outside, ill-tempered squalls rattled by. The portholes were battened down through the long hours of darkness for fear of submarines and yet the icy winds seemed able to whistle through the ship. Could it get any worse? Oh yes! Three or four days later she developed acute appendicitis, the pain so extreme that the ship's young doctor blanched with panic. *Aquitania* was not well placed to deal with an emergency of this kind, its hospital full and the nurses already fully employed. At least Freya found herself excused from the daily boat drill: 'I could now,' she thought, 'drown in a quiet independent way by myself.' It was proving a dire experience: the cold, the movement of the ship, the stench of oil and paint, and the grim attempts at entertainment – the deck tennis and sweepstakes – and the disconcerting mechanistic way the officers had of turning their attentions off and on as if by a switch.

On the fourth evening the ship docked at Halifax, Nova Scotia, and at eleven that night, swaddled in blankets and carried on a stretcher behind a flickering lantern by four sailors, Freya was taken off the ship in solitary splendour; it was, she thought, 'like the funeral of Sir John Moore at Corunna'. Above her, the ship's side soared into the darkness and drizzle, while thousands of men peered down, whistling and catcalling at the pain-wracked patient, 'the ridiculous little mouse' on her stretcher. At the infirmary, she was unfurled from her cocoon of blankets by a sympathetic nun and prepared for an operation in the early hours. At least, she thought, she had survived the grey and wind-torn ocean: there was nothing better for dispelling the dismal swell of the Atlantic rollers than the sense of dry, solid land beneath one's feet.

It was four days after the operation before she ventured out for the first time, taking a conducted drive around the town. She found Halifax peaceful with its rocky boulders and low ridges, birch and pine trees; it resembled, she thought, a cross between a pioneers' fort and a boat builders' city. It was 12 November before she left on the night train for New York. She thought the city thrilling –'delirious' shopping, its skyscrapers 'clustered rather like the towers of S. Gimignano or Bologna,'[9] the blue sky above 'pencil buildings'; the dark canyons of its streets; the incomprehensible patter of the taxi drivers. Still weak, and suffering from anaemia and low blood pressure, she anticipated that she would not be fit enough to begin her tour of the country until January 1944.

While New York City's energy and confidence was uplifting, the prospect of the lecture tour increasingly weighed her down, since she recognised the difficulties associated with her brief of presenting a convincing case for the British Government's pro-Arab policy. Freya saw that the terms 'Liberal' and 'pro-Zionist' were interchangeable in the city, and yet she considered herself emphatically liberal, but also passionately anti-Zionist. Unsurprisingly perhaps, her health problems continued, and by 6 December she was back in bed, depressed and laid low by a bout of flu; it was not, she wrote to Sir Sydney Cockerell, the best way to prepare for what lay ahead, facing up to both ignorance and malevolence. She concluded her letter by reflecting that, 'One doesn't write of all the events and I suppose if our war letters were read in time to come, people would say that we are as remote as Jane Austen from our time – forgetting the censor and the general uselessness of repeating newspaper news.'[10] Wistfully, she contemplated being in London's Kew Gardens amongst the azaleas, a far cry from the war, New York and the looming shadow of her traverse of the New World to sell the Old World's Arab policy. Invariably she felt restricted in what she could write in her letters. On 10 December, she wrote to Cockerell again, referring to a long letter that she thought would upset the censor. She would post it instead in the diplomatic bag, she told him. Freya reached the capital just before Christmas 1943, and was glad of the freedom of the embassy's diplomatic bag. She found a Washington bustling with US senators, journalists and 'influential ladies', and it soon became clear that popularising the Arab cause would be difficult, while promoting Britain's views promised to be even more problematic. At times she found herself dreaming of sitting in her garden in Italy just sewing. How she longed for 'the Civilisation of the East'!

* * *

The M. of I. boys have at last decided that they want me to do the same job for them in the Far East as I did in the Near East. My first stop is to be India and they want me there quickly.[11]

Cecil Beaton's diary, London, December 1943

In October 1943, the Ministry of Information had proposed that Cecil travel to the Far East to photograph 'the war effort in India and social services of all kinds', as well as sending back reports on the present state of Britain's Empire. His contract would run from 7 December 1943 to 9 September 1944. The departure from a cold, bleak Paddington station was inauspicious and Beaton was glad to stop en route at Lord Berners' exotic country house near Farringdon in Wiltshire. The next day he flew on to Land's End, where he was obliged to settle for a frustrating wait, only brightened by the dazzling good looks of the Canadian pilot who was to fly them south. Eventually the Dakota was cleared for take-off but crashed almost immediately, a tongue of flame licking through the cabin before the whole aircraft became swathed in a dense cloud of thick orange smoke. With an explosion likely, it was necessary to get out of the aircraft as soon as possible and Cecil found himself by the open door, observing others on board jumping out into the darkness. It was clearly better than burning to death, but there was no knowing how far he might fall. At all events he found himself 'upside down in a grassy field covered with hoar frost and patched with snow'.[12] There were flames all round. The handsome pilot was initially thought dead, but survived, badly hurt when the joystick pierced his stomach. Cecil flew back to London, in a state of shock, subject to sudden bouts of tears.

The experience did not stop him flying out to India soon afterwards. The Parliamentary Under-Secretary of State, Lord Balfour, remembered him 'limping and bandaged' coming to him 'with just one request. Could I fix as soon as possible another flight passage?'[13] So Cecil was in Delhi for the Christmas of 1943, exchanging the 'grit-grey' weather of London, a flu epidemic and the city's general air of forlorn gloom, for the Viceroy of India's house, a palatial pile built in tongue-pink stone, and with gardens where fountains played and birds shrieked, bugles sounded 'and sentries cleared their throats with a resounding rasp, spat and stamped their bulbous boots on the gravel.'[14] There were long marble corridors, salaaming servants and some 150 gardeners. After a family dinner party, notable for the numbers of red and gold liveried servants in obsequious attendance, Cecil tried to find his way back to his bedroom but got lost and, for half an hour, wandered through the palace's marble floors.

* * *

Though I am so far away from you in body, today especially my mind, spirits and thoughts are with you all.

Syd Croft to his parents, Libya, 25 December 1943

Christmas Day 1943: Syd Croft is in Libya enjoying a traditional Christmas lunch of 'ample turkey and pork, apple sauce, potatoes and vegetables, followed by Christmas Pudding with white sauce and rum', not to mention cake with icing and marzipan, beer and cigarettes. Freya Stark is in Washington, on her bed, writing a letter in pencil and feeling 'frail'; Cecil Beaton is in Delhi being cosseted by the same servants who ministered to Freya Stark not so long before; Noël Coward is also in the States, where, the previous week, he had lunched with the Roosevelts, serenading them with *Don't Let's Be Beastly to the Germans*, and struggling with flu – perhaps the same virus that has brought Freya low. By the time he reaches New York, he has lost his voice. On Christmas night he dines with Bill Stephenson, Head of British Security Coordination, who admonishes him for working too hard, insisting that he take a break, drawing attention to his evident ill health and the fact that he has clearly been overdoing it.

My father, Jack, spent Christmas 1943 contemplating his imminent departure from Habbaniya and organising the drinks for his mates. I know this because of a photograph I found in his house: it shows four men at a bar, all of whom are waiting with evident impatience for Jack to serve some cold beers. Perhaps, on this occasion, he is the man behind the camera? He has written 'My Little Effort for Xmas 1943' on the back of the picture, which shows lines of bottled spirits and beer, and overhead a sign reading 'Binder's Bar'. My brother remembers he was known ⁚   ⁻ ⁺ ⁻ 'Binder' Knott, adding, 'I am blessed if I can recall who told me that – I have to say I rather think it was Mum! Probably on the quiet after some bad behaviour on his part.' It is true to say that Jack could 'bind' – complain – at the drop of a hat. As for the bar, it looks anything but festive: it's in a drab room and the curtains are drawn against the sun. This is Iraq, after all.

By 6 January 1944, Jack had arrived at RAF Ein Shemer in Palestine. I imagine him complaining bitterly, aggrieved at being shifted like a pawn on a chessboard; in this, his third year of exile, he must have lost all sense of permanence and certainty. He was not alone in enduring such a long exile: Syd Croft observed that it was his '4th War Christmas and the 3rd overseas'. It was, however, 'quite the best I have had since arriving out here, except it rained heavily and at five o'clock on Boxing Day morning, water started dripping into the bivvy and within a few minutes became a torrent, so we

Binder's Bar, Habbaniya, 1943. (*Author*)

had to evacuate our dugout and make for the back of the truck. Fortunately, only my blankets and great coat got wet.' It is doubtful that Jack would have been quite so positive.

Being exiled during the war brought with it an acute awareness that foreigners thought and felt differently: both Freya Stark and Noël Coward, for example, were disturbed by the mood in America. Noël thought New York gave little sign that there was a war on – the street lights shone and there were large steaks on dinner plates, chilled glasses of orange juice, bananas (they had titillated Tommy Davies too), all of which he bitterly resented. Moreover, there was a widespread view amongst many Americans that the British Empire was in its death throes, its economy irreparably damaged; to cap it all, Americans' knowledge of the war, Coward thought, was appalling. Eventually, faced with yet another diatribe about the wrongs that Britain was committing in India, he found himself tersely pointing out the faults in America's own backyard: its treatment of its black population.

Freya Stark also had to face intransigent opponents of the British Empire: at one dinner, for example, she found herself sitting next to the former Danish Consul in Tel Aviv who was 'so shockingly anti-British' that she longed 'for a pet pogrom of my own before we were through the soup'.[15] Not everything was so negative: when she lunched with Mrs Roosevelt, the President's wife told her 'that what she dislikes in the Zionists is their Nazi principles.'[16] Freya confided that, as a propagandist, she derived great pleasure from her own words and ideas being voiced by someone else.

Noël Coward flew to Miami on 2 January 1944, heeding Bill Stephenson's advice to take a fortnight's rest cure in the West Indies, where Stephenson had a villa. It was a turbulent flight through bad weather, and soon after, he left for Jamaica, where he stayed at the 'Admiral's House' in the hills above Kingston. Instead of winter in New York, chilled by the undercurrent of anti-British feeling there, Coward could 'sit out at night on the terrace in my pyjamas sipping a rum punch and looking at this breathtaking view'; he enjoyed the use of the Chrysler saloon; being feted by the 'ravishing coal-black servants'; and the absence of phones, snakes and mosquitoes. It was truly, he thought, 'a stolen paradise'.[17]

* * *

At first it seemed such a <u>quite</u> hopeless task, so <u>huge</u>; but I have got a reduction of <u>our</u> line of argument down to a few basic principles, and got agreement on it; and have got into touch and had some little effect on the State Department of our part of the world, and the senators and journalists and social ladies I met have been sympathetic and interested: and today a man from our Ministry in New York said 'Thank God for your coming' – so I feel it may not after all be such a fearful waste of public money.[18]

Freya Stark to Sir Sydney Cockerell, on a Chicago-bound train,
6 January 1944

From Washington, Freya began the long rail trek across America, to Chicago first, then on 'the Chief' to California, arriving in Los Angeles on 3 February 1944. She found the landscape more heart-warming than the Americans who inhabited it; indeed, she thought the country 'monstrous', unduly materialistic and godless – 'and their hats are frightful.' From LA, the train followed the line of the Pacific coast, vast blue ocean to the left and green mountains to the right. San Francisco was 'casual, tawdry, theatrical, opulent', but undoubtedly beautiful, 'with hills so steep that houses and cabs look like a sampler stitched with no perspective, and the bay quite ravishingly lovely, so big that all sorts of weathers can shine and shower upon it.'[19]

Work, however, remained deeply unpleasant and left her wondering whether her health could stand the strain. The reason she was in America was to secure support for the British Government's pro-Arab policy, a stance that clashed with the principles of Zionism, the powerful movement towards establishing a Jewish homeland; to some this was nothing less than a 'wartime propaganda campaign' against Zionism.[20] The Jewish community in America opposed Britain's policy to such an extent that an official at the Washington embassy reported that 'Britain-baiting has become a vile sport, unworthy of a self-respecting movement.'[21] Freya Stark was not the first to be considered for the role: earlier discussions involving Lord Moyne, Anthony Eden and Leo Amery had come up with the name of Sir Leonard Woolley; Sir Ronald Storrs' name was also mentioned, but in the event it was Freya who was given the task, enthusiastically backed by Sir Kinahan Cornwallis in Baghdad, who declared that 'Miss Stark's proposed tour of America [is] more important than anything she is doing here at the moment.' Freya had reluctantly agreed to undertake the task, still smarting that the Ministry of Information's clothes allowance was so paltry that she had felt obliged to spend £300 on clothes out of her own pocket; they were 'not even very nice clothes: American fashions are all Hollywood.'[22]

Without fail, Freya was sick with nerves before each one of her pro-Arab lectures. Right from the outset she had been daunted by the size of the job and convinced that mere facts would not be enough to counteract deeply felt emotions. It was then a huge relief to discover that the Canadian leg of the tour would be less confrontational. She headed north in the spring and arrived in Vancouver on 27 February 1944, moving on to visit her late father's ranch at Creston some 450 miles to the east, where she spent a week struggling to sort through his papers and business affairs stretching back over the years: he had left for a new life in Canada in 1912 in the aftermath of the break-up of his marriage to Flora. On 4 March, she was on a train heading for Kootenay, writing letters as she often did when travelling, and intensely relieved that her audiences were now Canadian.

The train trundled on through a snowstorm howling across the prairie, reaching Winnipeg on 17 March. Freya continued to warm to Canada and its people, not least because audiences were less judgemental and fierce, she thought, with 'none of that awful opening of beaks like unreasoning fledglings who expect the punctual worm to follow' and which had been all too evident in the US.[23] She was back in America towards the end of March, and in Washington by the 26th of that month. The official view at the embassy was that her tour had been a success – the talks had gone well and Freya had handled both the press and key contacts with considerable skill. For all that, however, the fundamental issue remained: there was no escaping the intensity of the antagonism between Arab and Jew, and the intrinsic sympathy in the USA for the Zionist cause. Freya sensed that time was running out: the Zionists, she wrote, were 'gathering their ammunition. They are out for a fight to a finish and it is this year or never.'[24]

Chapter 12

To Palestine

A most unusual event occurred this afternoon, with a light shower of rain in the middle of a Palestinian July. It lasted for about a quarter of an hour.[1]

Operations Record Book, Ein Shemer, Palestine, July 1943

My father is on a flight to Palestine. He is sitting bolt upright on a narrow metal bench, surrounded by kitbags, bottles of water and rifles, talking to no one, and looking down at Habbaniya disappearing below him, the lake, plateau and cantonment soon replaced by wastes of desolate sand. The transport plane lumbers west across the desert, skirts the Sea of Galilee before turning towards the coast of northern Palestine and the low hills beyond.

Jack's posting to Ein Shemer was a step into unknown territory. Newly constructed and undermanned, the base was some 30 miles inland from Haifa. Opened on 23 November 1943, its first personnel were in place from 1 January 1944. There Coastal Command crews would learn to fly anti-submarine operations, using the Leigh Light searchlight to identify resting U-boats on the surface and how to fire torpedoes. Wellingtons and Ansons would periodically take off, each aircraft a dark blemish in the cloudless blue sky, and circle prior to setting off on patrol.

When Jack arrived he would have been glad that he had left Iraq behind. Moreover, for once in his life, he was in on something at its beginning, though he would not have welcomed the uncertainty and confusion. On New Year's Day, 'all ranks of the Opening Party were messed in one building – a sergeants' mess,' and by the time Jack arrived on 6 January, the numbers of men at the station were still very few – just fourteen officers and eighty airmen.[2] In time, Ein Shemer would resemble most other RAF stations: razor wire, guard on the main gate; white wooden pole stretched across the entrance; an air of watchful caution; and behind the barrier, a measured, rhythmic order. A posting here must have seemed idyllic initially – blue sky, dry heat, biblical country; the station was to have its own poultry farm, while gardens were to be established near to the airmen's huts. Moreover, the grass was a lush green, and Palestine, seemingly, a land of plenty. There were orchards of oranges, trees heavy with lemons, grapefruit, grapes and olives. There was even entertainment for the men, one-act plays performed by an ENSA company, and the station's own amateur drama group, the Astra Players, putting on a show. Jack's name was a notable absentee from the programme: not in the cast or stage crew.[3]

On the face of it, the camp exuded a sense of calm readiness, but there were enough problems to make the airmen wary: there was, inevitably, the threat of sandfly fever and the men were told that 'coating yourself with a light oil will give you some protection from them.'[4] The sun too was an enemy ('keep your head covered'), but mosquitoes were successfully thwarted by spreading oil on any standing pools of water. In time, other, more mundane disadvantages of the posting began to emerge. For example, there was the loud nightly chorus from the army of frogs in the wadi, which kept the men awake, and later, in high summer, it became uncomfortably hot. Men would dread the sun beginning to rise in the morning. The station was 66 feet above sea level, battered by gales once or twice a month in winter, and thunderstorms more frequently than that between November and February. When the weather was less furious, it was often plagued by haze and dust. In the driest summer months the soil was fissured with deep cracks, made worse by rain erosion. 'Heavy aircraft have been known to fall right through the perimeter track.'[5]

There were, though, greater dangers than the sun, weather or flies. It was soon apparent that 'no British official, from High Commissioner to policeman, slept calmly in Palestine.'[6] Beyond the perimeter wire – and the reassuring presence of heavy bombers lined up in the blazing sun (when they eventually arrived)[7] – there was a rebellious, angry country. There were secret caches of weapons, illicit target practice, gun-running and theft from British military bases, centres holding Jewish detainees overseen by British guards, growing hatred and suspicion, the proliferation of resistance cells against the occupier, whispered plots and treachery. In that sense, at least, it was much hotter than Iraq.

There had been mounting trouble in Palestine months before Jack arrived at Ein Shemer. For example, on the night of 15/16 November 1943, a remote police outpost some 20 miles away had been attacked. No one was killed but the incident provoked riots and angry confrontations between police and demonstrators. Three weeks or so after Jack's arrival, there was an explosion at government offices in Jaffa; in February, an attempt was made to blow up Jerusalem's cathedral, while the Stern Gang attacked Department of Immigration buildings in the city, as well as in Haifa and Tel Aviv; two British policemen were shot and killed and there was a series of bomb outrages. Things got worse in March: a British policemen was shot in the back; a Jewish constable was murdered; a terrorist was killed in Tel Aviv. Attacks on policemen continued: the headquarters in Jerusalem was attacked; four policemen were killed when the CID building was blown up; another was shot dead in Tel Aviv, gunned down from a passing car; and so it continued.

Then, on 8 August, there was an assassination attempt on Sir Harold MacMichael, the British High Commissioner. His car, under police escort, was ambushed by men with tommy guns on the road between Jerusalem and Jaffa, and the police driver and MacMichael's ADC were both seriously hurt. Jack, for the first time in the war since the long sea voyage east, was clearly in real danger. Was he aware that his arrival in Palestine coincided with the declaration by Irgun – the Zionist paramilitary organisation – that it no longer felt itself to be in a state of truce with the British? Irgun took the view that 'every Jew had the right to enter Palestine; only active retaliation would deter the Arabs and the British; only Jewish armed force would ensure the Jewish state.'[8] How much did all this register with my father? One of eleven RAF policemen on station, Jack would soon have been caught up in the day-to-day routine: the two warrant officers reduced to the rank of sergeant for fighting; an airman illegally wearing officers' insignia; a search of an Arab's hut in a neighbouring orange grove, looking for stolen blankets and sheets.[9] All straightforward enough, but on the other side of the perimeter fence, British policemen had become prime targets for the gunmen and the politics were toxic: 'The Polish Jews hate the German Jews, and the Russians hate the Polish and the Germans.' Worse, 'all the Jews combine in hating the Arabs and the Arabs and Jews combine in hating the British police, and the police hate the government officials who look down on them and won't let them join the Club. What a place! God knows who'll get it in the end but whoever it is, I don't envy them.'[10] I'm sure Jack's view would have been, 'Let them fight amongst themselves and just let me go home!'

* * *

My father was someone who always liked to be on the road to somewhere else, though he would have preferred the English seaside to the desert sands of Arabia! Much later, he and my mother would drive through the night to far-off Portugal in his polished second-hand Vauxhall Victor, Jack stoked up with caffeine, Greta recording events in a reporter's notebook. In their sixties they moved house four times and never felt settled again after that first move. In the early days of the war they were similarly keen to move, in this case, away from the English midlands to somewhere less attractive to the Luftwaffe.

They moved in with my aunt, the headmistress of the village school – the house was the schoolhouse. There were also some evacuees from Croydon in south London. A naturally busy woman, my mother will have done her bit – made blackout curtains; packed the china away; tried on her gas mask; dug for victory; made do and mended; did her physical training in time with the radio – ten minutes a day; knitted and sewed; painted lines down the back of her legs to simulate stocking seams; struggled with the washing; eaten things she didn't like (soya-link sausages and salt cod, for example); tried out some of the Ministry of Food recipes broadcast on the wireless; scoured the hedges for blackberries; turned frying pans into Spitfires; collected wood; pinched and scraped; and cut out careless talk. There is a photograph of her dressed like a land girl, holding a spade, accompanied by other women toting sacks of wood and with a broad smile on each face; there are trees in full leaf, distant, rolling hills and stubble on the ground; piles of hay. It wasn't all a rural sanctuary, however. My brother, Peter, remembers the villagers at night trooping into the dingy shelter on the school allotment, its rough walls invariably damp and sometimes running with water. On one occasion Peter saw a doodlebug scudding past the window at tree-top level; another time he was pushed into a ditch when a doodlebug's engine cut out. 'It crashed harmlessly a

The women at Little Hadham, 1944. Behind is the schoolhouse where I was born. (*Author*)

mile or so away.'[11] Occasionally, fighter aircraft from RAF Duxford swept south to defend the capital.

But, despite her conventional wartime wifely behaviour, there was a mystery to my mother's 1940s' history too. Apparently she 'went out a lot', I was told, and it is not difficult to imagine her enjoying some young man's attention in the smoky heat of an airmen's dance hall, followed by a lift home in his mud-spattered jeep. Jack was so far away and he need never know. There are other photographs that suggest a dalliance, or perhaps a love affair: was Ron the man behind the camera that day in Broxbourne on the river Lea in midsummer 1944? Peter is there, smart in short trousers

Mother and son
before Jack's return.
(*Author*)

and tie, while my mother looks happier than I ever remember her. In one photograph, you can almost make out where the man – for it must be him surely? – had sat in the boat, but there is nothing that marks him out, no evidence, apart from my brother's distant memory of the day out, and this shadowy figure who has disappeared from view.

Looking at these photographs now you cannot tell there's a war on, except perhaps for the absence of men. There are two snaps of women in the village school's yard. It is another summer's day in 1944, evidently warm, judging by the thin frocks. Mother is there, a gust of wind blowing her hair away from her forehead. A mournful dog on her lap holds her attention more than the camera. On this occasion, she looks thin and careworn; despite the sun and breeze brushing the trees, she is clearly worrying about something. How will this all turn out in the end? What had happened to cast such a shadow?

And what of the letters posted in wartime, from Iraq, Sharjah and Palestine to rural Hertfordshire? Peter remembered receiving occasional letters from our father, perhaps monthly; and the six-year-old child that he then was wrote back, beginning, 'Dear Bugwhiskers', the unflattering nickname that Jack had been accorded in his absence by my aunt and her housekeeper. I cannot imagine that Jack would have seen the joke.

Peter also remembered a poignant story about our father's wartime medals. 'I remember him getting a letter about them,' he said. 'I think it was the Africa Star or something. He couldn't be bothered with them and he never sent off for them. But I can definitely remember Mum and Dad talking about them.'

'What did Mum think about it all?' I asked, half expecting him to say that she wanted him to get his dues.

'Well,' said Peter, 'It wasn't as if she was proud of him or anything.'

Chapter 13

Where Were You on D-Day?

It's been a dreary wait, for so long without news of you at home, for I haven't had a line from you since the letter you wrote on 21 August. Nobody has any mail so I am not by any means an isolated case! We did recently call at a port but on advice I didn't write from there as the mail facilities are none too good nowadays. I did however send you an EFM, which I hope you will receive safely. You will at least know by that, that I am quite well and in the land of the living still.[1]

Captain Thomas Davies to Dorrie, SS *Samthar* (at sea), 24 November 1943

By mid-January 1944, Captain Tommy Davies was in Aden. *Samthar* had pitched and rolled south and east through the previous autumn and winter, initially bound for Hobart in Tasmania. She had arrived there at the end of October (when Freya Stark was still recuperating in the Halifax Infirmary) and then made for Colombo. Tom was hopeful of a return home and a spell of leave, but after leaving Aden and passing through the Suez Canal and the Mediterranean, he was required to set course for the USA. It was early April 1944 when *Samthar* arrived in Hampton Roads, Virginia. There was to be no respite from shuttling east and west. Instead of a return to England, it was another sequence of Middle Eastern ports – Suez, Port Said, and through the Red Sea to Aden once again.

* * *

Through the spring of 1944, while Tommy Davies was at sea, Freya Stark remained – reluctantly – in America. There were constant reminders of the differences between American and British values. Early in May, at a supper party in Washington, she was sitting next to the Governor of Barbados, whose English public school charm was impeccable, his confidence serenely untroubled. Freya thought him overly hearty, with a tendency to talk in a way that conformed to what the Americans regarded as typically English behaviour; worse, he seemed to believe it was the way to charm his American neighbour. The scene 'was much more like a Noël Coward play than real life' and the Governor's neighbour lapsed into a wounded silence.[2]

On 22 May, Freya took the train to Boston. Beyond the carriage windows, the countryside was a vivid green, the trees extending right down to inlets of placid water, but she did not warm to it; there was, she thought, 'too much green, there is no line, no sense of the bones of the land, no delicate pencil line of ridge or down or field.'[3] Behind her dissatisfaction was the sense that she was too far from the imminent shift in the fortunes of war, the invasion of mainland Europe. She could sense the intense preparations despite the secrecy and caution, and felt forever preoccupied with how it would all turn out. By the end of May, the interminable criss-crossing of America was over, her last lecture gratefully concluded, and with it, her foray into public life. She longed to be home, but instead was obliged to pass time in the idyllic peace of a Rhode Island summer, a world away from the invasion preparations on the English south coast. Five days before D-Day, she wrote to Jock Murray: 'I am sitting on a balcony smothered in wisteria; breakfast is still here and it is ten-thirty. A man is digging in a green field just below – all one hears is the click of the spade and drone of aeroplanes.'[4] She swam, rode around Nanshan Island off the Massachusetts coast, her horse pushing through thickets of sage, the scent filling the air, and planned a new book that she proposed writing when she returned to Devon later in the summer.

It was almost a month before she eventually flew back across the Atlantic. The aircraft's accommodation, 'reserved for Prime Ministers and such', was 'a little boudoir with beds and a divan from which one looked bang down on the Atlantic shining with icebergs in the sun'.[5] She was back in London on 4 July, glad to be back, however briefly, to see the city in its wartime garb; pleased too that the lecture room nightmare was past. Later that summer she left for Devon by train, its carriages full of evacuees escaping the doodlebug raids. She had mixed feelings, aware that she was running away from a capital under fire, but driven too by the fact that she had a book to write.

* * *

On D-Day itself, Tom Davies was at sea, sailing between Colombo and Madras. Towards the end of June, Dorrie Davies received a reassuring letter from a friend in Calcutta who had seen *Samthar's* skipper 'looking ever so well', though struggling with a dose of prickly heat. It wasn't until 4 July 1944 – the day Freya finally reached London – that *Samthar* turned for home; Captain Davies had already been away for nearly a year.

Freya Stark still in America; Tom Davies still at sea; my father in Palestine – all far from home during the early summer of 1944. Cecil Beaton too was a long way from Europe, having exchanged 'the black drabness of bomb-damaged South Kensington in the depths of the fifth war winter, [for] the sun, glitter, and *bhari tamasha* (splendour) of imperial Delhi'. It was like another world altogether,[6] although peopled, Cecil found, with recognisable British stereotypes. General Auchinleck, for example, with whom he dined, and whose wife lobbed almonds over the dinner table at her husband, he found to be 'the sort of heavy, clottish male soldier that I don't understand or admire', and the Acting Governor of Bengal, Sir Thomas Rutherford, he held to be 'a charmless rodent'.[7] The Indians, on the other hand, stunned him with their haunting beauty. 'Women's faces peep from tinselled draperies and remind me of doves; their bodies as compact and firm as bronze statuettes.'[8]

To his surprise, though, Cecil hankered after an India far from the imperial palaces and exotic gardens; he put this down to the way undue comfort eats away at peace of mind. Away from the capital and deep in the backwaters of India, he felt much better, 'impervious and serene'.[9] Despite his brush with death by aeroplane in the previous winter, he now found himself frequently flying into danger. For example, he was the sole passenger on a flight to Peshawar, in what is now northern Pakistan, the aircraft assaulted by lashing, torrential rain. He sat in the co-pilot's seat, acutely aware that the pilot was straining to peer into an impenetrable sky, half an evil black and half a dirty grey. When they did briefly emerge from the thick cloud, the land below was largely under water. Eventually the pilot judged that conditions were too dangerous to continue, so he turned back towards Lahore. Once they had reached relative safety, the pilot revealed that the engines had completely cut out at one point. 'I didn't say anything as I didn't want to alarm you.'[10] Beaton was alarmed anyway. Flying in India invariably proved hazardous, thanks to bad weather, widespread mountains, rudimentary landing strips, and on at least one occasion, an undercarriage that refused to budge from its locked position. Cecil had been obliged to 'take the stick' while the pilot fiddled in increasing panic, trying to release the undercarriage mechanism. When they finally landed, the aircraft bounced high in the air as if made of rubber. On another flight, this time in a Dakota, he was obliged to hold the hand of a terrified nurse, aware of the sweat in his own palm, while trying to exude a casual nonchalance.

There were compensations to these flirtations with catastrophe. In Rawalpindi he was given what he thought was the best dinner he had eaten since the war began. 'The steak,' he wrote, 'was as thick as a dictionary.'[11] The aircraft had floated down into a valley deep in the Imphal mountains, entering into an idyllic climate: 'sun all day; cold at night; the cherry trees in blossom, rhododendrons ablaze.' He was glad to have avoided the monsoon season, which shrouded the troops in a dank, fetid world, where 'boots are never dry, so that your toes begin to rot. Supplies suffer; the coarse flour breeds bugs. Mud reaches up to the thighs. Everything grows mouldy; even the bamboo poles grow internal fungus, and the smell of decay is everywhere.'[12] Mosquitoes teemed in the elephant grass. Small leeches would swell to the size of a man's thumb when they had slaked their thirst on human blood. Cecil travelled constantly, often in army trucks tentatively perched on ridge-top roads with perpendicular, deep drops on either side. When, after hours of laboured rolling over rutted mud tracks, they finally reached some remote base, perhaps poised on a fir-covered precipice, the atmosphere of missing home amongst the troops was acutely painful, so much so that 'it is almost more than one can bear to ask for news of England.' The appearance in their midst of this diminutive Englishman, complete with neat tweed jacket and his photographic paraphernalia, would have been a surreal reminder of the English capacity for the quirky and individual. These benighted servicemen – this forgotten army – were so far away, and inevitably, mail was spasmodic, arriving in clusters (or not at all) and long after they had been written, during which time so much at home might have changed. It left these exiles fearing the return to the familiar and domestic – if ever the war would end, and of course, if they were to be spared. One RAF officer confessed to Cecil that he was already feeling a sense of fright at the thought of going home. It was disturbing: 'After years of separation from the life they knew,' Beaton wrote, 'how could they hope to pick up, when they returned home, a thread of continuity?'[13]

The troops Cecil photographed were there for the duration, it seemed, or until they were wounded or killed, while he had merely to cadge a flight home when his contract ended, or the job was felt to be done. For all that, it was no cushy number. India was physically and mentally demanding, and Cecil's work was invariably beset with problems. For example, on one occasion he entrusted a consignment of some 250 rolls of photographs to be sent by air, only for them to disappear, never to be seen again. It saddened him that the subjects of those photographs, who despite what they were enduring, had smiled into his camera lens, would never see the outcome. Day after day, India tested him, whether it was the truck convoy back to Delhi during which they covered just 30 miles in six hours; the leopard hunt in Jaipur; the 'dazed trance' after smoking hashish in Benares; the way at night insects clustered in impenetrable clouds around the electric lights; or the chilling shock of urban poverty. Although he warmed to Bombay – 'I like this place more than any other town I have seen,' he wrote to Clarissa Churchill[14] – he was less than enthusiastic about other cities: Calcutta he regarded as 'a sort of oriental Clapham Junction', where men on leave from the front 'could relish walking on stone pavements.' India demanded a strong constitution and an iron gut – the latter emphatically not a Beaton strength. At one point, he came down with food poisoning after eating some malevolent prawns. Then his anticipated trip to China was necessarily postponed after he fell victim to a bout of dengue fever and was confined to bed for a week, his leg inflamed and throbbing, the whole experience being 'a crescendo of pain, sweating and general misery'.[15]

By early April he had recovered enough to set out on a ten to twelve-week tour of British military missions in China. It began with a hair-raising flight over the 'Hump', the range of mountains dividing India from its northern neighbour. Once in China, he travelled some 5,000 miles by train, sampan, truck and plane, a series of excursions so grim they collectively put the Indian experience into a more positive light. He visited the forward areas, slept on wooden boards, travelled uncertainly along narrow, mountainous paths, cast weary eyes up to skies heavy with 'pitiless' tropical rain, chased fleas around his skin, shivered at an observed case of bubonic plague, and to compound it all, was starved of books and music throughout. It all left him 'rather morbid and introspective'. In late April, he wrote to Diana Cooper, 'I hadn't realised quite what it means for a country to be cut off from the rest of the world for so long.' It was all so squalid: in a letter to Clarissa Churchill he described how bouts of dysentery meant that his stomach was a constant preoccupation: 'I am a victim of a major firework display within my stomach; rockets, Catherine wheels and a few merciful squibs make my days and nights very unsettled.'[16] All those mad scrambles to the outside lavatory in the relentless rain! He was still in China as D-Day came and went, and when he finally flew out of the country, fearful and with trembling hands, 'it was like coming out of jail, of being free of the Gestapo.'[17] Eventually he returned to Delhi, where he saw newsreels of D-Day, which made him long for home. The return to the west, however, was getting closer: after visiting Simla and Karachi, he flew to the United States – a journey punctuated by a seemingly endless series of stops at Aden, Cairo, Brazil, Trinidad and Miami amongst others. He reached New York on 4 August 1944, to be greeted by the news of the death of his close friend, the artist and tank commander Rex Whistler, who had been killed during the Normandy Campaign. Cecil 'sobbed uncontrollably.'

* * *

Eventually, Cecil Beaton's and Noël Coward's paths would cross in India, but first Noël was committed to visiting South Africa, as a guest of Field Marshal Smuts and the South African government. Back in 1941 there had been doubts about such a visit: 'Bobbety' Cranborne had even written to Duff Cooper suggesting opposition at the highest levels: 'the powers that be tried to prevent him going to South Africa.'[18] Now, in February 1944, under the auspices of the South African Forces Entertainment Unit, Coward spent nineteen days in Cape Town doing nearly forty shows. Noël was very conscious of the racial and political tensions in the country, while the concerts proved a considerable strain, with Coward harbouring 'a lurking fear' triggered by the rows of anonymous, sunburned faces and the sea of drab uniforms. What made it worse was learning that not everyone was willing him to succeed: at one point, he was pursued by a dogged English reporter who had been 'ordered to attend all my troop concerts until he was lucky enough to see me booed off the stage.'[19] The future Labour Government minister Tony Benn saw Coward perform in Bulawayo on 4 May 1944: 'He was very smartly dressed in a khaki shirt and tie, light brown soled suede shoes.' Benn thought him 'first rate', admiring the entertainer 'being so low despite the ladies present. He used the words "bloody, bitch, Christ, bastard, short arm inspection, sexy" and so on despite them.'[20] However, not everyone was won over by his performance. One soldier in East Africa Command wrote a letter to the press about what he had seen in Noël's Nairobi concert in early May. He was concerned that Coward had earlier performed for the 'civil population', and hoped that the show for the troops was 'a good deal superior' since 'there would be many who resented the large amount of vulgarity and filth which was gibbered forth through the medium of the microphone.'[21] Unperturbed by such idiosyncratic views, but troubled by the press's relentless pursuit of him, Noël moved on, all the while contemplating the relief of an imminent return to the UK. A telegram put paid to that, a 'bombshell' communication from Lord Louis Mountbatten, Supreme Allied Commander, South East Asia Command, inviting Coward to 'come out and entertain the 14th Army in Assam and Burma.' Could one turn the mighty Mountbatten down? Well, Noël couldn't, anyway: so on 16 May 1944, he sailed from Mombasa to Ceylon on board the destroyer HMS *Rapid*.

For Noël it marked the start of an unforgiving itinerary that echoed Cecil's troubles in India: the 'mosquitoes and mud' of the monsoon season; an aircraft crashing in flames just in front of them on the runway; the appalling daytime heat of Calcutta, often surpassed by the temperatures at night; a near-fatal collision with a naval lorry – all giving the 'authentic taste of hell and damnation'. The camp of bamboo huts at Chittagong was a typical concert venue; there, in warm rain, he gave a performance 'at a small gun emplacement on a rain-sodden hilltop'. Noël was there to entertain the 'Forgotten Army', the 14th Army under General Slim, which was fighting the Japanese in the Burmese jungle, as well as the monsoon, the snakes and insects, and an apparent lack of interest from the Allied press. He would sing, perhaps *Mad Dogs and Englishmen*, *The Stately Homes of England* and *London Pride* in a large, soulless warehouse – so Dennis Newland of the

Royal Corps of Signals remembered: 'a memorable night' in Comilla.[22] Noël flew to Imphal, on the India-Burma border, with a cargo of food and ammunition, through a ferocious electrical storm, and only left the day the siege was finally lifted. On the borders of Assam, in a fierce rainstorm that lashed the tin roof, he gave a concert to an audience largely made up of black GIs who 'had never heard of Noël Coward and were getting soaked.' Coward could not be heard above the noise of heavy trucks and torrential rain.[23] Predictably in such a testing climate, he fell ill with a fever, but he was reassured to note that his 'stool was as fresh as a daisy and [his] urine cloudless as a summer day.'[24]

Coward was learning that an artistic temperament did not sit easily in a war zone – but such self-knowledge did not ease the tension that arose when he and Cecil Beaton's paths crossed in Calcutta, two aesthetes up for a fight. At a dinner party, Coward 'played the piano, stealing the show and leaving Cecil out in the cold.' When, on the following day, Beaton looked out of the window to see Coward being photographed with a large group of Indian journalists, he took the view that Noël was making far too much of the trappings of success. He was somewhat mollified when one of Wavell's ADCs, John Irwin, commented that, 'It is not so interesting to see what Noël Coward has done for the world as it is to see what the world has done for Noël Coward.'[25] Later, in Delhi, Coward and Beaton quarrelled again. Artistic temperament might have been to blame, but so too was the persistent hardship that they were encountering and which was wearing them both down. Indeed, Noël eventually succumbed to a nervous and physical collapse, and when he returned to England after nearly a year away, he was 2 stone underweight.

* * *

Not everyone travelled overseas to the war with a heavy heart. Lieutenant Donald Macdonald, proud possessor of his medical degree from Glasgow University, and now a junior officer in the Royal Army Medical Corps (RAMC), was contentedly at sea in the winter of 1944, writing home and relishing the prospect of a new life somewhere other than Scotland. He was unsure of where exactly the ship was bound but the uncertainty did not trouble him unduly. Could it be Haifa, perhaps, or Italy? At all events, he could not 'for obvious reasons, speak of places and routes.' He had missed the D-Day landings by a whisker, arriving at Base Depot, Crookham in Hampshire three days before, on 3 June 1944, feeling 'as new as a peeled egg'.[26] This was emphatically another country, with its 'air of sunlit peace and calm prosperity', lush meadows and majestic trees. While Donald was enchanted by the adventure he had embarked upon, he felt relief that he had arrived too late to be faced with a blood-stained scramble up an invasion beach, dodging bullets, bodies and barbed wire. Instead there were the comforts of a simpler life: 'from dawn to dewy eve we marched, exercised, walked the 2 miles to and from the officers' mess at least four times a day, ate prodigiously, and even introduced our virgin palates to the warmish English beer.' The first night after the invasion, Donald went to the cinema in Aldershot.

There were occasional reminders that there was a war on: for example, 'a flying bomb or doodlebug landed uncomfortably close, the concussion switching on my bedside lamp,' startling him so much that he 'thought [he'd] arrived in the heavenly realms.'[27] But the overriding mood was soporific and Donald began to think that it was all a deliberate brass hat ploy to render the men both numb and willing to conform. 'Someone has suggested,' he wrote, 'that the purpose of keeping us here for a time is simply to make us GLAD TO GO ANYWHERE. How psychologically sound!'[28] Donald grew increasingly suspicious of the army's motives: when they were fed on real ham and eggs at the transit camp, he was sure it meant they would soon be on the move. It was to get them 'fattened for the kill', he thought, and indeed his wariness proved prophetic. It wasn't long after the ham and eggs initiative that he found himself aboard the troopship *Cilicia* in Liverpool Docks. The rare sight of white bread and butter 'which can be plastered on' suggested that sailing was becoming ever closer; then, on 16 December 1944, breakfast stretched to three courses. They set sail almost immediately, with Macdonald smiling to himself at the predictable way the military mind worked – give the men marmalade and all will be well.

I have done a lot of work, mostly bad. My brain has become addled by

1. overeating, gorging.
2. the hot wet climate.
3. trying to take in too many things and getting exhausted.
4. getting accustomed to not listening to bores, and being unable to attend when some interesting person talks.
4a. not quite hearing or understanding all that is told one (native English).
5. hearing too much about places, things and people that one has not heard about previously.

Cecil to Clarissa Churchill, the Far East, 20 March 1944

I was good and exhausted by South Africa even before I started. I know you understand all that, so I am not going on about it, and though I may have been rather petulant and irritating with you, I do believe, as far as the troops are concerned, that my tour was a success on the whole. I have had several pleasant repercussions from 14th Army men who have come up to me in the street and wrung me by the hand, which comforts me a great deal.

Noël to Lord Louis Mountbatten, London, 3 July 1945

I am now no longer a Government Servant so I can confess to you that one very hot morning in Baghdad I took eight files away from my assistant and burnt them.

Freya to Field Marshal Lord Wavell, Devon, August 1944[29]

Chapter 14

'All of the Very Best for 1945'

I am writing this on the 'other side' darling and it will be posted when we get in again. When you come up to town darling I am afraid you won't be able to come on board though. Women are definitely forbidden on these ships, and for that matter, all people who are not directly connected with shipping.

Tommy Davies to Dorrie, on board *Samzona*, 29 October 1944

It was early September 1944 when Captain Tommy Davies finally returned to the UK. When *Samthar* docked at Dundee in Scotland it had been some fourteen months since he and Dorrie had last seen each other. They had just four weeks together before he was sent to London to assume the captaincy of a new Liberty ship, the *Samzona*. He put up at the Mandeville Hotel in the West End, preoccupied with the fact that his new ship was still in the river having missed the tide – 'much to my utter disgust.' The hotel had been damaged in an air raid, as well as being 'full of Yanks all the time' – Tom seemed to think both facts equally irritating. His mood was soured further by a night of broken sleep, courtesy of the air raid sirens, and the rain 'piddling down' on the drab, bedraggled city. *Samzona* was required to operate a shuttle service between Tilbury Docks and France, a routine that meant seven to twelve days' absence, with no letters to be sent from the French side, 'owing to putting additional pressure on the mail service.' At least there would be more frequent short leaves, and the crew was a happier one than on Tommy's previous ship. There was comfort too from the two cats who had decided to share his cabin; he woke one morning to find 'a white and tabby cat which belonged to the last captain' fast asleep on his feet.

The weather in late October had been very cold, and as the series of cross-Channel trips began and winter closed in, it got worse with permutations of persistent rain and squalls, ice and frost, fierce gales and thick fog, which prevented them seeing the French coast. In mid-November, Tom was obliged to anchor off the Isle of Wight 'in full view of Southsea' while the wind howled all day. On another occasion, the weather was so bad that he wasn't able to change his clothes for days on end, or to sleep, other than the occasional stolen catnap in the Captain's chair. Eventually, in thick fog, *Samzona* anchored off the coast, her captain concerned about shallow water, and where he could hear 'the sirens and whistles at the works in the town'. All Tom could see, however, was a dense blanket of fog.

On the days when he docked on returning from France, Tom would find a phone box to ring home, desperate to talk to Dorrie, who, for her part, was worried about the unpredictability of the German flying bombs. Those phone calls home were often unsatisfactory, emphasising distance, the seemingly unending passage of the war, and the overriding chaos of the times. One night in early December, for example, Tom rang from Southampton, but the call was disrupted, his voice drowned by the uproar from troops returning home. 'A troopship had disembarked,' Tom explained in a subsequent letter, 'and the shed was full of lads, home from Italy I suppose, all full of the joys of spring, all shouting and whistling – a ruddy band playing further up the quay and an engine shunting into the shed too!' Tom felt too wintry to share their pleasure.

* * *

My uncle murdered! I went to sleep last night with strange emotions. Walter Moyne was an extraordinary man, colossally rich, well meaning, intelligent, scrupulous, yet a viveur … He collected yachts, fish, monkeys and women.[1]

Chips Channon's diary, 7 November 1944

A less secretive man than Jack might have described the way the countryside near Netanya Leave Camp reminded him 'of Devon, with the cliffs and the sea below crashing against the large rocks'.[2] But he could not bring himself even to speak, let alone write, about what he saw or where he went. He left no record of the promenade at Tel Aviv, for example, or the soft breezes off the Mediterranean; the cinema in Haifa; the pretty girls with dark eyes and olive skin; languid games of tennis; cabaret shows in the open air; pink-faced men drinking cold beer and talking of wives or girls back home, and – a darker memory – shady houses where trouble lurked.

For most of the war, my father's postings had him arriving just when the action had moved on: arriving at the Reception Centre in Cardington just as the battle for France was being lost; deposited in Habbaniya once the siege was over; exiled to Sharjah where sandflies and sunstroke were the enemy, not Germans. It was only when he reached Palestine that things were different: he arrived just when Jewish terrorism emerged from the shadows. Then, when he was moved on to Army Headquarters in Cairo in November 1944, he found himself right at the centre of events. Sometime after he died I was asked if he had been one of the 'Other Ranks' invited to Minister of State Lord Moyne's house in Cairo to listen to opera in his lordship's opulent, chandeliered drawing room. Naturally, I was floundering in the dark since this was precisely the kind of information that my dad never revealed. I knew that Jack's taste in music was more Gilbert and Sullivan than Verdi, and I suspected that he would have been very uncomfortable and resentful sitting there, being 'improved' by the Moynes' worthy record collection. But the question was asked by the son of one of his wartime colleagues and he seemed to think it likely that both men would have been there, uneasily patronised by the Moynes.

Until 1942, Lord Moyne had been Secretary of State for the Colonies and Leader in the House of Lords, but in January 1944 he had been appointed Minister of State in the Middle East. He was in his sixties, blue-eyed and dapper, quiet with steely grey hair. At one o'clock in the afternoon of 6 November, Moyne's official car, a sand-yellow Packard 120, numbered M 101180, its official pennants fluttering, drew up outside the front door of his villa in a leafy Cairo suburb. A glass screen separated him from his official driver, Lance Corporal Arthur Fuller. With Moyne were his secretary, Dorothy Osmond, and an aide-de-camp, Captain Andrew Hughes-Onslow. Fuller was only there because the regular driver, Sergeant Lamb, was ill. The villa garden was patched with shadow and avenues of bright sun; there was a smell of lunch and the early afternoon was heavy with heat. Hughes-Onslow stepped out on to the running board, clutching his cap and papers, while Lord Moyne leant forward to brief the driver on his next engagement. Hidden in the bushes were two men, trembling fingers on guns. They knew the significance of 6 November 1944: it was the 27th anniversary of the signing of the Balfour Declaration.

Fuller got out of the car and moved to open the rear door; Moyne eased himself forward from the comfort of the leather seats; Hughes-Onslow meanwhile was already striding up the drive. Suddenly a voice shouted, 'Don't move!' Immediately, Fuller was shot in the chest and crumpled on to the gravel, which slowly began to turn red. The previously languid Moyne hurriedly tried to get out of the car, but was immediately riddled with bullets. Horrified, Hughes-Onslow turned, saw both the minister slumped on the ground, and the two terrorists intent on their getaway. Fuller was already dead, but Lord Moyne was still breathing. Despite being given four pints of blood and undergoing surgery at five-thirty in the afternoon, he did not survive, and when his corpse was examined, there were eight bullet wounds puncturing his neck, abdomen, back, chest and fingers.[3]

After a frantic chase across the city, the terrorists were arrested and then brought to trial. One of them, Eliahu Hakim, was only seventeen years old. The trial took place in an Egyptian military court and both the accused insisted in speaking Hebrew throughout. Hakim sought to justify the killing of Lord Moyne, arguing that he was a legitimate target, but he 'regretted very much that Lance Corporal Fuller was killed because he was a soldier fighting the Germans.'[4] The funerals of Moyne and Fuller took place at the All Saints Cathedral in Cairo, and my father, it seems, was one of the servicemen marching behind Moyne's coffin, part of the sombre entourage symbolising an affronted empire.

As a crime it served the terrorist cause perfectly: politicians were stung into making angry speeches and exiled British soldiers grew ever more watchful and resentful. The Prime Minister talked of changing his mind over Palestine 'if our dreams for Zionism are to end in the smoke of an assassin's pistol, and the labours for its future produce a new set of gangsters worthy of Nazi Germany.'[5] Churchill was determined to see that the sentences passed upon the killers were executed, despite 'pressure from Zionist and American Jewry'.[6] If not, he wrote in a note marked 'Personal and Top Secret' to the British Ambassador in Cairo, 'it will cause a marked breach between Great Britain and the Egyptian Government.' Tension in both Egypt and Palestine grew. On 30 November, Field Marshal Gort cabled a summary of the status quo: 'Terrorists arrested and detained in custody – 950. Terrorists presently detained in Palestine – 310. Terrorists killed in action against the police – 6. Terrorists prosecuted and convicted – 21. Materials seized: 1 shotgun, 26 pistols, 43 bombs, 22 land mines, 38 gelignite bombs, 276 matchbox bombs, 705 sticks of gelignite, 2,296 rounds of pistol ammunition, 405 rounds of rifle ammunition, 115 detonators, 2 booby traps.'[7] It could have been a snapshot of the Middle Eastern world taken any time in the subsequent seventy years.

* * *

London looks very battered, crowded, tired but no flagging at all and everyone rather grimly disposed to go on for another year or whatever it may be.[8]

Freya Stark to Mrs John Marriott, 3 December 1944

Freya Stark, Cecil Beaton and Noël Coward were all struck by how the war had changed the face of London. The city had acquired a grey, dishevelled look, while the people seemed tired, and to Cecil, 'touchy', even 'quarrelsome'. The V1 'doodlebug' bombs that had fascinated my brother in Hertfordshire and disturbed Dorrie Davies as far north as Mansfield added to the edgy mood and the tarnished fabric of the capital, where even the trees had turned yellow, the green leaves coated in a thick layer of cement dust. To Noël, the V2 rockets, which began falling on London in September, were worse than the V1s: at least with the latter it was possible to hear them coming and take refuge if the engine cut out directly overhead. In contrast, the V2s 'dropped without warning and seemed to shake the universe.'[9]

Freya had returned to London from Devon towards the end of November and was contemplating a trip to India to establish in that country a similar pattern of propaganda to that she had pioneered in Egypt and Iraq. She occupied the time either side of a cold Christmas in the capital, catching up with old friends. ('It is a country of such dear, dear souls.')[10] Noël, meanwhile, was recovering from his time in the Far East, slowly putting weight back on. He visited Paris and Brussels for ENSA, appearing on 15 November at the Théâtre Marigny in the French capital, but found the experience tiresome and ENSA's organisation slapdash. Moreover, the atmosphere in Paris saddened him; it was, he thought, full of 'recrimination, shame and bitterness'.[11] His Paris flat had been occupied by two members of the Gestapo, whose unpleasant personal habits had left the apartment in a filthy state. The carpets, Coward noted, provided graphic evidence of the meals, the booze, and worst of all, the turbulent digestions of the two Nazis. Coward, who had been staying with Laurence Olivier and his wife during the preceding days, performed at the Stage Door Canteen on Christmas Day – a show that lasted from eight o'clock until one-thirty. He emerged into a fogbound Boxing Day morning, and would long remember the night's abiding atmosphere, the thick haze of cigarette smoke and the smell of beer.

The Ministry of Information continued to commission work from Cecil Beaton and he travelled widely as a result – Jarrow, Nottingham, Bradford – taking photographs for various propaganda jobs. Criss-crossing the country revealed the full extent of the nation's exhaustion. The trains were freezing and the food unappetising, not fit for animals, Cecil thought. He saw little to lift his spirits in the prospects of the post-war world and when he looked back he recognised how much the war had changed him. The prevailing mood that autumn was weary pessimism, and that was true of mainland Europe too, where hunger and demands for retribution had supplanted the short-lived euphoria of liberation. Cecil saw that first-hand when he was asked to put on an exhibition of his war photography in Paris, an initiative designed to enlighten the French as to what five years of war had meant for the British. Towards the end of November he visited the front line in the Vosges Mountains, travelling in the same train as Churchill and General De Gaulle. The weather – typically for that winter – was bleak, cold and grim, and Cecil, caught out by the unexpected invitation to travel, was ill-equipped, wearing thin shoes, a dark blue overcoat and a black Homburg. The train's front carriages carried the politicians and their hangers-on, while the journalists – more than 100 of them – were at the rear. As the train steamed east through the night, Cecil could see 'every few yards a soldier at the salute all along the railway track towards Strasbourg'.[12] He returned to Paris with a 'Brie cheese the size of a farm-cartwheel', but there was little else to enthuse over. The city seemed 'stunned' in the aftermath of the German occupation, and life remained hard: 'only a small proportion of people have any heating in their rooms and many have not enough to eat.'[13] Travel was strictly curtailed and feuds were commonplace, with many old scores being settled. Steeling himself, Beaton toured the former headquarters of the Gestapo, whose basement prison walls were scratched with despairing messages of defiance from prisoners long since dead.

* * *

Whatever be the fortunes of war, however long I may be away from home, among strangers and unknown, remember only one thing: I wouldn't have missed this for the world!

Donald Macdonald to his parents,
on board the MV *Cilicia*, Christmas 1944

The *Cilicia* manoeuvred its way down the Mersey on a gloomy December day, with fog settling over the city and away to the west. From the deck, Lieutenant Donald Macdonald watched Liverpool's docks 'rapidly fading into the obscurity of the sea mist'. His sense of excitement was tempered by the fact that he was required to share cabin A15 with ten other men; it had been designed to accommodate two. *Cilicia* was overcrowded and top-heavy, forever at the mercy of a heavy swell. Two bunks down from Donald was Patrick Woodcock, later to become Noël Coward's London doctor. 'I can't paint or write or act,' he wrote to Donald many years later. 'I love people who can – so my practice is a way of living vicariously. (Noël Coward, John Gielgud, Lauren Bacall, Marlene Dietrich etc. – if you don't mind a bit of name-dropping.')[14] This was reminiscence in old age. Now, on this day in mid-December 1944, the two young army doctors, Patrick and Donald, stood side by side on *Cilicia's* deck wondering what lay before them. Ships' sirens blew mournfully, while at the margins of the far horizon, destroyers cut the grey ocean. The Atlantic swell heaved, and fittingly, left men doubled up with *mal de mer*, including Donald, who later, in a letter to his parents, described how 'one meal had reappeared, course by course'. Further out to sea, the wind increased; so too did the surge of the waves.

Much further south, the clouds lifted and the universal grey monotone fell away. The Atlantic now had flecks of green and blue, and the 'ships achieved the whiteness they knew in peacetime.'[15] Porpoises rolled by the ship one evening, and not long afterwards they saw the coast of Spain. Donald could see snow on the distant mountains. Gibraltar proved a disappointment, but once into the Mediterranean, what had seemed a penance now acquired the feel of a pleasure cruise. He was 'breathless, ecstatic', beguiled by the brilliant sunshine and the 'miraculously beautiful nights', the distant shapes of the Atlas Mountains and the Sierra Nevada. Before arriving in Egypt there was even the comfort of a traditional Christmas dinner, the menu for which, signed by others on his table, and written in a style more suited to an ivy-clad country hotel in the Scottish borders, comprised cream of tomato soup, fillet of sole, braised American ham, roast Vermont turkey with sage stuffing, garden peas and roast potatoes, plum pudding, cheese and biscuits, all presented with 'Compliments of the Season and a speedy return home' from the ship's master, Captain Smart.

My father on his ship's voyage around the Cape years before had played endless games of pontoon; in room A15 of the *Cilicia* Donald played bridge, rubber after rubber, he and his roommates sitting, cramped and huddled, on the top bunks with a board resting on the bedding, the playing cards and bottles threatened by the confusion of confined knees and feet. But, cramped as the officers were, the lot of Other Ranks was far worse, Donald likening it to life on a prison ship. My father's card schools – the only glimpse he ever offered of his long confinement on the *Capetown Castle* – would have been infinitely more hindered by lack of space, a guaranteed recipe for argument and fist fights, particularly given the absence of air, activity and responsibilities. Lieutenant Macdonald at least had the dubious privilege of conducting FFIs, or Freedom from Infection Inspections, which entailed an 'examination of pubic and axillary regions'. These should have been meticulous but often were conducted in the dim light of a torch, the medical man squeezing with difficulty through the narrow confines below decks. Jack would have revealed his nether regions with great reluctance! Donald was also charged on occasions with the 'unenviable' task of censoring the men's letters. I doubt that Jack's letters to my mother would have required much in the way of excision. I cannot, for example, imagine him penning his first impressions of Egypt as Donald did so diligently, his mind still racing from the first sight of Port Said harbour as he stood on deck, leaning on the ship's rail, glad of a sea breeze in the heat. A freshly trained medical man, it amused him that 'the first words to introduce us to the mysterious East were the 6-foot rooftop legend "Dewar's Whisky" closely followed by "Craven A does not affect your throat".'

* * *

We've had no fresh orders yet, and here we stay. I don't know why it's all been altered dear, but it may be because of the enemy thrust into our lines, or maybe because of that convoy being attacked off the Scheldt this morning.

Tom Davies to Dorrie, Barrow Docks, Christmas Eve, 1944

The Davies family was separated for Christmas 1944, just as it had been the previous year. Tom was required to return to his ship before the festivities began, travelling to Barrow Docks by train, a singularly unpleasant journey. It arrived nearly six hours late and it was one-thirty in the morning before Tom was back on board ship. To cap it all, he was obliged simply to wait until fresh orders were received. There was no knowing when, or to where, *Samzona* would sail. In the event, she sailed immediately after Christmas, initially through fog, and had docked in Glasgow by New Year's Eve. It was 'colder than charity' there and Tom was anxious about the labour situation once the celebrations were over, anticipating that after the holiday the men 'will be working off the methylated spirits they had been drinking.' The bleak weather brought out the earnest lover in him: 'Well my darling,' he wrote to Dorrie on the last day of 1944, 'if for nothing else, this is to wish you all of the very best for 1945, with complete happiness, and may this and all succeeding years be the happiest you have ever had. In the years to come my love, my love for you will be steadfast and strong as ever.' No sooner had he penned the words than he imagined her reaction, 'I suppose you will say to yourself "Silly old bugger – and him nearly fifty!"'

Mansfield was deep in snow when he snatched a few days' leave at the beginning of the year and he was back on board for his fiftieth birthday on 13 January 1945; coincidentally, my mother turned thirty-two on the same day. There is no way of telling what sort of birthday she had; but Tom Davies listened to a play, *Mary Tudor*, on the wireless, and had a few 'gargles'. At both ends of the country, Glasgow and the Home Counties, the weather was raw and bitter, windows starred with frost and the air still. Tom's cold had gone to his chest, always a weakness for him, and a particular worry given that *Samzona* was shortly bound for Canada. On 15 January, Captain Davies spent the day steaming round the Firth of Clyde, adjusting compasses and preparing for yet another Atlantic crossing. 'I adore you my love and always will do,' Tom wrote that evening. 'You will know when I am on my way home in the way you can usually tell.'

* * *

We have left behind much of Europe, and with it the blackout, and lamps strike wriggling reflections from the muddy water, which seems animated by their brilliance. And as I retire for the night, the port is busy with light.

Donald Macdonald to his parents, Port Said, 26 December 1944

Donald Macdonald arrived in Cairo soon after the assassination of Lord Moyne. I like to think that he and Jack might unwittingly have passed each other on an Egyptian street, though clearly not in one of the places in the city where 'Other Ranks' were unwelcome or forbidden. To Donald, after weeks at sea, and years of blackout darkness, Egypt's extravagant lights and riotous noise were a revelation. Everything about Cairo was a shock to the system, be it the 'utterly oriental' railway station – 'yellow ochre in colour, with turrets, battlements and grilles, it might be a sultan's palace'; the continual hooting of horns; the Nile 'busy with feluccas and the old paddle steamers'; the street Arabs who 'actually cultivated Glasgow accents,' the better to ingratiate themselves with the troops; the city streets 'strewn with orange skins, loud with street cries, [and] the drone of tramways.' And then there was the food! 'It would be cruel of me to describe it to you,' he wrote to his parents, the envelope stamped 'Passed by Censor', but he did so anyway. He soon developed a passion for Jaffa oranges, eating 'four or five a day as a rule, not to mention an odd two or three bananas'. At Groppi's he gorged on fruit sundae, a Cairene mess of ice cream, bananas, cherries, and 'a vast gob of whipped cream'.

On New Year's Day 1945, he taxied out to the pyramids, barely a month after my father had made the same trip and had posed nonchalantly on the crumbling stones, looking into the middle distance. Donald thought the ancient monuments were 'vaguely reminiscent of the conical coal heaps of Fife', but this was not a typical reaction; overall he thought the city was the Paris of the Middle East and he revelled in its energy and turbulence. He savoured an expansive dinner at the Casino Opera and visited the Tutankhamen exhibition, which had been placed 'in cold storage when Rommel's advance threatened to engulf the city'. Behind the excitement, however, he was disturbed by the extreme poverty suffered by many of Cairo's population.

Through the early weeks of the new year he was obliged to wait for an onward posting. He sat in a wicker chair in the officers' compound under a January sun; wrote letters home; or read (*The Vicar of Wakefield*), conscious of the lily whiteness of his legs in his new shorts. He could hear the hum of voices and occasional sounds of glass and bottle from the nearby officers' mess, a long, low-slung building with a rattan fence surrounding a sandy tennis court. Occasionally, a fresh breeze disturbed the heat and nudged him into thinking of home, fond memories of an onshore wind blowing on the Fife coast. Large ants scurried to and fro in the sand around his feet and kites whirled overhead. He put on weight, unsurprisingly since 'double cream and double chins are inseparable' and he joined the Gezira Sporting Club, thinking that its swimming pool might tempt him to exercise. The heat prompted other, more salacious thoughts. 'I never thought I could be so obsessed with sex as I am these days.' He reassured those reading his letter in a dark, freezing Scotland, that his thoughts had remained just that, since he didn't have 'the courage of my immorality!'

It was a good thing, evidently, that the Army's bureaucracy soon caught up with him: he was posted to 15th (Scottish) Base Hospital, Middle East Force, a hospital whose wide sunlit corridors and polished parquet floors seemed a kind of paradise to the impressionable young doctor. At the end of January he travelled to Palestine for an anti-malaria training course. His first reaction to that troubled country was wholly positive – the landscape, 'green to the skyline', the tall cedars, and pink and cream villas, all so very different from the brawling chaos of Egypt. Later he realised that there was another side to the country, evidenced by hardship and political tension. He was conscious too that, while he could buy five large Jaffas for 2½d, there were people in Europe who were starving, and whose numbers would grow as the war entered its final phase.

He flew back to Cairo, reading Huxley's *Point and Counterpoint*, occasionally looking down on the bare desert, and contemplating what his future might hold. Emigration to Canada, perhaps? Exchanging his medical career for a life as a writer, an idea he tried to sell to his disapproving father: 'Please admit that you think I might make a go of it. Please do not discourage me.' If he resented his father's austere disapproval, it did not show in his devoted letter writing: he wrote home with disciplined regularity and once, on 16 February 1945, he enclosed some pressed flowers, labelled 'To Daddy from Palestine.'[16] When he wasn't on duty, he settled himself in the officers' mess, where he and others snored in armchairs, listened to the tick of the clock and rustled newspapers. When the urge to write home became too great to ignore, he would sit on a balcony overlooking the tree-shaded garden, notepad resting on his lap, and begin to describe a world apart from his beloved Fife. 'At my elbow the wireless is playing a minuet; outside the trees are swaying as though in time to the music.' Doves cooed in the eucalyptus trees; roses were in bloom; and Donald's pen scratched away under an unforgiving sun.

Towards the end of February, the Egyptian prime minister was assassinated in parliament and Cairo was declared out of bounds to British troops. Denied the city, Donald cycled around the camp on an 'old speed-iron, a ramshackle green bicycle with a too-easily-detachable saddle', noting the 'Texan' skyline with its 'sandy yellow bluffs'. Later, he explored the desert by jeep, releasing clouds of swirling dust before stopping on a cliff 'overlooking the citadel and the Dead City [with] all Cairo and the Nile spread like a magic carpet at one's feet.' While such exploration was rewarding, the same could not be said of work: it was mundane, often tedious or unedifying. Neither the Army bureaucracy and protocols, nor the machinations of those seeking an escape route from the Army, impressed him: there were those who preferred to 'go sick rather than spend the time in the profitable and enlightened tasks of polishing refuse bins', while others swallowed 'foreign bodies' to get themselves admitted into hospital.

Beyond the hospital walls, the war seemed inescapable and unremittingly brutal. At the end of March, Lord Moyne's two assassins were hanged. Both Jack and Donald were in the city at the time and would have heeded the tinderbox atmosphere. The grimness of the world of 1945 was brought home to Donald through a chance meeting with a Palestinian ATS girl. Originally from Bessarabia, she described her recent past to him. She hated all Rumanians, she said, and was now homeless, and her brother was her only surviving relative. He was fighting with the Russian Army, a fact she struggled to come to terms with, since she felt the Russians had committed even worse atrocities than the Germans. Donald asked her how she could ever smile again, having seen such things. She replied, 'I smile now only for others.'

* * *

I have been marooned since Tuesday and if we don't get un-iced by tomorrow I shall go mad. The flying boats lie like great mammoths hung with ice in lumps and all the poor men who spent day and night hacking chunks off have gone sick.[17]

Freya Stark to John Grey Murray, Poole, Dorset, 28 January 1945

The flying boat in Poole Harbour was encased in ice. Freya Stark, holed up in a hotel in Bournemouth, never wanted to see the town again; she was waiting impatiently for a thaw, which would free the aircraft for its flight to India. Growing sheets of ice littered the harbour and each day the aircraft looked ever more flightless, while Freya would be wakened before dawn, taken to the harbour in an icebox of a bus, and given a sombre, unappetising breakfast. Then the flight would be postponed for yet another day. Eventually, after a week of waiting, the weather relented, and once its coating of ice had been chipped away, the flying boat took off and headed south and east. It was an unpleasant flight. Banks of heavy cloud hid France from view; there were ice storms in the Mediterranean; the passengers picked at a miserable meal cooked by Italian prisoners of war on a grim island off the North African coast; and when they finally arrived in Cairo, there was a dust storm raging. The following day, things got no better. Habbaniya was having its own sandstorm, and to cap it all, Freya sprained her ankle. The only consolation was that she had been accorded a very high priority as a traveller. Once in New Delhi, at the Viceroy's residence – where Cecil Beaton had stayed the year before – Freya's anxiety about the nature of the proposed work increased. The Wavells were presently away from Delhi, but Lady Wavell had left an unsettling message about the task ahead, something that was made worse by the clutch of files with which Freya was presented for her perusal. Files? She would burn them given half a chance! She had, after all, managed to survive five and a half years of war without any files worthy of the name. Until she could discuss the situation with the returning Wavells, Freya tried to relax as best she could, learning a little Hindustani and exploring the old city, preferring its labyrinthine alleys to the lumpen, imperial splendour of the buildings Sir Edwin Lutyens had built to overshadow the old India.

Eventually, towards the end of February, Freya had a long, unsatisfactory conversation with Lady Wavell, which highlighted the very different views the two women held on the work to be done. The overriding fear for Freya was that it would all boil down to giving formal lectures to large audiences of women. The beauty of India went some way towards compensating for such an unsettling prospect: she was fascinated by the landscape, the pervading scent of flowers, the Mogul tombs, the light and colour, the picnics and point-to-points, the pomp and ceremony of these dying days of Empire.

With the situation still unresolved, she travelled south, accompanied by an Indian bearer, to Hyderabad, Madras and the distant southern coast of India, and by the end of March, she was in Trivandrum looking out at the blue waters of the Indian Ocean, watching baby sharks some 2 feet in length with 'angry blue eyes, like furious old colonels'.[18] Away from Delhi, she felt somewhat easier in her mind about the task in hand, optimistic that the scheme might indeed work with a small inner group acting as the means by which the message would be enhanced and broadcast widely. She was back in Delhi by mid-April, and in the days that followed her return, she found herself longing for Italy, for home in Asolo, while contemplating magical evenings of lingering mist. Beyond everything, she was tired of the war, the propaganda and sightseeing, and the enervating heat. On the day war with Germany ended she was still travelling, this time on a train to Simla, 'a bees' nest on the top of several hills joined by ridges'.[19] When she reflected on the outbreak of peace, it seemed to her like 'walking along the shore when the huge waves are subsiding and the whole place littered with wrecks.'[20]

* * *

> Isn't the war news good now darling? Thank goodness they are getting it really good and strong now. It gives one such a feeling of intense satisfaction when you think of those dark days of 1940, and in my innermost mind I used to wonder when I left you when I would ever see you and Angela again.

Tom Davies to Dorrie, Digby, Canada, 16 February 1945

On the bridge of *Samzona*, Tommy Davies peered for days into the teeth of heavy blizzards battering the Atlantic. 'Blizzards at sea are a curse dear,' he wrote to Dorrie, 'the visibility is nil.'[21] The weather didn't improve on arrival in Canada, and Tommy, charged by Dorrie with finding her some stockings, muttered gloomily to himself as he trudged through grubby heaps of snow in a series of small towns. The very idea of stockings provoked laughter and regretful shrugs from dozens of shop assistants. Denied the gift of New World nylon, he searched instead for tinned food 'to help restock the larder bench' at home, but even that proved problematic, since food was scarce. Such shortages did not deter *Samzona's* crew, who, with the ship's hold being steadily filled with cargo, shopped remorselessly, 'coming on board with every darned thing,' Tom observed, 'except the galley stove.'

By the time *Samzona* had re-crossed the Atlantic and docked at Southampton, it was spring and 'all the fruit blossom and may trees were in full bloom.' After a brief leave, he returned again to Canada, where the weather remained wintry, permutations of snow, rain and fog. The last few days of the voyage, when the visibility was particularly bad, left him drained. 'I didn't have a decent fix for days dear and was very worried and anxious about the ship.' Another captain in the convoy ran his ship aground, incurring what was thought to be a total loss. 'I'd face,' Tom wrote, '5,000 submarines and go into action gladly, rather than have another three days like I had before we arrived here!!'[22] The return trip coincided with the ending of the war with Germany on 8 May 1945, and Tommy's celebration was a muted affair, just a couple of extra gins, fairly abstemious, but enough for a warm glow to infuse his bedtime letter, which he signed off with a sigh, beneath the sharp glow from the naked light bulb in his cabin, 'All my love to you darling, your adoring Tom.' Not for the first time, he found himself looking back over the war years, to the time when a German invasion seemed inevitable and he had been away at sea, not knowing 'where you both were, and whether even if you were alive or dead'.

By the middle of the month, *Samzona* was back in Southampton Docks, her captain smiling at the treasure he had accrued from across the Atlantic. Dorrie, he knew, would be thrilled: the frocks, henna, Yardley's shampoo, face powder, chocolates, combs, tinned food, honey, maple syrup ('worth its weight in gold now'), starch and some cake doilies. Her list had acquired a series of buoyant ticks in Tom's neat hand. Despite the largesse, he worried about what lay ahead. 'I rather imagine that you are going to have a thin time with rations during this coming winter,' he wrote.

On 19 May, *Samzona* was 'anchored off Deal waiting for sufficient depth of water at Antwerp', its hold full of wheat for the starving in Belgium. The mention of specific locations was a novelty; at one time, if the censor objected, a letter might have arrived, 'looking like a piece of lace curtain'. Things were different now: 'You notice in this letter darling I am disregarding all precautions about security! I take it it's quite in order to do so now, now that we have no enemy here.' There might have been a change to the rules surrounding wartime correspondence, but those routine crossings of the high seas showed no sign of ending. The wheat for Belgium unloaded, *Samzona* re-crossed the Channel and Tom snatched a brief leave at home before embarking on a slow train journey across country to Swansea Docks. Morosely, he stood in the corridor, pondering on the future, both what life had in store for him and Dorrie, and also the prospect of yet another sea passage, thirty days this time, to Vancouver, and then a return via Panama and the all-too-familiar Atlantic Ocean.

* * *

I do wish we could look forward more hopefully to a war-less future.

Donald Macdonald to his parents, Cairo, 9 May 1945

Like so many others, Freya, Jack, Tommy and Donald were far from home when the war with Germany ended. Freya was on a train in India, looking out of the carriage window at the smoke drifting past, and beyond to the blue hills near Simla, while Tommy was at sea, nursing a tumbler of gin and frowning over an air letter, not for the first time struggling to find the words to bridge the distance between his ship and his home in middle England, and to keep his beloved Dorrie sweet. Cecil Beaton was at Ashcombe, where the news of peace when it broke felt like the onset of spring, as if the world was suddenly bathed in bright, warm sunlight. For all that, the wastefulness of the war years still haunted him. Noël Coward was also in England on VE day; he visited his mother, and then wandered through London's streets in the May sunshine, strolling down the Mall before standing outside Buckingham Palace, which, by then, was floodlit, dispelling six years of darkness. The crowd there was 'stupendous'. Later that night he went to a party at Chips Channon's house. Despite the euphoric ending to the fighting, Coward felt apprehensive about the future.

Donald Macdonald was in Cairo, freshly released from hospital after an attack of dermatitis caused by the city's sticky, humid heat. In his hospital bed, he had been soothed by the gentle sound of men playing cricket in the field close by the hospital, the curtains at the open window stirring in a soft breeze, tall hollyhocks swaying gently to and fro, and the heavy smell of roses. When he looked up into the cloudless 'bare blue vault of the sky' there were, without fail, aeroplanes competing for airspace. The sound of their engines had become so commonplace as to be unnoticed. It was 3 May before he was fully discharged from hospital, with the declaration of peace very close; he imagined his parents 'quaking with excitement beside the Macdonald Console Radio while the news of "unconditional surrender" is expected hourly.' For his own part, he heard the news at 6.57 pm Cairo time, 'lying contemplating the ceiling and the two lizards which hung there like grotesque spiders.' He could hear the distant howls of cheering from the city and considered how he would like to celebrate: a 'binge of ice cream and assorted fruits', perhaps, or a luxurious nap. Somehow the weather did not lend itself to wild celebration, with Cairo choking beneath a hot wind and thick dust blown in from the desert. The next day, there was 'a violent electric storm [like] a celestial air raid'. Suddenly it was all over and the world began to change. There was an end to censorship, for example, and the arrival of the first Victory Mail from the UK. Donald wrote promptly back while he listened to Dinah Shore on the radio crooning the most fitting of songs: *You'd Be So Nice to Come Home To*.

> The evening that Victory was proclaimed – Monday – some of the rowdier spirits in our mess, inflamed by other varieties of spirits, went out in a body and tolled the bell of the little church next door. This apart, the only public acclamation of Victory is the beflagged state of many of the buildings in the Garrison. The water tower which stands by the gate of the Reception has its Union Jack, unfolding limply now and then as the over-fresh breeze strikes it. We heard Churchill's pronouncement yesterday afternoon. It was relayed from Britain on the Cairo Forces wavelength. Not as inspiring a show as I would have expected.

Donald Macdonald to his parents, Cairo, 9 May 1945

> I have found the orders all changed now darling and we are bound to Vancouver (thirty days' passage). From there we shall load lumber for home, I hope. That's what it looks like, I should think – but these days darling we may go anywhere from anywhere. We go through the Panama Canal of course dear, but that is sixteen days away and air mail will take about ten days back, so it will be about a month before you receive my first letter darling.

Tom to Dorrie, on board *Samzona*, 4 June 1945

* * *

And Jack, my father – where was he? Was he back in England – at home by VE day? Many years later, I asked a cousin of mine, 'Can you remember exactly when my father got back from the war?' All he could recall were the bales of straw at the Victory celebrations, and the chain of fiery beacons from hilltop to hilltop. He wasn't sure if the man in the bonfire's flickering shadows was Jack, newly arrived home and with his sunburned arms around my mother's waist, or someone else entirely.

Chapter 15

Homeward Bound

I have received one letter only from you this voyage dear, written the day after we departed. I suppose lack of mail is more or less understandable this time though, having had our orders changed so much and being generally messed about! Although I cannot be reconciled to the fact. I shall be glad when we will be able to give you an address and posting dates like we used to in peacetime.

Tommy Davies to Dorrie, on board *Samzona*, 12 July 1945

For Tom Davies, Donald and Jack, the peace did not signal an immediate return to normality. Neither Tom nor Donald were in England when the Germans surrendered, and as for my father, I still did not know whether he was in Cairo, on a troopship home, or struggling to ease himself back into his marriage in that house of three strong-minded women. Was old Bugwhiskers back?

It is tempting to make a glib comparison between the uncertainties of post-war life for those 'ordinary' men posted in wartime and the rapid and easy return of home comforts for the celebrated – the Freyas, Cecils and Noëls of this world. In fact, nothing was straightforward. Coward, for example, was unable to return to Goldenhurst, his house overlooking Romney Marsh in Kent. He had purchased the property in 1927, but in the early stages of the war it had been requisitioned by the Army, unsurprisingly, given its strategic position on the edge of a potential invasion beach. Returning to the house in May 1945, he found it deserted, empty and padlocked; he was surprised that he hadn't been told that it had been vacated. When he eventually found an open door and could wander sadly around the rambling corridors and rooms, he was mildly encouraged to see that it had been left clean and in reasonably sound condition. The garden, predictably, was a wild, choked confusion of uncontrolled plants and weeds. It was all 'a bit heart-breaking,' he wrote in his diary, 'but what is past is past.'[1] At least with the Germans defeated he could contemplate a future: it had emerged that Coward was on a Nazi list of people who would have been 'disposed of' had the Germans invaded. He was in good company: soon after the list appeared he received a telegram from the novelist Rebecca West: 'My dear, the people we should have been seen dead with!'[2]

The past, in truth, was not so easily set aside, while the immediate future worried him. The war had been 'too long and too stupid and cruel,' but a settled peace seemed almost out of reach and the prevailing mood was one of wearied anti-climax. His 'mind and hands [felt] heavy,' he wrote in his diary on 15 May 1945. He thought 'England would be bloody uncomfortable during the immediate post-war period', and days after the atomic bombs had been dropped on Japan, he noted that this new weapon was 'going to revolutionise everything and blow us all to buggery', adding that that wasn't such a bad idea.[3] A week or so after the bombs were dropped on Hiroshima and Nagasaki, he invoked the ghost of Neville Chamberlain in a letter to Joyce Carey: 'It looks like we've finally got what dear Neville promised us – "Peace in our time" – sort of.'[4]

The war had changed everything, and although Noël was proud of his contribution to the war effort, it troubled him that gossip columnists in the press retained – and articulated – 'a certain distaste for Coward's wartime activities'. He sensed 'sooner perhaps than did many other actors and playwrights returning from the war, that the demands and conditions of his profession had altered drastically.'[5] He worried about what that change might mean for his own career, conscious that the war years had altered him, as well as stealing six years from his life. Through the summer and autumn of 1945, he was busy enough, presiding over the final stages of *Brief Encounter* and rehearsing the revue *Sigh No More*, which ran for 213 performances; it was reassuring that he had lost none of his decisiveness or certainty about the quality of his work. On one occasion in September, having watched a matinee performance, he decided the understudy was unconvincing, so he took over the role himself for the evening show.

But the continued denial of the neglected Goldenhurst was a constant reminder of the uncertain new world; it meant too that he must look for an alternative home. Eventually he acquired White Cliffs, a house at St Margaret's Bay, near Dover; it was aptly named and ingeniously situated below beetling cliffs where Channel storms sent sea spray spinning over the roof. Occasionally, flaking chunks of the famous cliffs crashed down into the garden. There were mines still floating in the bay, and on foggy days Noël could hear the mournful bleat of the foghorn on Goodwin Sands. His first visit to White Cliffs had been inauspicious, the car breaking down in the remotest and bleakest part of the Kentish Weald. It was bitterly cold and had begun to snow, but Noël was not to be put off: the house was available on a twenty-five-year lease and he decided to take it, and was soon convinced that he would be happy there. The autumn proved to be a relatively mild one and Coward, fortified by a bottle of champagne brought by his partner Graham Payn, warmed to the house. It was peaceful and warm enough to sunbathe and they walked on the downs, did up the house and motored into Dover for supplies.

* * *

Cecil Beaton's homecoming was blighted in similar fashion, in his case by the loss of Ashcombe, his house deep in the Dorset countryside. Just before the war ended he learned that the lease would soon expire and not be renewed, meaning that he must leave the house by September. It was a blow, since he loved the house; it had proved a great solace during the war years and its position high above the sea, yet protected on three sides by a barrier of wooded downland, gave it a magical tranquillity. It had not been undamaged by the war: for some part of it, a searchlight had been located there, together with a dozen soldiers; and one winter's night, a German bomber returning from a raid on Bath or Bristol had ditched its final bomb 'in the Ashcombe valley and destroyed the small cottage in which my landlord's gamekeeper and family slept.'[6] It also blew out some windows of the main house and brought down a ceiling. It could have been worse: at one point, an army officer came to the house to reveal that there was a scheme to blow up the whole of Ashcombe since the house obstructed the mortar practice of the commando units that were based there. Cecil 'pointed out that, as so many houses were still being demolished by the Germans, it seemed perhaps a little overzealous to do the enemy's work for him.'[7] In the event, the house was spared, but gunfire frequently echoed around the valley and Cecil's favourite trees regularly suffered damage while idle soldiers with time to kill threw stones that chipped pieces from the garden's statues.

Like Coward, Cecil was busy during the summer, in his case designing the costumes and set for John Gielgud's production of *Lady Windermere's Fan*. He worked single-mindedly on the project at Ashcombe, relishing his last days in the house, its sleepy grandeur, the blowsy weeds, the dark trees. He also began work writing a book about it. There was a blue haze to the summer heat; the trees looked gloriously majestic and he felt a deep anguish at the prospect of leaving forever, a grief that grew as the deadline for departure came nearer. One May evening, Chips Channon 'drove over to Ashcombe to dine with Cecil Beaton, a long melancholy beautiful drive through isolated country. The house is romantic and amusingly arranged, and Cecil received us in Austrian clothes.'[8] Three days later, the general election having been lost, Churchill had resigned and by September, Beaton had left Ashcombe, never to return. He had been unable to face the final stages of emptying the house, the gradual dismantling of what he had shaped with such dedication, and the consigning of it all to fallible memory. Instead he went abroad and thereby avoided watching the removal vans taking away 'into storage my somewhat tarnished and garish furnishings'.[9]

* * *

I must tell you that a few days ago we had a change of destination by wireless, and I am now bound to the place I was originally intended to go. That may mean anything darling – Europe, Mediterranean or the East. I can only say I hope and trust that it's not the East as another long spell in that intensely hot weather would about put paid to me for a while. I have only really just about recovered from the last lot.

Tommy Davies to Dorrie, on board *Samzona*, 18 June 1945

There was always something perverse about a sailor living so far from the sea, Mansfield being many miles from the coast, in the heart of England. It had the small and dubious advantage of being equally inconvenient for every possible port of departure for Tommy. Now, with Germany defeated, he hankered after a return to Southampton, where the family home had been before the war. But he knew too that the city had changed: 'The new Southampton which will arise out of the ruins may never be such a delightful place as the old one was.' How many other correspondents across Europe could say the same about their own broken cities? Moreover, property prices in Southampton and elsewhere were beginning to rise fast – three times pre-war values, Tom thought – reflecting the shortage of housing caused, in part, by war damage. Like many others, including Cecil and Noël, Tommy shared the dilemma of where to live once the peace was fully established. To make matters worse, this was a time of intense activity for the merchant marine, manifested by sudden and unexpected changes of orders – a course to be set for Baltimore instead of Vancouver perhaps; or long, meandering sailings to a series of here-today, gone-tomorrow, far-flung ports. Tom suffered greatly with the heat too: for example, when he was in New York in mid-June, he found himself 'wallowing in the throes of a heatwave'; typically, although he complained of it in his letters home, neither his well-schooled, careful penmanship, nor the thin blue paper, showed any trace of his cabin's 90 degrees.

Samzona was charged with 'running food and essential products' as fast as possible into 'British Liberated Areas'. In early July 1945, this meant yet another crossing of the Atlantic, thankfully in perfect weather for once, so good that 'we were in whites until a couple of days ago' when 'good old English rain' began to fall. As well as supplies for Europe, Tom had brought back his usual trove for Dorrie: stockings, zip fasteners, tins of food – but, alas, no butter this time. They docked briefly at Falmouth on 13 July, before continuing on to mainland Europe, not Antwerp as anticipated, but Morlaix, a French port 'only used in an emergency when the big ports are all smashed up.' The Bretons 'could not do enough for us as we were British,' Tom reported, but the shops seemed empty and the prices were sky-high. He was hopeful of the ship returning immediately to the UK, since the crew had to be paid off and a new one engaged, and indeed, there was a brief stopover in Newport towards the end of July, long enough for he and Dorrie to have a 'godawful row', largely about daughter Angela's schooling – Tom baulking at the prospect of paying £3 a week for private education. He had reached that age when you look back with surprise at the rapid passage of time and can see the prospect of retirement not so far beyond the horizon ('it's only eleven years next January'). He wrote to Dorrie telling her that he wanted nothing other than 'to spend the evening of our days by the sea', and yet, on his last leave, he had been startled by a suggestion out of the blue from his wife: 'You were quite a sport to offer to have another baby darling.' At fifty, he thought he was too old. How often he must have dwelt on the reasons for Dorrie's quixotic suggestion as *Samzona* moved beneath him in the reaches of the night.

The long stretches of time at sea were beginning to take a toll. Tom's health was not good and his patience was wearing thin too. Glumly he envisaged the present set of working arrangements continuing for two more years, working 'in these Ministry ships', which meant that 'with the Pacific war still in progress, I am likely to go anywhere and do anything!' He found much in the post-war world to resent: the 'lousy' postal service; the proposed reduction in wages; the continuing secrecy about intended sailings and destinations; the way the country was being governed. He spent a low-key VJ day in New York, presiding over a lunchtime cocktail party for his officers to celebrate, but never far away was his despond at the increasingly remote prospect of a rapid return to the UK. His fears were borne out: he sailed from New York on 26 August bound for Karachi and Bombay with 'one of the last Lend-Lease cargoes', wryly commenting to Dorrie that the Americans were 'fairly slick about stopping Lend-Lease'. It took just twenty-nine days to reach Karachi, since, with convoys now a thing of the past, *Samzona* was able to sail at 11½ knots rather than 8. The stopover at Karachi was for 'a few hours' only and 'the noise and the racket of cargo being discharged' was enough to prevent him writing home. 'The mosquitoes have worried the life out of me at nights,' he wrote later, signing off, 'Ever your devoted Tom.'

* * *

Clothes – shirt and shorts – are sticking to me, the skin-folds at the back of my bent knees, even under my pretty little chin, are clammy with accumulated sweat.

Donald Macdonald to his parents, Cairo, 25 May 1945

It was hot in Cairo that May, like being cooked 'under the grill', and by the end of the month, temperatures exceeded 100 degrees in the shade. The newly promoted Captain Macdonald ('an automatic promotion which has no honour attaching to it') settled into a comfortable routine despite the heat. He swam, deciding 'to risk the myriad infections' in the water; rummaged through Cairo's bookshops; continued to deal with the 'swallowers' (the succession of detainees at the barracks who tried to wangle an early return home by swallowing a variety of indigestible objects); saw *Gaslight* at the air-conditioned Metro cinema, and *Gone With The Wind*, which he greatly enjoyed; admired Cairo's difference – the mosque, for example, 'dominating Cairo's scene with all the slender frailty of a theatrical property'; and went sailing on the Nile, 'coming back to port under the wings of great BOAC Flying Boats.' He did not anticipate a return home any time soon.

In July, he was cheered by the outcome of the 1945 General Election. 'Jubilant over the first of the Election Results – fourteen Labour seats out of twenty!' The despondent gloom of his fellow officers – 'Conservatives almost to a man' – added to his pleasure. These same officers, Donald thought, all too readily talked to native batmen as if they were dirt, while, more generally, he was unimpressed with the attitude of the British in Egypt, suggesting that they exercised 'a despotism quite comparable to Hitler's New Order'. He disliked unwarranted subservience too, since it was 'beneath the dignity of one man to brush another man's clothes, unless from motives of good will'. He evidently enjoyed the likely middle-aged shivers of his parents at such radical opinions, so out of step with his comrades in the officers' mess, cavalierly signing off one letter with a sketched self-portrait and the tag 'Anarchist, 1945 Edition'.

He was greatly out of step with my father, I suspect, although it struck me that while I knew how Donald had voted, as well as Beaton, Coward and Tom Davies, my father's choice between Churchill and Attlee was yet another mystery. I knew though that, for most of his post-war life, my father never voted other than Tory. In 1945, I suspect he may have refused the opportunity to vote, adopting the same principle he had taken when he had refused to claim his medals. For his part, Noël Coward was staunchly pro-Tory, believing that Labour had behaved disgracefully throughout the war years; he had warned Churchill that he should not 'descend to the arena' to face the 'shoddy lot of careerists' that he believed the Labour Party to be. Before the election, he had fervently hoped they would be trounced. The Labour landslide appalled him. Cecil Beaton thought the Labour Government 'horrible', a view that never wavered as time went by and post-war winters grew more brutal. It was, Cecil thought, 'another ice age', with coal and gas both in short supply.[10] He blamed the relevant Labour minister, noting in his diary that the country was 'enjoying a peak of the Shinwell winter season'. There were, he thought, few joys in post-war England, and he blamed the Labour Government: 'Mr Attlee's gang has brought disaster.'[11]

Tommy Davies too was scornful of the Labour Government, believing that its reforms 'don't seem to reach the average middle-class person' and blaming it for rising prices and rationing. He rarely talked about politics but could not resist on one occasion challenging his chief engineer, who was prattling on 'about nothing but ruddy engines and Socialism', and who thought the Labour Prime Minister, Clement Attlee, was 'a wonderful man'. Tom was scathing: 'I should have thought that the only person who would ever have thought that would have been his wife!!'

* * *

Naples so miserable I took one little walk and found myself weeping and fled back to the hotel not to see these heart-rending children listless in the streets. But here it has gone back to the eighteenth century, living today, for tomorrow one dies.[12]

Freya Stark to Nigel Clive, British Embassy, Rome, 21 July 1945

* * *

For Freya Stark it was the post-war damage to Italy in general, and her home in Asolo in particular, that mainly occupied her thoughts in that summer of 1945, rather than the seismic shift in British politics. It was the end of July before she left India for Europe. She flew from Karachi to Cairo, looking down at the familiar desert before heading north, thrilled to see Europe's 'wicked but civilised curving shores' again and church spires emerging from huddles of narrow streets and houses.[13] She travelled via a desolated Naples,

Rome and Venice, then from Padua to Asolo by a lorry that slowly picked its way along potholed roads, over a temporary bridge and past wrecked army vehicles, including a German tank half-submerged in a canal. Village by village, crowds of peasants dressed in black stood in forlorn groups while the church bells tolled, sights and sounds that seemed to symbolise Italy's plight, its chronic shortages of transport, fuel and food. It was clear that the prospect of famine was very real. At her feet in the lorry were bags containing three bottles of olive oil and twenty-four lemons; coffee, tea and sugar from Cairo; and two Indian cashmere shawls and a pair of slippers, all comprising the comforts with which she could face whatever chaos greeted her when she finally reached Asolo.

To her great relief and surprise, Villa Freya proved to be largely intact, although there were unexploded shells in the garden, and all the chairs in the house needed repairing – Freya surmised that 'Fascists must sit much more roughly than we do – they have rubbed bare places with their arms.'[14] The house had been occupied by senior enemy commanders, and towards the very end, the SS had threatened to make a last, desperate stand at Asolo, a plan overtaken by the speed of the final collapse. The town now resembled a medieval backwater, Freya thought. A system of barter flourished, the postal service no longer functioned, and there was no disguising the damage done to Italian morale. News was hard to come by and no certainty for a time as to whether peace had finally come. Then the atomic bombs were dropped on Japan, the two raids having a Frankenstein quality, she thought, and reinforced the mood of fear, pessimism and uncertainty. Finally, on 26 August, a tired and faded Union Jack was hoisted over the villa to mark the peace.

More normal times slowly returned. Security was improved when a contingent of Polish troops was deployed to provide protection from the threat of partisans and bandits spilling down from mountain hideouts, although there were still frequent house break-ins and a thriving black market. Government as such did not exist. After a while, the railways started to run again, albeit without windows or heating, and mail began to trickle through at last, although the resumption of correspondence led to anxieties about what may have transpired over the intervening years of war: 'One has a fear now in writing to one's friends, like Pandora opening the box, not knowing what is going to come out.'[15] A letter from Wavell in India was delayed by more than six weeks, despite the crown on its envelope, while other letters were simply lost – Freya estimated that half went astray in those early months of the peace. Home at last, she pottered in the garden; chopped down poplar trees for firewood; and located the silver from where it had been hidden at the start of the war, and dug it up.

Despite the hardship, she retained her optimism ('Oh Nigel, what a lot of things the world is full of, in spite of all'),[16] but she was yet to feel free or rested. The Ministry of Information was reluctant to let her go and she eventually agreed to work for them for a six-month period, teaching the Italians about the values of democracy by reading British newspapers. She received a £100 month 'allowance' and a German car, an Opel, which she christened *Gretchen*. She thought it exquisitely beautiful, but its frequent tendency to puncture took away some of its magic. Freya found herself driving the crumbling highways and back roads of northern Italy, trying to establish English reading centres, 'rolling along these wet and pasty roads filled with holes made by armoured vehicles, with rows and rows of poplars and wet fields and mist caught in the trees.'[17] As the first peacetime Christmas for seven years approached, she was in Milan, oppressed by the never-ending rain, the dripping ruins and the city's graveyard atmosphere.

* * *

After proclaimed date of ceasefire in Europe (known as VE day) a period of six weeks will elapse before releases commence.

TOP SECRET, Air Ministry to AOCs-in-C, All RAF Commands overseas,[18]
Whitehall, London, 22 April 1945

I am certain that Jack would have been more exercised by when his return home would be scheduled than about the post-war election result. But exactly when had he taken his last backward look at Port Said harbour and steeled himself for whatever might face him in post-war England? Could I track down the paperwork that defined who would travel home, and how – and when? It seems that as far back as March 1941, a government official with an optimistic turn of mind had defined how the demobilisation process might best be conducted, and in particular, who might be released early. Given that Jack wasn't required for reconstruction work, wasn't a prisoner of war, nor, presumably, an 'extreme compassionate case', I doubt that he would have been prioritised for an early return.[19]

Then, in an Air Ministry cable, I read that it would be six weeks after VE day before releases would begin. It was a sentence that stopped me in my tracks. SIX WEEKS! VE day was 8 May 1945, and six weeks after that would take the beginning of what would be a protracted process until well into the summer. With my birth date being in February of the following year, it surely meant that Jack was most unlikely to have been home in time to father me. At first sight, the evidence seemed conclusive.

But then the rest of the telegram revealed a series of caveats, unsurprisingly given the complexity of the exercise, the sheer numbers of men to be transported and the limited number of ships available. Soon after, I discovered another significant document in the National Archives: it defined different release dates for different groups of airmen; specifying, for example, that 'RAF Police, Groups 43 and 44' weren't to be released until November 1946. Clearly I needed to find out which 'group' Jack was in. There was a formula – a 'Table for the Calculation of Service and Age Groups'. In order to work out the group, it was necessary to 'add the last two figures of the year of birth to the number shown below the month of entry'.[20] Jack's 'year of entry' was 1940, in October, when he was posted to Topcliffe. It put him in Group 27. What, I wondered, were the implications of that? Was this the key to the puzzle? At all events, I seemed closer to some sort of answer.

I had hoped that there were archived passenger lists for returning ships and telegraphed orders from the Air Ministry to Allied HQ (Middle East) defining which units would be moved and when. Initially I was encouraged to find a file with the names of returning members of the Palestine Police.[21] Their ship had arrived back in the UK on 27 January 1945, and the associated paperwork was remarkably detailed: long lists of names; then port of entry, profession, age, originating port, address in the United Kingdom and so on. Slowly I scanned each line, before finally accepting that my father's name wasn't there. It couldn't be, surely, although a chance remark from the son of a former colleague of his had suggested that Jack had wanted to join the Palestine Police at one point. I turned to other ships' lists and other consignments of returning troops, looking through passenger list after passenger list, starting with the most likely months in the early summer of 1945, and on into the winter of 1946, gradually realising that, without knowing the name of the ship at least, locating an individual in all this paper bordered on the impossible.

I seemed to have reached a kind of ending, at least while Jack was still alive.

* * *

Like Freya, Donald Macdonald was deeply disturbed by the atom bombs unleashed on Hiroshima and Nagasaki: he thought they marked the beginning of the end – 'Is it to be world peace or world pieces?' he wrote. The VJ celebrations in Cairo were muted, 'almost as dull as those on VE day'. When the welcome prospect of a posting (on 'garrison duty') to Europe was dashed, Donald decided to hitchhike to the Holy Land during a spell of leave. It was 30 August 1945. His first lift, in an army truck, took him out of the city and into 'a sudden, wonderful green belt which I scarcely knew existed', passing through lush fields of sugar cane. The swing bridge over the 'Sweetwater Canal' was up, and a cavalcade of laden barges and feluccas was gliding through, while a long line of traffic waited. His second lift was in a Humber Snipe, with an Army major at the wheel who drove like Toad, at speed, in a flurry of klaxons and exhaust smoke, past waterwheels slowly turned by blindfolded buffaloes and strings of camels trudging east.

At Ismailia, Donald was dropped off at the junction of the Port Said and Palestine roads, which he had been told was normally a good spot for hitchhiking. He decided to try his luck at once, although it was already 12.30 pm and he knew that 'one hour after midday is late for transport crossing the Sinai Desert'. He sat under a rattan canopy on the roadside and waited, but there was nothing at all travelling towards Palestine. He watched a carrion crow scrabbling in the dust while time passed and it grew even hotter, until the heat finally drove him into the shade of the railway station, where he decided to wait for a train. It proved a fateful decision. 'The first familiar face I clapped eyes on was quite a pretty one,' he wrote, 'that of an ATS girl who used to be in

Morelands Camp, near Portsmouth.'[22] The pretty ATS girl was searching for an ice cream when she bumped into Donald; it was a moment he would never forget. The letter he wrote home so long ago he headed in scarlet ink to mark his red-letter day: 'Journeys start in lovers' meeting.' It was to be a chapter heading for the autobiography he never wrote.

It was midnight before the train left, hauled by an engine with a plaque on the cab, which said 'Schenectady 1942'. Donald thought its imminent return to the Americans typified the unseemly haste with which the American government had curtailed the Lend-Lease programme whereby the United States had provided aid to Britain during the war. The Americans, Donald thought, were 'not taking long to take in the spoils!' His view was widely shared: 'the end of Lend-Lease was undeniably brutal' and was typified by the fact that the British Food Mission, bent on sending substantial supplies of food from the States, only discovered the truth when one of their ships was refused leave to sail.[23]

Donald had 'smoky bacon, a chunk of bread and some char' for breakfast in Gaza, and then travelled on to the leave camp at Nathanya, where he wandered along the water's edge, crooning in his soft baritone and picking up shells, thinking of childhood days walking the shore at Largo on the Fife coast. Later, he caught the Jerusalem bus, travelling east across the coastal plain at Lydda, through 'dark spires of cypresses', scrubby vegetation and then over the hills of Judea. What else to do but the tourist trail? Gethsemane, the Mount of Olives and Bethlehem, where, he wondered, 'what our Lord makes of it all', and then, like Jack before him, he decided to visit Damascus. Heading north towards Syria, he sensed Palestine's dangerous heart, observing that 'at every rail – or road – bridge there is a pillbox, manned day and night'. He passed through Beirut, crossed a mountain range, before winding slowly down to the plain and 'the green vastness of the Damascus oasis filling the valley'.

Leave over, he returned to Cairo, where the first months of peace were scarred by riots in the streets, with windows and neon lights regularly smashed. To reassure his parents, Donald played it down, blaming it all on youths and children. It rained for the first time in the eleven months he had been in Egypt, and he found himself reflecting on how different life had been from what he had anticipated. Instead of 'dust storms, drought and dirt', he had 'lived luxuriously, fed magnificently, and bathed dangerously frequently'. The prospect of Scotland's raw cold and insidious dampness did not appeal at all, but at the same time he did not relish staying a further year in Cairo. Like Jack and many others, his thoughts often turned to demobilisation, a distant prospect in his case. Group 31 under the demobilisation scheme ('Python') was due to be released very soon and that, he wrote, would 'break the back of the great exodus'. However, his own group number was an 'astronomical 54', making him pessimistic about the prospects of release any time soon: 'I MAY be out for NEXT Christmas. Even LIAP [Leave in Advance of Python] had its drawbacks: Captain Walker … has just been home on LIAP and says it "doesn't do you any good",' since it makes 'you more discontented and less well-adjusted to the Middle East'. Donald consoled himself with thoughts of Miss May Mott, the pretty ATS girl who had turned his head and stirred his heart at Ismailia station.

Chapter 16

Now That the War is Over

Actually ours is one of the last Lease-Lend cargoes to India, and was nearly stopped, as we left the USA after VJ day! They were fairly slick about stopping Lease-Lend, weren't they? I think it has rather caught us with our pants down. It was rather a lousy trick too, as it was done, I am sure, with the idea of getting in ahead of us on world trade. Things look very gloomy for poor old England at the moment dear.

Captain Tom Davies to Dorrie, aboard
Samzona in Bombay, 3 October 1945

With the war over, there were some signs that the mail was getting through faster. A letter from Dorrie had taken just nine days to reach India, something that cheered Tom greatly. 'It really makes one feel that we are again in the land of the living and not of forgotten men,' he wrote. There were suggestions too that *Samzona* might be used to bring men home from India: 'It wouldn't be the first time these ships have carried 600 troops!' Undoubtedly there was a need to speed up demobilisation: Tom described the situation as a 'vicious circle' since 'we can't have textiles and things until we have labour to make 'em – and the men are all over the world at the moment.' He was not alone in taking such a view: 'Mr Isaac, the Minister of Labour, has today made a statement that the men are being brought home by every conceivable kind of transport.' But instead of returning soldiers, *Samzona* was loaded with a cargo of ground nuts. By 4 November, Davies was in Port Said, glad that it had become 'much easier to write now that censorship is lifted', and that mail from home was proving more regular.[1] Tommy gently chided his wife when he realised that, for a time, she had been inadvertently sending mail to his old ship, *Samthar*.

Through to Suez all had been going well enough, but misfortune struck in the Canal when Tom had run the ship ashore, just 'one of those things' he declared on 14 November, writing from Haifa in Palestine. *Samzona* had been allowed to sail on from Port Said after an inspection, but a second check, this time with the cargo removed, was more troubling, revealing problems with the rudder mechanism. It meant a spell in Alexandria's dry dock and a lesson in what captaincy brought with it in terms of responsibility. 'I have been left practically on my own to make decisions regarding the repair work, which will involve rather a lot of money.' Tom found himself constantly worrying about whether he could have acted differently and prevented the damage. There was, though, no alternative to waiting patiently until the repairs had been completed, seeking consolation in the pictures ('Schnozzle' Durante in *Music for Millions*) and some 'four-bob-a-bottle' gin.

Palestine was simmering with 'trouble and bloodshed', but Haifa was mercifully quiet, 'a fine modern city', Tom thought. There was a temporary curfew, however, with no one allowed ashore at night, and recurring outbreaks of plague. Not everyone felt so positive about Haifa: in the files of the Imperial War Museum in London there is a letter from an airman writing home to England in which he describes Haifa as 'not a very nice town, what with the flies and the Jews and the heat'. My father was no more politically correct, often greeting any perceived sign of penny-pinching with a headshake and a muttered, 'They're not all born in Palestine, you know.' I think that may have been the only context in which he ever referred to his time in that country. Regrettably, I never once challenged him, beyond a tentative, 'Dad, you can't say that!' Oh, but he could, and did! He was of an age and time when it was commonplace – acceptable even – to say such things. Tom Davies observed to Dorrie in a letter written in November 1945 from Haifa, that, 'It takes an awful lot of getting used to in this place to see nothing but Jews all around you – all sizes, shapes and ruddy colours!' Both Cecil Beaton and Freya Stark provoked outrage at perceived anti-Semitic leanings; in Beaton's case a drawing he had done for *Vogue* magazine in 1938 referred, in small print, to 'all the damned kikes in town' and had significant repercussions, including the loss of his *Vogue* contract – his 'American career was effectively ruined, at least for the time being.'[2] Freya's Ministry of Information wartime trip to the US was intended 'to counteract Zionist propaganda, which was producing anti-British feeling to an alarming degree' and her statements on the issue could be easily misconstrued: 'I really can't see,' she wrote to her mother during the war, 'that there is any kind way of dealing with the Zionist question,' and she affirmed her preference for choosing to live 'uncomfortably ... in a hovel with the resentful Arabs.'[3] Donald Macdonald would soon find himself embroiled in the harsh realities of that same Zionist question.

At the end of November, Captain Davies received more bad news. 'However, my darling,' he wrote on the 25th, 'I am sorry to say that I have had a rude and disappointed awakening this morning, for a cable from London was delivered to me with instructions to proceed to Lourenço Marques in south-east Africa, and there to load coal for Buenos Aires. Halfway round the blessed world.' He had been hoping for a cargo of oranges for Europe and Dorrie's warm embrace within the month! It was a cruel blow: 'I am in the depths of utter despair,' he told her. How she must have felt for him, thousands of miles away and in such a despondent state, and to make matters worse, he was increasingly worried about his health. Through the war years, he had often expressed concern about his chestiness and he often seemed unable to throw illness off quickly. This time he wrote about a persistent heart condition, 'an enlarged heart' brought on 'years ago by some kind of violent exercise'. He needed to see a specialist, he thought, but he was so many days from the UK, and each day *Samzona* sailed further away. Six days to reach Aden, he calculated; twelve more to make Lourenço Marques; five days there, then eighteen for the crossing to South America. He might be home for February 1946, if he was lucky, but it looked as if the Davies family must face another Christmas apart.

* * *

Frankly, I don't know how I'm going to stand the cold of Scotland again ... One of the celebrated sword swallowers got up on the prison roof and threatened to jump off and has since swallowed another spoon.

Donald Macdonald to his parents, Cairo, 17 November 1945

At much the same time as Captain Tommy Davies was sailing, with great reluctance, south towards Lourenço Marques, Captain Donald Macdonald received a letter from Gilbert MacAllister, an old friend who had been a

Japanese prisoner of war for four years. MacAllister described 'the supreme joy of being home again, of the wonderful kindness and hospitality extended to him at every stage of his repatriation journey'. He had felt a sense of wonder at the world to which he had returned, and occasionally, a confused bewilderment after the horrors of the previous four years. It was an uplifting reminder of what home meant to those returning after years of war, but Donald could not contemplate being in that happy situation for a very long time. Moreover, Cairo, at the turn of the year, had turned decidedly gloomy and wintry, the mornings cloaked in a dank fog – a *shabora*. 'One wakes to find one's lumbago roused and one's garments ... damp and chill to the touch.' The mist was soon replaced by a cold wind, which blew for days on end. The temperature fell, tumbling to the mid-fifties – 'What is this country COMING TO!' Donald wrote to his parents back in a freezing Scotland. The political situation was just as cheerless: there were riots in the streets and at the university, and a former government minister was assassinated.[4] Donald downplayed the situation in his letters home, declaring that he should not be thought of 'as a second Sidney Carton about to be sacrificed to a howling mob'. If Egypt seemed troubled, the rest of the world was little better; uneasily, Donald noted the 'announcement in today's paper' about atom bomb tests in the Pacific producing 'freak weather in the USA for a whole year'.

* * *

But I am so fed up with this writing business; it is such a hopeless method of expressing anything at all. I think I am beginning to understand something of the mentality of people who write once a month. I am really very cynical, disgusted and bitter about what is happening to the Army in this demobilisation racket.[5]

Chris Barker to Bessie Moore, Italy, 9 March 1946

Not many people ask the question, 'What did you do after the war?' Or, 'How did you survive it?' Or even, 'What did you feel at the beginning of peacetime?' The upsurge of relief and joy surrounding VE day was certainly short-lived, and even then, not necessarily shared by everybody: 'VE day can't mean much to us,' one parent noted, 'as my daughter's husband is a prisoner, and we haven't heard anything since December.'[6] By the time the winter of early 1946 had set in, the hope and euphoria had gone, leaving many people physically and emotionally drained. Freya Stark began the first full year of peacetime at home in northern Italy, feeling exhausted, shivering with cold and all too aware that most people across Europe felt the same.

Noël Coward was also to find it a testing year, not least because it was clear that a reprise of his pre-war career would not do in this brave new world. At a party to honour Coward held in New York early in the year, Cecil Beaton observed that there were those who 'just can't bear to face Noël after the notices for his recent play' and had chosen to stay away. While Beaton thought Coward was 'in dazzling form', he was disturbed by the evidence of passing time and its debilitating effect on people, the way 'mouths [were] wider, eye bags lower, hair brighter, laughter louder' than before the war. Noël spent much of the year preoccupied with a production of *Pacific 1860* at a much-damaged Drury Lane, struggling with cold rehearsal rooms, labyrinthine planning regulations, leading lady casting problems and so on. Moreover, the press continued to pursue him with venom, to the point where he felt that his news value was 'higher than that of anyone in the world, with the possible exception of Stalin and James Mason'.[7] As if that wasn't enough, the state of the world in general troubled him, not least the atomic bomb: 'far too much cock has been talked about atomic energy,' he wrote in his diary on 1 July. 'I am convinced that all it will really do is destroy human beings in large numbers.' On a more basic level, a conversation with 'a young Flying Officer in the train' in March was sobering, the airman being 'very disillusioned about his reception in England'.[8]

On a late January day of bright sunshine, with a heavy sea pounding the nearby shore, Noël had been struggling to concentrate on work. He picked up a copy of Roald Dahl's short stories about wartime flying and began to read, idly at first, and then with increasing attention. Suddenly, he wrote in his diary that night, he recognised what was wrong. He realised the vital importance of retaining the deep feelings triggered by the war, which he could see he was in danger of losing. He knew that if he forgot those feelings or allowed them to be obscured because they were uncomfortable, he would be lost. He must not be diverted by the trivial or inconsequential, he thought, but focus instead on what really mattered. He needed to hang on tight to those moments or he could not be said to have survived the war unharmed.

Professionally, of course, mere survival was not enough. 'To survive the bleak years ahead, he would have to repeat what he had done twenty years before: invent another Noël Coward altogether.'[9] The sombre mood of post-war Britain did not chime with the dapper, witty crooner. Through the early part of 1946 he was working very hard and when summer came he elected to motor to the South of France in his newly acquired MG, relishing a leisurely drive and a relaxing break in the sun. The itinerary might have been borrowed from the 1920s – Biarritz, Cannes and St Tropez. He played the casinos and dined with the Windsors, a glittering place setting alongside the exiled former Mrs Wallis Simpson. For once, he was 'at that wonderfully convenient destination: incommunicado'.[10]

Both Cecil Beaton and Freya Stark spent much of 1946 on the move, although for very different reasons. Cecil set out for the United States, via Canada, during a 'dour, grey' February, 'crossing on a troopship filled with ugly GI brides and their horribly seasick children.'[11] Going to America, he believed, might mean finally achieving the longed-for breakthrough on Broadway. The war was a thing of the past, he thought, but there were two surprises in store when he finally reached the States. First was the glimpse of the next war – America's paranoia about espionage and its mushrooming obsession with the threat of Russia. Then, in March, Cecil was bewitched by 'the incredible eyes and lids, and blue, clear iris' of someone he had not seen since 1932, the exotic, reclusive Greta Garbo.[12]

* * *

You get everything in these places (except real coffee): loaves of white crisp bread, grated parmesan, every sort of meat: you pay immensely, feel happily benevolent and return sadly in the evening to the Military Transit Hotel where the Victors eat their dismal meal of margarine and camouflaged bully beef, suited to the poverty of their incomes. It is a strange world.[13]

Freya Stark to Jock Murray, Turin, 20 January 1946

Freya Stark spent six weeks early in the year criss-crossing Italy before returning home to Asolo. By 19 January, she had visited almost a score of towns, working to establish reading centres for the Ministry of Information. In that bleak winter, travelling was anything but pleasurable, involving, as it usually did, appalling weather – deep snow, wheels encased in clanking chains, or thick fog, or roads slick with mud. Strident red flags in town after town flapped in the bitter wind. The situation in Italy was fragile, its people floundering as if at sea in a small boat with no means of steering. The economy was adrift; politics seemed dangerously volatile; and services – trains, mail and the rest – were haphazard.[14] Freya travelled on through days of persistent rain – a damp day in Verona succeeded by others equally soggy in Parma, Siena and Rome. Writing to Christopher Scaife in Baghdad, she observed that at least he was 'out of the sadness of Europe'.[15] Once back in Asolo, exhausted and so grateful to be home, all she wanted to do was sit in the shade, forget politics, propaganda and persuasion, and think instead about the garden and where the plum tree might best be planted.

The debris of war was inescapable, the rusting coils of barbed wire; the crumbling white houses dismembered by artillery and bombs; and the undetected mines that made swimming hazardous. There was a disconcerting lawlessness too, not necessarily home-grown – it was an American Fifth Army deserter, for example, who stole Freya's beloved car. It all made for an exhausting existence, and by the end of April she was in need of a rest cure, both mentally and physically, baulking at the prospect of any more propaganda work. It gave her a headache just to look at pen or paper, or so she confided to Sidney Cockerell. She struggled through the summer of 1946. In June she headed for the Dolomites, where she lay in bed listening to the rain, or, when the weather allowed it, tramped through the hills. One three-hour walk reduced her to a volley of ferocious headaches and fits of shivering. In the autumn Freya travelled to London, stopping off in Paris to buy a hat and a new dress and staying with Duff and Diana Cooper. From the British Embassy there she wrote to Stewart Perowne on 4 December – 'My dearest Stewart' – wishing him a happy Christmas, sending 'ever so much love', but giving no hint of the change in her life that the new year would see.

* * *

At the sight of Garbo I felt knocked back – as if suddenly someone had opened a furnace door on me: I had almost to gasp for the next breath.[16]

Cecil Beaton's diary, New York, 15 March 1946

Cecil Beaton had first met Greta Garbo in 1932. It had been in Hollywood, and he had seen her through a window: she was sitting on a white garden seat, smoking, her cigarette held aloft. He had been overwhelmed by her beauty and then, on parting with her, distraught that they might not meet again – 'Then this is goodbye?' 'Yes, I'm afraid so. *C'est la vie!*' Four years later, the *New York Times* was printing rumours of an affair with Noël Coward![17] Now, fourteen years after Beaton and Garbo had first met, Cecil found himself looking at her with a kind of wonder: he thought her eyes resembled an eagle's, both in their blue-mauve colour and their intensity, while the lids had a mushroom hue. His forensic photographer's eye noted the texture of

Greta Garbo photographed by Cecil Beaton for *Vogue* in 1946. (*Getty*)

her skin, her hair colour, her waif's ankles and her grey clothes; her shirt had a highwayman's look to it. She was evasive, elusive and intensely beautiful. So sure was Cecil of his feelings and their shared understanding that he proposed marriage. 'I know all about you,' he said, 'I want to tame you and teach you to be much happier.'[18] She thought the suggestion 'extremely frivolous' but he told her, 'I know I shan't be happy until you make an honest man of me.'[19] There was a kind of wooing: they walked together in Central Park; he visited her at the Ritz Tower Hotel; they went to the gym together; lay side by side, enjoying joint mud packs. Throughout, knowing her intense dislike of publicity, her obsession with secrecy, Cecil set his camera to one side, resisting the urge to suggest she pose for him.

Then suddenly, in May, there was a bombshell: Garbo announced that she was leaving for the West Coast, before travelling on to Sweden from California. New York suddenly seemed empty, being there, pointless; so Beaton left for England to work on the design of a ballet for Frederick Ashton. It was to prove eminently forgettable, ephemeral compared to his passion for Garbo – wherever in the world she might be. Beaton returned to the US later in the summer, at one point walking down Bedford Drive, Beverly Hills, forlornly looking for Greta's house. She proved uncontactable, and in consequence, Cecil threw himself unrestrainedly into work. In time he learned that she was angry over photographs he had taken of her that had subsequently appeared in *Vogue*. It dawned on him that he had frightened her away, as if she were a beautiful bird that had settled on a tree in his garden, and then, startled by an injudicious movement, had flown away never to return. It felt like a kind of murder. Towards the end of the year they spoke on the telephone but she eventually told him that he shouldn't phone or write to her again. Professionally, 1946 ended with a sense of a new career path, Beaton signing a seven-year film contract with the director Alexander Korda – but there was no resolution in prospect of his obsession with the quixotic Greta Garbo.

Chapter 17

Two Returns

Our tame cynic says there will be no boxing contests on board as there would be no room for a man knocked out to lie down!

Homeward Bound, Magazine No. 1, 10 April 1945, Price 2d

Never a patient man, the last few miles from the railway station to the house where my mother – another Greta – lived, and I was born, would have had Jack muttering darkly about infuriating delays, the lousy roads, the miserable weather and the sheer bloodiness of the government for sending him away for so long. For certain he would have been breathless with anxiety. Did my brother see him first? He certainly remembers the moment when this stranger turned up, kitbag on his shoulder and carrying presents: a leather wallet for Peter, brass cigarette boxes inscribed with camels and pyramids; even something for the evacuee, Max, who had been in the house since the Blitz – random gatherings from Cairo street markets. I don't know whether he brought me anything; nor did I know then if I was actually there. That all depended on the date when the train stopped at Bishop's Stortford station and the tanned, balding airman stepped out on to the platform, clouds of steam drifting round him and his bulging kitbag. That date, I still did not know. At all events, Peter, who had slept in our mother's bed through the war, was banished to his own single bed while this whiskery stranger assumed his snuggling rights.

In his final years it was easy to forget that Jack could be the life and soul of a party. At the baked meats after the funeral of one of his five sisters, he took the nursing home's matron in his arms and danced with her, him laughing wickedly and her flustered and giggling, as if she quite liked his thin old man's arms around her waist. This from a man of ninety-one, with not much time left. For a brief moment he was young again, a gleam in his eye and a woman to clutch.

Within little more than a year, he had gone too, dead, finally, at ninety-two. It was sad, a relief too, if I am honest, since he had not got any easier to deal with, and part of me thought I might at last find out more about his past from whatever was left behind in his cold, lonely house. There were empty envelopes, old coins, faded news cuttings, tailors' scissors and pins; there was a sparse wardrobe, a few books (John Grisham, Michael Dobbs), a dusty stair lift, and no letters at all. But I did find something revealing, evidence of something he had never spoken of. It was the newsletter for the returning troopship HMT *Cameronia*. Entitled *Homeward Bound*, it consists of just four pages, limited by 'security, paper rationing, lack of office space and equipment'. It cost 2d, any profits to be handed over to charity, and opens with *Farewell Egypt*, a poem that reveals the typical mood of the exiled:

> *Land of romance, love and joy,*
> *(Fifteen girls to every boy!),*
> *Land where everyone's a friend*
> *Allies with us to the end*
> *Oh, Egypt – earthly paradise,*
> *You're a pearl; without a price;*
> *You're a land of sterling worth – and me?*
> *The biggest ruddy liar on earth.*

The ship was uncomfortably crowded but the general consensus was that 'a fortnight or so as a human sardine going in the right direction is better than a month on the beach waiting for the next ship'. While most men would have accepted that judgement, the insistence by the onboard clergyman, one Pastor Hill, might have attracted a more ribald response: 'It is not by the kindness of the Air Ministry or the War Office, or having completed our tour of overseas service that we are homeward bound, but rather, it is due to the blessing of God.'

* * *

Homeward Bound

No. I. | **10th APRIL, 1945** | **Price 2d**

FAREWELL EGYPT!

Fairest 'neath the heavens above,
Egypt, land we've learned to love;
Land that'll always have my heart
Locked in memories as we part;
Memories that will always last
Of scenic beauty unsurpassed:
Land of brains and land of wealth,
Land of cleanliness and health.
Land whose sons are proud to be
Upright, honest, strong and free.
Land of romance, love and joy
(Fifteen girls to every boy!),
Land where everyone's a friend
Allies with us to the end.
Oh, Egypt—earthly paradise,
You're a pearl without a price;
You're a land of sterling worth —
          and me?
The biggest ruddy liar on earth.

MEET THE MASTER

In case you should, in the days to come, start thinking that this ship is being steered anywhere other than towards land, may we introduce the Master?

Captain G. B. Kelly, C.B.E., is a Coleraine man, and started his apprenticeship in 1900 on the sailing ship "Lord Templeton." After serving for six years under sail, he gained his Master's Ticket and then changed over to steam.

In 1915, Captain Kelly became Lieutenant-Commander Kelly aboard Britain's first "Q boat," the "Perugia." He has been a Captain for 20 years, has commanded ten different Anchor Line Ships . . . . . the "Cameronia" for five years.

Here's to a good voyage Sir, we're sure it is hardly necessary to remind you that we're right with you.

"For Sale—Retired Lieut-Commander's jacket, trousers and overcoat. Make excellent doorman's uniform if rebraided."
          —*Advertisement.*

OUTWARD BOUND

Dear Reader,

You must have been soliloquising as follows:—

"Who is this black fellow we see on board?". "Where does he come from and what is his destination?". "Is he civilized?" "If so, what are those cuts one sees on either side of his face, etc., etc."

Answer:— "I come from the Anglo-Egyptian Sudan and I am going to England on a four months' visit to attend a course in the Institute of Education, London.

The Sudan at present produces its own teachers, doctors, engineers, lawyers, etc., and is developing towards Self-Government. It has a 'Defence Force' which fought and is still fighting for the sound cause of Democracy.

Khartoum, the Capital of the Sudan, is a fine city to visit, especially in winter—Nov. to Feb. It has a magnificent hotel, The Grand, where the food is as good and the service as efficient as on board this ship.

The people are not uncivilised, although the fact that they have tails is not altogether untrue, but they make use of them. I quite remember how, as a boy, my tail helped me to carry my books to school, how I coiled it and sat on it comfortably when seats were not available, and how I moved it joyfully when I won a game of chess or a hand of bridge. Unfortunately our tails disappear when we reach a mature age. How, I do not quite know!

The story of the cuts is a simple one. Boys have them for tribal distinction purposes. Girls, for beauty. They are now dying out.

I am afraid I have written more than the Ship's paper can publish, but I hope the Editor will not cut it down. I shall be only too glad to answer verbally any questions you might like to ask.

Yours, Mr. Taha

Mr. Abdel Rahman Ali Taha is the Vice Principal of the Institute of Education in the Sudan.

The front page of *Homeward Bound*. (*Author*)

> As I write it is 6.00 pm and there is a scuffling of army boots in the corridors as legions of sorry wretches begin to queue up for yellow fever inoculations. An expression of implacable hatred sits on my placid countenance as body after body arrives, each wearing an outer semblance of casualness but at heart full of unnamed horror of the ordeal by needle. 'The Beast of Abassia' is what they'll soon be calling me.

Donald Macdonald to his parents, No. 1 Reception Centre,
Middle East Force, 24 May 1946

By the summer of 1946, Donald Macdonald was growing disillusioned with Cairo, partly because work and his medical training seemed to have little connection. There was, for example, the day in mid-June when he worked a twelve to fourteen-hour shift, of which three hours were spent at the prison. The gaol had 300 inmates and forty-six had reported sick, but Donald thought only two were genuinely ill. Then there were the bizarre emergencies: the soldier from 2 Detachment, REME who had 'accidentally shot himself while cleaning his rifle'. There was blood everywhere, gushing from the apex of his left lung, and he died later in hospital. In the immediate aftermath, Donald looked down at his arms and hands, sticky with blood, 'like those of a slaughter man', before the medical orderly casually commented that the man had been a VD case. Donald had scrubbed his arms and hands frantically before he learned the venereal disease thankfully wasn't syphilis.

On leave in early March, Donald travelled to Luxor overnight on the Aswan Express. He visited the Valley of the Kings, 'a most barren and forbidding place, ringed around with yellow rocky cliffs', like the badlands of Colorado, and stayed at Aswan's Grand Hotel, in a room with a ramshackle balcony overlooking the Nile. The location reminded him of the films he had sat through featuring 'whisky-sodden adventurers in soiled "ducks" lounging in similar situations'. The heat and light of Egypt made him 'almost dread the return to bleak Britain'. He found himself idly contemplating a life in the Merchant Navy and wrote enthusiastically about visiting South America, Mexico, the States and Canada. Many years later, when he was a father, he came to realise how such wanderlust must have been greeted at home.

Despite his feeling that it was time to move on from Cairo, Donald's posting overseas had given him the chance to look afresh at the world and his own life. In Egypt, he was 'revelling in a freedom only lightly touched by a certain attachment back in Lennox Castle Emergency Hospital', the tie being in the form of engagement to 'Nana', the 'tall, dark and willowy' Doctor Joanna Brunton. She wrote regularly – letters 'unencumbered by too much lovey-dovey stuff' – and while Macdonald Senior was 'enchanted with her', the young Donald was sure his own feelings did not match his father's. By March 1946, the engagement was broken. The true state of his heart was revealed one day in the surgery: 'Most touching among these far-from-home lads was a smartly dressed soldier wearing a black beret with a white cockade.' Donald asked him what was wrong. 'He broke down and cried, saying "I want my wife."' Donald was shaken: 'I remember almost envying him for caring so much, being so cherished by his distant lover. I wanted to be "in love" like that.' With that example before him, and citing the fragile state of a post-A bomb world, he wrote home unapologetically, 'the very minor matter of a broken engagement worries me not at all.'

By mid-April, Cairo's air resembled 'the breath of a bakehouse, muffling nose and throat in a warm stifling embrace'. Scotland, Donald knew, would hardly have emerged from its winter dreariness, the trees barely green, snow still on the high hills. He had been away some eighteen months. There was a possibility he might be posted nearer Europe, probably to Ankara in Turkey as doctor to the British Embassy and expatriate community; in anticipation, he signed a letter 'Mac Ataturk'. In fact, the posting went to a Major Cole, the son of a regular officer, an advantage Donald could not match. Instead, that August, he sailed for home on a short-term leave, initially disenchanted and chastened, although the first night at sea under a clear sky bright with stars helped restore his optimism, the Mediterranean stretching 'from horizon to horizon like a sheet of silver brocade'. His first sight of a Europe lashed by rain was grim, and arriving in the French port of Toulon on 18 August 1946, the 'wreck-strewn harbour and the much-bombed, empty, glum-looking town' underlined what Europe had suffered, as well as what still lay ahead. He found himself thinking of sun-baked Cairo and May, the pretty ATS girl from Ismailia station, with whom he had now fallen in love. Donald sent a postcard to May, addressed to S/Sergeant M. Mott, Chief Clerk, Statcentre, GHQ, Middle East Force. It illustrated 'a country of incomparable loveliness' – glossy turquoise sky and red-roofed houses in a valley of dark green trees.

The train journey from Toulon to a 'bomb-devastated Calais' took thirty-six hours. Used to the brilliant clarity of Cairene light, northern France seemed to be in a kind of twilight, while Scotland would already be showing unmistakeable signs of autumn. England at least had a neat orderliness about it, but the weather in Dunoon was 'unspeakable', and the people downcast and colourless. Everywhere he encountered a deep apathy, as if the end of

Donald and May, Port Said, 1946. (*Donald Macdonald*)

the war had drained the last of people's energy and removed all hope. In the second week of September, he left the 'glorious chaos' of home to spend time in 'the regimental tidiness of my Aunt's house here in Largo'. Roselea was a 'chic little villa by the sea' and the change of scene from west to east coast was 'like stepping from a garbage-pile into a surgical theatre'. Donald wrote to Sergeant May Mott from his grandfather's old room, its stillness and peace only broken by the murmur of the sea.

May was scarcely out of his thoughts as he began the return journey to Cairo: the train 'steaming out of London on a sunny Sunday afternoon' past the 'sweeping gracefulness of the Kentish downs' while he drank Southern Railway tea and ate 'stodgy NAAFI cakes' in the buffet car after a stumbling walk along the carriage corridor. The smoke from the engine drifted past the window, occasionally obscuring these last reminders of green English downland. Once out of Dover, the journey became less serene as the Calais-bound Channel packet rolled heavily on its crossing. He caught the night train to Toulon, travelling 'past strange empty stations and slumbering towns', and at one point, the dull glow thrown by the lights of Paris. They had reached Orleans by dawn, where he shaved and ate breakfast, looking out at 'spindly-legged and pale', malnourished children in the early light, and sad, derelict guns in the grassy sidings. Finally, the train pulled into 'the shattered shell of Toulon station'.

Toulon had its wartime ghosts, its transit camp had once been dubbed 'Belsen sur Mer', but by late summer 1946, there were worse places to spend twenty-four hours. When Donald finally left France it was on a 'fine sunny morning with mist in the hills and a haze on the water'. He was aboard the *Empire Mace*, a Liberty ship that had been involved in the D-Day landings, steaming 'out of Toulon into a still sea of dazzling gold', and heading for Port Said, past the wrecks of ships lying half-submerged in the harbour, 'sea-scarred ships whose rust and barnacles show how long they have lain rotting in shallow water.' Donald was fascinated by the ship – 'an all-welded American pre-fab' and sister ship to Tommy Davies's *Samzona* – in which one could 'look down to the water over a hull without a rivet in it'. Once the ship was at sea, a sense of timelessness descended. It proved an eventful voyage: sightings of the Stromboli volcano ('that smouldering mountain'); flying fish ('like a glistening wet swallow'); and 'a ship cut in half' with both halves still afloat. The sea became choppy and Donald was consequently sick, cursing 'the cook [who] goes out of his way to dish up greasier and more pungent messes when the ship is rolling heavily'. The ship's captain was demonstrably cautious about approaching the North African shore, worried about mines. Eventually, entering Port Said, Donald smiled wryly at the 'grotesque introduction to the Mystic East' overlooking the harbour, the sign proclaiming 'Johnnie Walker – Born 1820 – Still Going Strong'.

Chapter 18

Posted Home

This is the first number of the ship's newspaper for this trip.
  It is to be hoped that this modest effort may be a souvenir of a Happy Return from a job of work overseas, happy despite cramped conditions.

Homeward Bound, Magazine No. 1, 10 April 1945, Price 2d

Port Said under a glaring sun. It is April 1945. How different from that April day in Liverpool three years before; now there are no grey skies or sea, although the boarding rituals are the same: sailors leaning out over the ship's towering side, looking down at streaks of rust and the oily water, men carrying heavy kitbags, the gangplanks swaying under their marching boots, the search for space on a crowded boat deck. The ship, *Cameronia*, later the *Empire Clyde*, is crowded with nearly 3,800 returning soldiers and airmen on board. It is the same ship that Tony Benn sailed in when he was posted overseas: he was 'situated on D4 Mess Deck where, in an area not more than 80 feet square and not higher than 6 foot 5, 296 of us were accommodated.'[1] *Cameronia* sailed from Port Said on 4 April; stopped off at Gibraltar six days later and arrived in Liverpool on 17 April.[2] It was Jack's thirty-first birthday.

They must have decided to try for a baby straightaway: after all, Greta was thirty-two and both of them would have been all too aware of the time they had lost. So I was born on an unseasonably warm day in February 1946, and if my arithmetic is right, I am conclusively my father's son.

* * *

I have been on the bridge continuously since leaving the dock and it's a relief to get down out of the cold and unwind for a few minutes, dear.

Captain Tommy Davies to Dorrie, aboard *Samspring*, 8 May 1946

Tommy Davies was enjoying a long leave through the early months of 1946, and then took command of another Liberty ship, the *Samspring*. She set sail in the afternoon of 8 May, slightly delayed by the fact that some horses – part of the cargo – had been 'lost somewhere at Nine Elms Goods Station'. Emerging into the Channel, there was a nithering north-east wind blowing, bothersome enough to keep him on the bridge throughout the night. By seven in the morning, they were steaming past the Royal Sovereign lightship. Despite the weather, he did not neglect his letter writing duties, signing off as 'Your ever faithful and devoted although crotchety old Tom', before a pilot boat skipper took the envelope away to post in Dover.

By 23 May, he was in Curaçao, having survived a scare on the north coast of Venezuela when *Samspring's* keel scraped the sea bed. Although the ocean floor was soft mud rather than anything more sinister, it had happened twice, both entering and leaving port, and Davies was anxious about the strain imposed on his ship.[3] 'Ships,' he told Dorrie, 'are built to float and not sit on the land.' There was an irony about the incident, since he had been charged by the Company with ascertaining the depth of water in the Maracaibo Lagoon, where Shell were constructing new oil refineries that needed to be accessible by ocean-going tankers. To Tommy's consternation, the job involved an aeroplane flight from Curaçao to Maracaibo. Moreover, the task was potentially contentious since 'it's open to all kinds of criticism by captains who would follow me there.' There was a certain amount of risk too, enough for the Company to insure his life for £5,000, 'so if I do go and get plonked off,' he wrote to Dorrie, 'you will be quite well off, dear.' After discussions with the 'oil people', he elected to sail the 120 miles or so into Maracaibo in a small tanker – that way he could check out the two long sandbars and the twisting channels, and he thought *Samspring* would be too long to navigate the bends, that being more of an issue than the depth of the water. He planned to stay at the oil company's hotel and take launches out to various key locations before returning by small plane to Puerto Cardon. In the event, the take-off was terrifying, the aircraft shaking as if on the point of disintegration, and Tom was convinced that 'he would not live to tell the tale.'[4]

Puerto Cardon proved to be 'nothing but sand and cactus'. Rain was infrequent and a constant sand-laden force 6 wind blew over the scrub. It 'gets on one's nerves and wears one down,' although the near-gale had a cooling effect – without it, it 'would be just one Hades of heat!' The brooding sharks discouraged swimming in the ocean to cool down, while nearer the shoreline there were barracudas, which were prone to 'nip a piece out of your bottom [and then] whilst you're wondering what happened they nip back and have another piece!' It was the middle of June before he left Puerto Cardon, and early July before he could contemplate sailing for home.

* * *

I have just read *Sex Problems of the Returning Soldier* by Kenneth Howard, with a foreword by Rev Leslie Weatherhead. It is very good and sound, so far as I can judge. Amongst the points made is that of the welcome break that Army life is in some marriages; it says that married couples must develop the 'us' to be successful, and that then children may well follow.[5]

Chris Barker to Bessie Moore, Italy, 1 April 1946

At some point in that year, Jack took his young family, now blessed with me, away from the school house in Little Hadham, Hertfordshire. The first surprise was that the move did not involve a return to the Midlands – bear in mind that I had been given the middle name of the town – Dudley – where my father came from! The move was west, to Bristol, and there is no one alive now who would know why that apparently random choice was made. My brother simply remembers our father going up to London on the train for an interview: evidently Jack had met up with an acquaintance from the 'rag trade' who had invited him 'for a chat'. The next thing was a long, uncomfortable drive in a furniture van, arriving at the down-at-heel shop in Bristol's Old Market Street, where my mother had been appalled when Jack shamefacedly revealed that we were expected to live above the premises. It was dark, primitive, poky and more suited to rodents. I can remember the shop in the 1950s, when it had a Dickensian feel, upstairs being cobwebbed and musty. For Jack, the accommodation would have been little better than the huts at RAF Sharjah. My mother mutinied and the three of us went back to her sister's house post-haste, at least one of us in tears as the train pulled out of Temple Meads station.

Chapter 19

'For God's Sakes, Write!'

For the first time I am 'packing a gat', a venomous-looking 'Colt' automatic.

Donald Macdonald to his parents, in transit to Cyprus, 8 October 1946

Soon after returning to Cairo from his home leave, Donald Macdonald was ordered to report to No. 22 Reception Station at Famagusta in Cyprus. It meant a hurried ordering of his affairs since he was required to leave within the week: kit needed to be sorted, notably 'the heaviest bulk commodity' (his books), and even more pressing, some kind of resolution of his burgeoning love affair with May. How would separation be managed? When he wasn't on duty, Donald sat on the veranda, writing letters and reading, occasionally looking up at the constant stream of aircraft in a clear blue sky. He left Cairo on 8 October, initially for 'troubled Haifa', a journey sufficiently dangerous for Donald to carry a gun for the first time, although he spurned flaunting it in its shiny leather holster; instead it was secreted at the bottom of his kitbag. He left Cairo with mixed feelings, a backward glance at his cool, dark bedroom as he switched off the light for the last time, and the thought that 'we leave part of ourselves in whatever place we linger for a while.'

There was a further cause of regret. Arriving at Cairo station there was no May to wave him goodbye, unsurprisingly, since he had not suggested it to her. He watched the minutes tick by on the station clock, hoping that she would suddenly appear running along the platform towards him. Much later, he would learn that she had longed to be there too. Instead, alone, he climbed aboard and soon was asleep as the train rocked its way across an empty Sinai desert. He would wake up in time for breakfast in Gaza.

Palestine remained volatile, a fact symbolised by the doubts over whether the railway line across the desert would be intact, or blown up. Back in 1939, the British Government had proposed an independent Palestinian

Jewish migrants behind wire at Haifa. (*Donald Macdonald*)

state where Jews and Arabs shared power. The idea was that the number of Jews entering the territory would be limited to 75,000 over the subsequent five years and thereafter would be dependent on Arab consent. It may have been well-meant but the scheme proved flawed, divisive and unrealistic. It was bitterly opposed by the Zionists and it provoked a growing trade in forged visas and landing permits; clandestine night-time journeys in sealed trains, from Warsaw, Vienna or Bucharest; and desperate sea crossings in rusty tramp steamers. 'The vessels and their often ill and malnourished passengers presented a picture that horrified British consuls at ports along the immigration route routinely compared to the slave trade.'[1]

The situation worsened. The British persisted with the quota system, while the Royal Navy was obliged to try and forestall attempts to reach

Palestine by ragged fleets of crowded ships. Would-be immigrants were faced with being put in detention camps, or were summarily sent back where they came from. 'The day after declaration of war, a British coastal patrol vessel opened fire on the ship *Tiger Hill* as it landed 1,400 illegal immigrants from Poland, Rumania, Bulgaria and Czechoslovakia on a beach near Tel Aviv, probably the first hostile shots fired by British forces after the German attack on Poland.'[2] Anti-Semitism in the British Civil Service made matters worse; typified perhaps by an official minute by Sir John Shuckburgh, which coldly noted that 'the Jews have no sense of humour and no sense of proportion.'[3] Jewish refugees were sometimes regarded as 'an organised political invasion' with the potential for allowing significant infiltration by enemy agents. There were a series of regrettable incidents, including ships at anchor being sabotaged and sunk, with considerable loss of life.

Throughout the war, tension in Palestine grew – as my father realised when he was posted there in 1944 – and if anything, the outbreak of peace ensured that there was even greater scope for argument, protest and suffering. Donald was soon to find this out for himself, since Cyprus housed large numbers of would-be immigrants to Palestine. As soon as he arrived in Haifa, 'cluelessness began to rear its ugly head', with the result that he was forced to hang around the railhead for three hours, waiting for transport to the docks. There was none forthcoming, it seemed, and when he took matters into his hands he found himself 'answered languidly by a staff sergeant who didn't trouble to take his feet off the desk!'

He finally arrived in Famagusta two days later, in the middle of October 1946, and soon realised that the posting was likely to be problematic. 'Famagusta,' he wrote to May, 'has been chosen as the dumping ground for "Illegal Immigrants" and there are already about a thousand Jews in the "Concentration Camp" here.' Immediately, Donald could see the flaws in the chosen site for the camp: it was flat enough, but there was hard rock only a foot below the surface, occasionally emerging as white bony outcrops. Even to make a deep-trench latrine, it was necessary to use dynamite. Materials and labour were in short supply, and unsurprisingly, the internees were liable to cut up tents to make clothes. Donald's job was to cater to the medical needs of the internees in a camp that was 'large, sprawling and utterly disorganised', as well as establishing a reception centre. That

Sergeant May Mott, GHQ, Middle East Force. (*Donald Macdonald*)

presently consisted of a muddle of half-finished Nissen huts. It would have been difficult, Donald thought, to be assigned a more challenging task. It was 'a pretty predicament for a dreamy theorist to find himself in'. He was based at the King George Hotel – 'a ramshackle edifice' – a mile or so south of Famagusta, amongst bungalows with red roofs, water-pumping windmills and a landscape dotted with the clean stone of church spires. Famagusta itself lay surrounded by its city wall, while at anchor in the bay were several Royal Navy ships, including an aircraft carrier and the cruiser *Leander*.

A tour of the island's various internment camps was a depressing experience and Donald fumed at the way the situation was being handled, the 'usual old Army story of false economies and niggardly release of stores, of interminable requests and interminable delays'. The solution was obvious – 'the bulk issue of every necessary item to the interned Jews' – but evidently that could not be implemented. When he broached the subject in the Pig and Whistle, the officers' bar in Varosha, 'a rather jaded and cynical Garrison Engineer' dismissed the idea with a weary shake of the head. Woken early next morning by the crowing of a cock and the insistent murmur of the sea, Donald consoled himself with a swim, before returning to his desk, continuing to fill his 'out' tray with letters designed to get something done. Morale was too low, the atmosphere too tense and the internees too resentful to ignore. Moreover, the camp administration was in a state of chaos, 'positively beautiful if you have an eye for that sort of thing'. His desk drawers, he told May, illustrated the situation perfectly, 'a goulash of tennis balls, ladies' smalls and top secret scrawls'. On top of everything, the post was unreliable and frequently heavily delayed. For Donald, in the early stages of a love affair, these long, unexplained silences were cruel. 'Horrible and Deceitful Mouse,' he wrote to May on 16 October, 'for God's sakes WRITE!' When he heard from her the following day, it was a great relief. Such reassurance could only be temporary, however, until the next delay, when he would again begin to worry if he had lost her forever.

Chapter 20

Couples

Set sail at 4.30 am with a brandy. Calm sea, thank goodness. Jack OK as yet …
Shocking road – we shall take off any minute now. Mercedes sail past us. Jack
drives on the right like a veteran!

Greta's notebook, driving with Jack to Austria, September 1965

The only piece of sustained writing left in Jack's house after he died was
a torn reporter's notebook full of my mother's scrawled handwriting.
Occasionally I dip into it, and after forty years, it still evokes her voice,
breathy, urgent and anxious. I've often thought there was more than a touch
of the romantic novelist about her – she was a great one for building castles
in the air, to the extent that one couldn't rely on her version of the past. But
her descriptions of 1960s' holidays in Austria or Portugal are essentially at
the level of 'tea here; breakfast there; Jack getting cross with the traffic'.
It's a pity, since she could readily embroider a story and was not averse to
disguising the past. Her eyes would twinkle when she described her alleged
Romany past – descended from Spanish gypsies, she would say, citing her
love of the sun as evidence. Certainly she was dark-skinned, with a suntan
that never really faded and a preference for clothes in bold colours, with
vivid reds and striking contrasts.

After she died, however, Peter and I researched her family's origins
and discovered that for generations back they had scarcely left the flat
Lincolnshire fens. Moreover, she scattered untruths like a secret agent
laying a false trail: her parents, she told me, had both died in the Spanish
flu pandemic after the end of the First World War. Not true. In fact, she
was sixteen years old when her father Tom died in 1929. I also began to
wonder if the woman I had been led to believe was my aunt, my mother's
sister, was no such person. Known to me throughout my childhood as Aunt
Sis, was she in fact my mother's mother? After all, 'Sis' was eighteen when

Greta was born, and the use of 'Sis' for 'sister' has a kind of dodgy, insistent, 'protest too much' feel to it. It would not have been unusual: 'Some village families had complicated structures where grandmothers, mothers, aunts and elder sisters were indistinguishable.'[1] Now all the protagonists are long since gone, and the subterfuge, if such it was, was perpetrated very carefully, with my mother's birth certificate, for example, revealing nothing untoward.

Another mystery was why she married Jack in the first place. In photographs of them as a young couple, they look singularly ill-suited: Greta is poised, her dark eyes locked on whoever is behind the camera. Jack can look very handsome, dark and prowling, but somehow, even when the camera is most flattering, he gives the impression of being unsure and almost, well, rough trade. There is one portrait of Greta where she looks fit for Hollywood – it is a properly arranged studio picture: neutral background, artful lighting, best bib and tucker. She is wearing a crisp, striped blouse, buttoned high; her skin is clear and pale; her hair glossy and swept away from her face. One ear peeps out from her brushed-back curls. I am proud of her. But it is the eyes and mouth that hold you: that unflinching, brave stare and her thin, no-nonsense lips, emphatically closed and bright with the reddest of lipstick, like blood.

She and Jack had only been married three years when the war broke out. Separation like theirs was commonplace, but no less painful for those separated, and it is no surprise that many marriages did not survive: 'Couples who had once loved each other found they were no longer compatible. It was hard to sustain a relationship over years of separation; a commanding officer noted that it was often all right for the first two years, but troubles and infidelities tended to occur in the third year of separation.'[2] In an effort to keep the troops happy, the postal service between home and postings abroad was quick and cheap, but it was beyond the capability of many to keep love ardent and faithful through a stilted, censored correspondence. 'The overwhelming proportion of the population had left school at fourteen, so that they were not the most articulate letter writers.'[3] It was no easy task to sustain a relationship by post when writing was not a natural gift.

Divorce increased rapidly during the war years: of the near 25,000 divorces in 1945, 70 per cent were attributed to adultery. Women got married younger too: some 30 per cent of first-time brides were under twenty-one; living in a world where death was a daily risk, men and women dispensed with caution. Some 80,000 British women became GI brides. Noël Coward observed the consequences of growing distrust and separation by time and distance when he was in the Middle East in the middle of the war, referring to the 'seeds of suspicion and unhappiness in the minds of thousands of our fighting men who are isolated and far away and have no opportunity of checking up for themselves'.[4]

There is no evidence, apart it seems from the existence of me, to indicate how Jack and Greta sustained their marriage through the war. I possess no letters that passed between them during those years (or any other, come to that), and therefore have no clue as to whether he, like Tommy Davies or

The other Greta – my mother.
(*Author*)

Donald Macdonald, was a diligent correspondent, or not. When he died, why did he leave so many photographs and so few words? I had hoped to find bundles of dusty correspondence in the old man's loft, but his only words were terse, scribbled notes on the backs of photographs: 'The family including Judy the dog. Love Greta, School, 1944.' Jack's snaps, sent from the Middle East, were annotated with similar terseness, though he usually made a point of declaring his love for her.

When Jack, sun-scarred and anxious, approached the front door of the house where my mother had spent the war, what was he expecting to find? How would they both have changed? Was he still deeply in love with Greta, and she with him? I imagine the two adults smiling uncertainly, Jack looking mournful and Greta sniffing tears away. Then a perfunctory embrace, before my brother emerged from behind our mother's skirts. 'I adore you Cecil,' the other Greta, Garbo, would tell Cecil Beaton, but for the life of me I cannot see my mother's lips mouthing similar sentiments into my father's ear. They had been apart for three years, the same length of time they had been married before the war began.

* * *

I can book rooms, or perhaps a room? Och, yes, m'dear, please let's be bad for once in a while!

Donald Macdonald to May, Cyprus, 14 November 1946

Later that autumn, Donald drove into the mountains, to a resort near the summit of Mount Olympus, at the wheel of a grandly proportioned Chevrolet staff car, 'the sort of thing that Brigadiers and Generals ride around in.' A man raised his cap as the limousine progressed in stately fashion through a white-stoned village. 'Perhaps,' Donald reflected, 'he thought we were a hearse.' A series of hairpin bends slowly revealed clusters of red-roofed villages and churches with 'sugar-icing belfries' in the valley below. Vines clung to the precipitous hillside. As they climbed, poplar and beech trees were replaced by pine and juniper. Donald stopped for sweet Turkish coffee, and bought some apples, before travelling on towards Troodos. There, through a break in the cloud, 'round the hoary head of old Olympus', he could see the whole of the island spread out below him and the blue, glittering sweep of the Mediterranean. There was no barbed wire to be seen, or camp huts; just the winding road, the island's coastline and the occasional sprawl of people's homes. The weekend over, he drove back to Nicosia along a 'switchback highway', stunned by the island's beauty, its tree-clad hills, the golden sunset, and 'the intense rose and purple of the hills which shared the afterglow' as twilight fell. Back in the valley floor, speeding towards Nicosia, he soon began to think of what lay ahead, rather than the idyll of the past few days, and his return to the camp was as dispiriting as he feared. Officers in the mess were huddled 'around the blazing hearth in an atmosphere of choking cigarette smoke', and when night fell it brought the first chill of autumn. Soon after, 850 more Jewish 'illegal immigrants' arrived by sea.

He heard nothing from May for ten days and assumed the worst: 'My darling,' he wrote, 'I am getting really worried about your silence.' Two days later, a clutch of letters arrived, which he read and re-read 'in the cloistered silence of my tent', disturbed only by the idle flapping of the canvas, the noise reminding him of sails teased by a south-west breeze. He liked life under canvas and his routine: he would wake at six-thirty in the morning; then sit down to write with 'shafts of white sunlight slanting across the dusty air of the tent.' The morning light was pure and sharp, while the shadowy glimmer of the hurricane lamp at night made reading problematic; it brought to mind stories of his father as a boy, lying on his stomach, reading by the light from the cottage's peat fire.

Life under canvas was agreeable enough, but for those interned in the Karaolos camp it was anything but. When Major General Foote completed an inspection of conditions 'he was at the stage of holding up his hands in dumb appeal.' General Oliver came the following day and simply 'retired in horror and confusion' at what he saw – the overcrowding, the evident unrest, the shortage of medicine, food and water. Moreover, the prospect of an outbreak of disease was never far away. Donald watched the *Eolo* 'filling up with wretched voyagers en route for Haifa and home,' the ship rocking in the teeth of a freshening onshore gale. In early November, two more ships from Haifa docked, with nearly 1,300 would-be immigrants. 'Many of them came ashore with their eyes streaming or closed up from the effects of tear gas,' while British soldiers were subjected to howls of 'Gestapo! Gestapo!'

and 'Hitler! Hitler!' There were scuffles and a number of troops came under attack, with the result that they opened fire. Although no one was killed, the atmosphere remained tense. A truck carrying a group of Jews returning from Nicosia in the early evening overturned, with a significant number of serious injuries. They were taken to Donald's ward, where he struggled to cope in dim light, with the wounded shrieking with pain, and with no orderlies to help him.

It was difficult work at the best of times: often Donald would conduct delicate medical procedures while hemmed in by internees who chattered like 'a shower of magpies'. He was cheered by seeing small bands of immigrants marching between camps singing lustily. 'They look fit and reasonably happy, and I feel we are slowly and laboriously rebuilding their faith in the possible goodness of humanity.' A few days later, on 8 November, Donald discovered that he was to be temporarily promoted to Acting Assistant Director Medical Services (ADMS), making him 'the next most senior officer on the island!' The man he was replacing was going on leave. On the surface he was 'quite an agreeable soul, rather pompous and very anxious to appear efficient and

Would-be migrants to Israel. (*Donald Macdonald*)

very peremptory', but Donald knew he had a secret life involving regular Friday trips into Famagusta and a lovers' tryst with a 'popsie'.

Donald, of course, was a committed lover too, writing to May on a near-daily basis. He would find an isolated spot, perhaps 'overlooking the sweep of Famagusta Bay and the mountains beyond,' or, sitting alone at dusk in his tent under the wavering light of a fitful paraffin lamp, and write to her. At other times, he wandered 'aimlessly in the moonlight, over empty fields stretching to the horizon', thinking of May on the other side of the Mediterranean and striding through brittle scrub or down an avenue of eucalyptus trees marking a deserted highway. When he wasn't in camp, he frequented the nearby George Hotel with its 'usual assortment of retired Army officers and their quite intolerable wives spoiled by long residence in India or elsewhere'. Camp 63 – 'home' – was not a place for the faint-hearted, however, with its scabies epidemic and fears of typhoid. There were 'sights which would make the stoutest hygienist quail': the latrines were filthy ('vomit-making dens of iniquity') and there were flies everywhere. In the absence of anybody else – 'Evasion of work is almost an honourable pastime in HM Forces' – Donald gathered all hands to help clear up the camp, which soon looked 'a little less like a public refuse-tip'. As a reward, he led a party to the beach for a collective swim.

Camp 63 might have been neater and tidier, but the bigger picture was less hopeful. Donald was convinced that 'the latest Government statement on entry permits which allows the "Illegals" detained here 300 certificates this month and 750 a month in succeeding months' would cause serious trouble, and sure enough, it emerged that a breakout from the camp was threatened, provoked by 'confirmed agitators'. Donald consoled himself with the prospect of May's proposed Christmas visit to Cyprus, and worried instead about problems that he could do something about – should they share a bedroom when she came? What should they do? Where should they stay? What should they do about the bad winter weather in the Troodos Mountains? They were 'feet deep in snow', Donald wrote, 'and utterly inaccessible.' Above all, he knew now how much he cared for her: 'I hope someday,' he wrote, 'I shall be able to say, "Let's be a comfortable couple."'

The deadline for the attempted Jewish breakout came and went with no sign of an uprising, although the atmosphere remained tense and a hunger strike was expected to begin on 17 November. 'Never,' he wrote, 'have I heard the name of Britain so oft reviled as in the last few months.' He booked two single rooms for May's visit and reminded her of the September day in Ismailia when their relationship had begun and their first kiss in Qasr-el Nil Square. A few days later, he wrote her three letters, emphatically love letters. Sitting in a staff car speeding towards Nicosia, with snow-capped mountains in the distance, the lovelorn doctor was soothed by reading poetry (Osbert Sitwell), though he suspected that May would deem it 'a sign of grave mental decay'. He would never forget that road from Famagusta to Nicosia: the orange groves flourishing behind tall fences of bamboo; the windmills; the wide prairie landscape, treeless and brown; the 'blue range of mountains away to the north'; the jagged peaks; mud-brick villages; dogs bounding alongside the car; 'flocks of fat-tailed sheep'; and then the first sight of Nicosia from some 10 miles distance: twin minarets standing 'like sentinels against the skyline'.

Chapter 21

The King of Cyprus

> Along the road behind my tent as I write, led by an indifferent bugler, a straggling cohort of Jews marches along with the odd torchbearer lighting their way with an oily flame.

Donald Macdonald to May, Famagusta, Cyprus, 15 December 1946

Christmas 1946: I was, I imagine, on the point of crawling, scrabbling commando-like across the floor. But whose floor, and where? I do not know. Had Jack already moved the family to Bristol or were we all back at my aunt's/grandmother's (!) house in the Home Counties? As for the rest: Freya Stark was in England too, staying with Jock Murray for some of the time, running 'his wife ragged with her hairdresser, theatre, luncheon, and dinner appointments'.[1] Noël Coward was struggling to cope with the critical reaction to *Pacific 1860*: 'a blast of abuse in the press', but spent 'a peaceful Christmas Day' at home in bed 'talking to people on the telephone.'[2] Cecil Beaton was in New York, planning to return to the UK on the *Queen Elizabeth* in a few weeks' time. Tommy Davies was at sea, having missed yet another family Christmas at home. And Donald? In Cyprus with May.

On 4 December, Donald wrote a long letter to May, 'The Concubine in Special to His Celestial Majesty King Karaolos I', sustaining the joke through seven pages – 'It has been whispered among the ladies of the court (whom God preserve!) that the coming of your exquisite self will be the signal for dreadful orgies throughout the kingdom, and it is even rumoured that His Majesty purposes kissing you upon the mouth in a public place.' He signed off as 'Procureur without Portfolio at the Court of HCM Karaolos I'.

Back in Cairo, May warmed to his letters; they caught the very timbre of his voice, laid bare his heart, and made her laugh. He might be describing the background noise as he was trying to write, the Jewish immigrants singing *La Marseillaise* as they walked on the road behind his tent, or the packs of dogs barking; he might have enclosed some money to be spent on food parcels for family back home; or he would be remarking the fact that his skull looked 'like a rather poor quality turnip', or protesting loudly about being press-ganged into playing football. She laughed at the way he described his newfound role as Acting ADMS, making him 'in a small way the King of Cyprus'. She liked his humanity too, the genuineness of his concern for others, for example, the time he wrote about swimming in a boisterous Mediterranean, unable to forget the *Eolo* making heavy weather of far angrier seas.

December brought heavy rain sweeping across the island. Another 4,000 Jews arrived from Haifa amidst ugly rumours of brutality prior to embarkation, while on Cyprus itself, troops and camp internees were obliged to wade through thick red mud and endure a sudden cold snap. Where just weeks before, uniform had consisted of khaki drill – bare knees and shorts – now the troops were back in battledress. Donald was struggling to cope, with just two RAMC officers in a camp of more than 10,000, and he got little sympathy from GHQ, which contended that 'the Jews must be made to work', while insisting that any form of coercion was unacceptable. A new camp at Dekhelia opened in an ominous cloudburst.

Towards the end of the year, Donald was 'suborned by the SIB [Special Investigations Branch]' for a secret mission designed to extract an Israeli informer from the internees' camp.[3] It involved driving an ambulance into the compound to deal with a suspected case of appendicitis, tenderly lifting the supposed 'victim' into the back of the vehicle, and then slowly motoring beyond the wire towards safety. It proved problematic, not least because the informer was no actor – indeed, sixty years later, Donald would remember it as the worst performance he had ever seen. As his compatriots anxiously swarmed around the ambulance, the duplicitous agent persisted in sitting up, while Donald, sweating profusely, kept pushing him back down. Finally, despite everything, the mission succeeded; however, when he handed the man over to the SIB major in charge of the operation, he blurted out that he had taken the precaution of hiding an unloaded pistol in his battledress. 'Are you mad?' the major said. 'If they had caught you with that, you would have been lynched!'

Still the migrants came: on 14 December, a cold, damp and cheerless day, 750 more arrived, survivors from a ship that had foundered off Rhodes. They docked in the early afternoon next to the *Eolo* in a vessel normally used for offloading tanks, and when it was realised that they were not in a Palestinian port, the passengers staged a sit-down strike, which eventually required tear gas to break up. Looking down into the hatches, Donald was reminded of slaves in a galley. The Zionist national anthem and chants of 'PAL-EST-EEN' drifted across the harbour; so did the tear gas. British soldiers drove them away in a convoy of 3-ton trucks. The next day, the British Foreign Secretary, Ernest Bevin, declared in the *Cyprus Mail* that 'The Sun of Peace is rising'. 'I hope he is right,' Donald wrote, 'Mr Chamberlain once said something similar and World War II began a year later.'

Chapter 22

Before the Russians Drop their Bomb

It was the first time that I'd ever seen you wearing lipstick – and I told you it looked like a child had been to the jam cupboard.[1]

Cecil Beaton to Greta Garbo, Wiltshire, England, 9 March 1947

Cecil Beaton sailed for the UK on 3 January 1947, travelling with Alexander Korda. Just over two months later, he started work with Korda at Shepperton Studios on two films, *An Ideal Husband* and *Anna Karenina*. It meant getting up at dawn in the continuing bitter weather, and often staying at the studios until the middle of the evening. England in early 1947 was a sombre, austere place – Cecil blamed 'Mr Attlee's gang' – and the winter seemed endless, with week after week of ice and snow, sleet and slush. He felt that 'the British Empire has gone down the drain.'[2] Throughout that time Cecil was searching for a new house after his tenancy at Ashcombe had ended. That had been a cruel blow, one that he likened to hearing his own death knell. He was set on remaining in Wiltshire and when he first set eyes on Reddish House, having driven through the village of Broad Chalke, it was enough to make him pull up outside in a raucous squeal of brakes. 'I had once seen the house long ago,' he wrote to Greta Garbo, 'and thought it one of the loveliest I had ever seen.'[3] He was ravished by the house, he wrote; it was 'a small Charles II house … a treasure' with its yew trees sculpted into the shape of poodles and its near-mauve brickwork, stone pilasters, and an unknown poet's bust in the crumbling stonework over the door. The inside of the house was more underwhelming, but when he took his mother for a second opinion, she had few doubts, beguiled by the warmth of the lilac-shaded brickwork; the way the garden stretched up to a paddock; the long lawns tapering away between double rows of trees, both limes and elms. The kitchen garden was surrounded by a traditional Wiltshire chalk wall topped with thatch. He made an offer of £10,000 for it and the bid was accepted;

only afterwards did he wonder how he would find the money. He signed the lease on 4 April 1947, and took possession on 21 June, his 'lucky day'. It was the first time he had seen the place without snow on the ground.

Happy with being 'a country squire', the acquisition of Reddish helped reconcile him to the loss of Ashcombe. His first full day there, 24 June 1947, proved 'serene'. He sought to persuade Garbo to visit, describing the daffodils, bluebells and violets, the 'lyrical weather', the glorious views from every window of the house. 'I suggest a visit to Europe,' he wrote, 'before the Russians drop their next bomb on us.'[4] The work with Korda and the delights of Reddish both absorbed him – but Garbo remained his obsession. In his letters, he bombarded her with reminiscence ('and you told me you hated wearing underclothes'), and questions: ('Do you like avocado pears?' and 'Do you wear a pair of red pyjamas? All these things I wonder.')

* * *

London was bitterly cold, snow, sleet and slush, and Mr Shinwell cutting all the warmth (though there is still far more than in Italy).[5]

Freya Stark to Stewart Perowne, Paris, 9 February 1947

Early that year, Freya Stark left London for Paris, which proved marginally less cold, but where coal was even scarcer than in Attlee's England. Reflecting on the hardship there, she wrote, on 9 February 1947, that most of the population of London had had their pipes burst, while there was 'general gloom over Palestine, India, coal and everything else'.[6] She was convinced that the British Government needed to give serious thought to an oil boycott or even air landings in the Middle East. The political situation might be depressing, but on a personal level there was some joy: before she left London Freya had agreed 'a wonderful deal with Jock Murray: my copyright when I die with a mink coat now!' She preferred 'a mink on my back to a copyright in the tomb'.[7]

By the end of February, she was back in Asolo, having travelled by rail, a journey reminiscent of the ease of pre-war journeys, the train bursting through the tunnel and out into the glorious light of Italy. While the journey might have been a pleasure, the return to the house itself was by no means trouble free. The winter in northern Italy was cold and there was little electricity, and throughout 1947 the house remained a financial burden, its boiler broken, for example, and needing to be replaced. There were leaks and chaos, and the house seemed forever to be filled with masons and carpenters, this at a time when Freya was absorbed in trying to write a new book. The creation of *Perseus in the Wind*, with its intense concentration on worthy issues such as 'Service', 'Love' and 'Sorrow', and its tight prose, did not come easily in a house echoing with hammering, sawing and workmen's booming voices. It was, though, better than the thought of resuming her lecture tours – these she hoped never to repeat. Italy too was still suffering, symbolised by the familiar house at L'Arma, with its walls chipped and stained during the years of war, damaged by careless soldiery, the blistering sun, or winter rains. Forgetting the war would take years; the Italian countryside could seem serene and beautiful, on those days, for example, when she went out walking, carrying her picnic lunch in a red and white spotted bag. When she stopped for lunch, eating it as she sat alone under an olive tree, she was careful to keep to the paths, since stepping off them could easily detonate one of many hidden mines.

* * *

Off I went in a frenzy to Waterloo, only to find that owing to the cold the train was two hours late starting. Gladys and Bert with me. We perished, and finally arrived at Southampton at two-thirty. Waited in a queue for ages. Finally got on board and had a fantastic lunch, with white bread and every luxury.[8]

Noël Coward's diary, 29 January 1947

Noël Coward remained in London through most of that January, but often in a sour mood: sensitive to criticism; frustrated by the slow progress of his writing and by seemingly interminable backstage rows; as well as being depressed by the grim weather. He watched the novelty of television one evening and dismissed it as a ghastly innovation. He was edgy and malcontent, finding it hard to settle to anything: 'Tried to paint; couldn't. Tried to compose at the piano; couldn't. Tried to sleep, could, but without pleasure.'[9] So, at the end of the month he left for America, 'fled for a Cunarder and New York.'[10] The New World provided him with some comfort, and a welcome diversion from the bleakness of post-war Britain: he lunched with the Kennedys and serenaded the future president and the rest of the family at the piano; enjoyed parties characterised by 'pyjamas and dressing gowns and steak and caviar and that wonderful feeling of long friendliness';[11] as well as languorous Turkish baths and games of rummy in smoke-filled rooms. He was back in England by the middle of March, and in common with many others, including Freya and Cecil, found himself preoccupied with re-establishing home life.

* * *

Pancakes and butter (real) – what a perfect flatulence it all was! Dammit! Why do women ALWAYS want to marry me?!

Major Donald Macdonald to his parents, Cyprus, 6 January 1947

In Scotland, Donald Macdonald's parents were enduring an appalling winter: 39 degrees of frost in some places and a sea that froze. They 'have little or no coal left and have taken to spending longer than usual in bed, with hot water bottles for comfort.' He proposed that they come out to Cyprus for some respite, but he recognised that life on the island was not without its drawbacks: sickness, traps for the unwary, and bad weather. He knew that there was little prospect of them taking him up on his offer. Sergeant Mott, however, had come for Christmas, arriving on the morning of Christmas Eve and staying until early January 1947. As she left for the return to Egypt, she slipped a letter into Donald's coat pocket, which he read with a heavy heart, in a room where her perfume still lingered. 'At that moment,' he wrote, 'I should have given anything to hear your footstep behind me, your comforting hand on my shoulder.' She meanwhile was leaning on the ship's rail looking back at the island and wondering what life might hold in store.

In the internment camp at Karaolos there was another outbreak of scabies, and Donald could not resist talking to the press about it – 'Today at Dekhelia I shot my mouth off to some reporters' – and he became very worried about the man from Reuters, 'a particularly nasty piece of work who twists every statement'. Heavy rain frequently fell from deep grey regiments of scudding cloud that swept across the island. The camp became a morass of mud and deep puddles, and Donald's tent revealed a serious leak. When he saw a bulge in the canvas roof, he 'gingerly palpated it', only to disturb a cat that was sheltering between the inner and outer skin of the tent. He shared the leaking tent with a brooding fellow major, a man 'not given to over-indulgence in anything, unless perhaps gloom' and whose only visible passion was stamp collecting. Thankfully, Donald also had the use of a cottage 'a few yards from the grumbling sea' at Dekhelia. It had a bath, a fireplace and a Mediterranean view. During January he would scour the beach for driftwood, 'picking up armfuls of twigs around the shores of my little peninsula.' It was often bitterly cold and there were gales too, which whipped up 'immense grey rollers' that crashed on to shore. On one day, 30 January, there was 'thunder and lightning, sudden hail storms, grey skies … brilliant sunshine … in short, a mad March day in January'. Then, soon after finally getting a Cyprus telephone number at which May could ring him (Famagusta 324), he was urgently and unexpectedly summoned to the airport.

He was there within half an hour, excited by the prospect of a flight in a Lancaster bomber, although the pilot, 'a weedy looking youth with stained fingers', did not inspire confidence. They took off for Egypt around two in the afternoon, and looking down, Donald was mesmerised by the aircraft's shadow as it passed over the Suez Canal and the Bitter Lake, 'where seafaring ships stand smoking idly in the midst of the desert.' The sudden posting to Port Said as Embarkation Medical Officer (EMO) had meant leaving his kit behind in Dekhelia, as well as unsettling him, but the work – looking after the medical needs of crews and passengers in port – was interesting at least, and the role came with a car, a launch, and, 'after years of ersatz margarine and National bread', there was the luxury of real bread and butter. His new office, 'a high-ceilinged room [with] tall and shabby windows', looked out over the port, a sun-bright panorama of oily water, wharves and rust-stained warehouses. He was 'not merely Major Macdonald but also SMOLEM – Senior Medical Officer Levant and Eastern Mediterranean.'[12]

There were matters to be settled on Cyprus, however, and early in March, Donald sailed for the island, via Haifa, on the *Empire Rival*. She was transporting more 'illegals' and Port Said's new EMO was obliged to spend the night in the ship's hospital. At one point, the engines failed, leaving the ship becalmed for more than an hour in an uncomfortable swell. Eventually they reached Haifa, the *Empire Rival* docking 'while the heliotrope mist of searchlights played over the harbour, and flares, like errant stars, drifted down over the serene and sparkling city.' Sirens boomed; young soldiers in 'cerise berets and camouflaged sky-jackets' bellowed orders and 'the ring of steel upon stone' added to the tumult. Long queues of the dispossessed stared sullenly at soldiers who, in turn, patrolled to and fro, their nerves taut, their faces sombre.

The ship sailed for Cyprus at first light with some 300 refugees on board. Donald talked to a Jew once from Antwerp but now set on a new life. 'Why in Palestine?' Donald asked. 'Why not somewhere else, America, for instance?' In two – three – years,' said the man from Antwerp, 'America as bad as Germany.' The sea was calm, almost glassy, and the ship's progress was slow, its skipper intent on arriving in Famagusta at the best time for disembarkation – six in the morning, when passenger exhaustion minimised resistance. At that hour, in a glorious morning light, Cyprus looked like paradise, winter's bare foreshore had sprung into new green life; crimson poppies bent in a gentle breeze and a sprawling yellow carpet of buttercups stretched down to the sea. The morning, however, soon turned sour. Off Famagusta, another ship of illegal immigrants from Haifa was hove to, its onward passage forestalled by the Governor of Cyprus, who had initially refused permission to dock. When they eventually reached port, some passengers refused to disembark; tear gas was fired; officials in Cyprus and Palestine exchanged angry cables, which resulted in a ban on any further disembarkation for the foreseeable future. The migrants meanwhile looked out over the blue Mediterranean and despaired.

When he returned to Port Said, it soon became clear that Donald's posting as EMO was to be no sinecure. Rather, it meant 'playing nursemaid to an assortment of arriving and departing Colonels, Brigadiers and even Generals', acting as their obsequious travel agent and information clerk; ensuring that kit was stowed on board ship; finding 'special accommodation'; booking hotel rooms; providing transport; organising red carpets for visiting generals; and baling out those who had gambled their money away at the Casino Palace. Fussing around such 'privilege-seeking bigshots' brought out the 'Bolshie' in him. A more obviously medical role was his responsibility for 'the orderly evacuation of invalids'. It all meant that there was no time to rest, weekends being fleeting at best and often non-existent, with the result that he was 'almost as irritable as my maternal grandfather'. To make matters worse, the weather was unseasonably stormy, with thunderstorms, rain and high winds. The days passed in a bleak routine: awake at six-thirty and up an hour later; a cup of 'loathsome tea' courtesy of Ali; a shave, and every second morning, a hot shower, followed by greasy eggs and bacon. Prompt at 8.45 am, a rickety Austin 7 – affectionately known as *Tilly* – would pull up outside the mess and he would drive to the guardhouse, where he stalked round the cells, inquiring after the health of their occupants. Then, he would conduct a short sick parade before sitting at his desk trying to remain calm in the face of the rising insistence of the telephones. When enough was enough, he would escape by launch across the harbour to one of the ships in port, the *Otranto*, perhaps, or the *Arundel Castle*. 'I live half my life on the water like a Venetian,' he wrote.

It was nothing if not varied, and sometimes he needed a thick skin, and at other times, an unctuous bedside manner. One minute he might be the butt of a 'brusque admonition' from an irritable senior army officer over what was deemed Donald's cavalier attitude to time, or receive 'a right royal "bollocking"' for 'not being sufficiently attentive to the baggage of Major General Harris', or be required to cope with the repatriation of two merchant seamen who had been involved in a wild brawl on the quayside. They were both judged mentally ill and Donald had been obliged to lead one of them, a diminutive fireball 'less than 5 feet in height', like a child by the hand up the gangplank, while he shook and muttered, convinced that he was heading to his death. Donald's day, which began at 8.00 am, might end after midnight.

There was even some conventional doctoring: the captain of a seagoing tug, 'one of a small fleet towing several large sections of a floating dock from Bombay to Malta', required 'a preliminary skirmish with a thermometer and some unskilled labour on his abdomen'; the 'not-so-good ship *India Victory*' arrived in harbour 'with the skirl o' the pipes' and cases of suspected smallpox aboard; and Cunard White Star's *Scythia* arrived from India with 2,000 troops bound for home, and no medical staff or equipment. He was not beyond some mild vengefulness: the odious Colonel Davies, who had taken the liberty of addressing him as 'Mac' as if they were bosom pals, was consigned to the isolation ward of the *Tusculum Victory*, situated between decks, with steam pipes running along the walls rendering the ward 'as hot as the place I am mentally consigning him to!'

At the beginning of May, the USS *Toledo* arrived in Port Said with two escorting American destroyers, and Donald was piped aboard 'with all manner of white-clad Yankee sailors standing to attention at the top of the gangway.' It made him feel like Lord Mountbatten. With May still on leave in England – she had sailed for home in mid-April – he read a lot (*Kidnapped*, Somerset Maugham's *The Razor's Edge*, *A Portrait of the Artist*); saw *Kismet* (he was bored) and James Mason in *The Seventh Veil*. He fell victim to Port Said's spell: 'the bougainvillea and the jacaranda trees against the white porticoes of our handsome buildings, the bluebells blue and cerise like a cloud of coloured smoke'; the advertising hoardings with their spidery writing reaching up into the wide cloudless sky; 'the rash of brass plates' at the shipping office doors; and 'the domed green and white splendour of the Canal Company Building'. There was, though, no escaping the seamier, grimmer side of the city – the view from Donald's window, for example, comprised coils of barbed wire to deter thieves; regimented lines of army huts; a forlorn clump of trees; and two large black gasometers. The noise was loud and incessant, and included the 'constant and immoderate whistling of trains' – this from a man who loved railways. The landscape was 'flat, barren and empty', and the tidal flats to the south smelt foul – 'They stink, oh! How they stink!'

Nonetheless, there were days when the joy of being alive overwhelmed everything. Take the afternoon when he sailed out to the harbour's outer basin and the second mate of the *Empire Rest* treated him to an expansive meal of liver, kidneys and eggs. He headed back to shore standing in the bows of the launch and singing happily, lungs full of the clean breeze and revelling in the gentle rock and swell of the boat. 'In short,' he wrote to May, 'I feel elated, free, optimistic.' Best of all, 'You will be with me in a week or two!'

* * *

This is really a continuation of the last letter but I have to split them because of the weight – which reminds me talking about weight darling ... I have maintained my very rigid diet since leaving England and haven't touched potatoes or bread or sugar once! My only indulgence has been a small bit of marmalade to help push down a bit of Ryvita at breakfast, and a morsel of butter. Sugar I haven't touched since I saw the specialist.

Captain Tommy Davies to Dorrie, on board *Darro*, 17 May 1947

Captain Davies had taken over a new ship, the MV *Darro*, in April. She was 'a lovely ship', sufficiently superior to *Samspring* that he feared he would not keep her permanently. She was air-conditioned and Tom's quarters comprised a day room with a 7-foot desk, a lounge seating four, a bedroom complete with settee, a 'bath and bog', and an entrance porch and vestibule. The panelling was in a tasteful dark mahogany. He was bound for Buenos Aires, carrying both cargo and some thirty passengers. 'It blew heavens hard as we went down the river,' he wrote to Dorrie, 'and the sea was so bad that I couldn't change pilots at Gravesend.' Instead, he anchored and rode out the storm. By mid-May, *Darro* was heading south under blue skies in calm seas. Despite the good weather and placid ocean, he found it difficult to rid himself of anxieties about his health, sufficiently worried to cut back on what he ate, substituting Ryvita for most of the things he liked! He couldn't settle in the ship: 'It is because I have had so long at home and miss you and Angela so very badly.'[13] He wrote to Dorrie from Montevideo on 28 May, evidently dwelling on what the future may hold, and on death. 'I only hope we shall go within a few weeks of each other.' By the time he had got to the end of the letter, however, he had cheered himself with descriptions of the food he proposed bringing home. The return was blighted by curtains of heavy rain, poor visibility off Ushant and long hours at a stretch on the bridge, the conditions too dangerous to turn in for the night. He was glad when a cable from the owners informed him that he would be relieved on arrival in Antwerp, not least because the passengers had been 'the lousiest bunch of grumbling baskets'.

* * *

Dearest of all
My father says he supposes you will have the idea that he is a kind of unconverted Eskimo with bunches of heather growing out of his ears.
    If you haven't got all your trousseau, dousseau!

Major Donald Macdonald to May, Port Said, 8 May 1947

Both Freya Stark and Donald Macdonald were married in 1947, she in October and he in July. Donald's last night as a bachelor was spent in a fifth-storey hotel room in the Eastern Exchange in the centre of Port Said. Cairo was sunk in blistering heat, but Donald was fighting a cold, obliged to sniff and snort, while the strains of two competing dance bands drifted in through the open window. 'It seems strange,' he wrote, 'that none of my own kith and kin will be present.' The family in distant Fife, denied the chance to see the young Macdonald getting married, had to be content with a long letter, written in the immediate aftermath of the great day. The bride looked 'queenly' at the wedding, he reported, but was seasick on the crossing from Egypt to the Cyprus honeymoon. The hotel in Limassol was 'so new that the washbasins still bore their packing tapes and were not piped for water', while the young lovers both suffered from stomach bugs.

Once they had recovered, they hired bicycles for two shillings a day, heartened by the fact that 'the hirer didn't even ask our names.' Such trust and the island's 'golden silence' were both uplifting. One day they cycled over the Kyrenian Mountains to Nicosia; it took two hours to reach the top of the pass, the two of them peddling hard under an unforgiving sun. They stopped by a spring for a drink of cold water before sweeping over the brow of the hill, stopping eventually at a ramshackle café halfway down for slices of water melon. On the sun-baked plain, the air was like an oven and the tarmac softly melting. In the afternoon, they returned to the summit with their bikes roped together on the top of a local bus, before a triumphant descent, freewheeling ever faster. At the Pine Tree Holiday Camp, Troodos, the air smelled of pine trees and the hot water boiler was fed with burning pine cones.

Returning to Egypt, the newlyweds moved into Caffé's Pension, initially occupying a large room on the ground floor. The food was good, and although a curfew was now operating in Port Said, Donald reassured his parents that

Donald and May's wedding, Port Said, 19 July 1947. (*Donald Macdonald*)

he couldn't 'imagine Egypt getting REALLY uncomfortable like Palestine'. It did, however, remain noisy. Writing on 7 September, he could hear a barrel organ outside playing *I Belong to Glasgow*; ducks complaining, rhythmic hammering; the 'rattle of passing gharries'; and the shrill klaxons of taxis. Port Said had, by now, begun to lose its attraction: there was an outbreak of cholera; riots and disturbances became more serious, the pavements often littered with broken glass. The fanlight over the front door of their pension was shattered. A curfew was imposed, which led to an unhealthy confinement, accompanied by the sound of the 'drunken voices of young soldiers' pent up in the Britannia Club. 'It is all very tragic,' Donald wrote, 'to see these youths (of eighteen to twenty) staggering about the streets quite oblivious to the impression they are giving.' He and May could still enjoy walking hand in hand along the Rue Kitchener, the 'long palm-lined boulevard' that runs west from Port Said, unease spirited away by a refreshing wind off the sea, but, for all that, it was becoming clear that it would soon be time to move on. Even the Rue Kitchener had its limitations, being 'about the only road in Port Said worth walking along, and then only in twilight'.

But where to go? To his parents, Donald wrote: 'we get the impression that the "spivs" and "drones" are rapidly ruining the UK,' while Captain Walker, of the *Snowden Smith*, told him that 'one half of the country's filling up football coupons and the other half's checking them.' With the novelty of peace rapidly losing its shine, and the Iron Curtain having descended across Europe, disillusion had set in: there was a much-resented slow-down in the demobilisation of troops in the Middle East; the cholera outbreak in the delta got worse; there was 'a cessation of tobacco imports from America', and a swing to the right in the municipal elections. All that hope and promise of the summer of 1945 seemed to be fading fast.

Chapter 23

Not the Marrying Type?

Such a peculiar thing has happened: I have promised to marry Stewart ...

It is one of the happy things that Stewart likes the people I like. We have a common world to set out in. He is being sent to Antigua. I believe he just couldn't bear to go alone and had to have a wife among his tropical kit.[1]

Freya Stark to Nigel Clive, Asolo, 14 September 1947

Stewart Perowne proposed to Freya by telegram and they married in early October 1947, a few months before he was due to take up a diplomatic post in the West Indies. She was due to follow him there in the new year, when she

Freya Stark and Stewart Perowne on their wedding day. (*Getty*)

would begin 'domestic life as a Colonial Officialess in the Spanish Main'.[2] Freya was a few months short of her fifty-fifth birthday, and Stewart was forty-six. For both of them it was a trip into the unknown, in terms of their marital status and his new posting. Freya anticipated that the house in the West Indies would be equipped with electric light and a fridge, but the rest of the forthcoming experience was shrouded in mystery. Towards the end of the year she fell ill with 'a headache that you could cut like cheese', an affliction that she attributed to a kind of collapse brought on by the intensity of her work on her new book. Her 'blood pressure', she wrote, was 'even lower than the bank balance'.[3] It was some consolation that Rebecca West had once told her that she ended 'every book with an illness'. Certainly Freya approached the new year unwell, with a raging cold; she was also worrying about money and her new husband, who 'slept so much – staying in bed until noon, then returning to his room after lunch for a nap that lasted until teatime.'[4]

* * *

My darling
May I call your attention to the date, darling – twenty-eight years ago! Happy Day! …
　We shall be arriving in Los Angeles by next Monday.

Captain Davies to Dorrie, RMS *Teviot*, at sea, 19 August 1947

In July 1947, the month that Donald and May were married, Tom Davies assumed captaincy of a new ship, the *Teviot*, and sailed from Cardiff for America, Guatemala and Panama. It meant another English summer missed. By 3 August, he was off the coast of Virginia, increasingly wary of his new crew and disturbed by the chief engineer, a 'queer bloke, teetotaller, non-smoker, never goes ashore, never spending any money'. On 19 August he wrote to Dorrie from San Jose in Guatemala, its four towering and active volcanoes casting shadows both over the bay and Tom's imagination: 'Having just passed through six years of war safely, I should hate to depart this life by being hit on the bean with a lump of pumice stone.' They passed through the Panama Canal and sailed up the American West Coast towards

Vancouver, with Tommy growing ever more worried about the behaviour and attitude of the crew, 'all young fellows and a drunken ruddy lot at that'. Four had recently deserted, and Tom had 'clamped down' on the rest as a result. 'They think I'm a basket!' he told Dorrie. Nevertheless, things still deteriorated: by the third week of October, the ship was nearing Norfolk, Virginia, when six of his firemen refused duty, in effect, an action 'bordering on mutiny'. Five of the men were eventually prosecuted, while a sixth ('a proper bad lot') was in hospital at Cristobal suffering from a nasty dose of VD. Tom was sufficiently worried about this incident escalating into mutiny that he slept with a gun under his pillow.

* * *

I'm not so sure that your silences are very kind.[5]

Cecil Beaton to Greta Garbo, Reddish House, 24 March 1947

Cecil Beaton returned to New York in October 1947, hoping to see Garbo, but disconcerted initially by her calculated evasions. Later, in her hotel room when she had finally relented, he noticed that 'all the mail was addressed to a Harriet Brown'. Previously, when he had rung Greta's number he had often been told by the operator that 'Miss Brown' no longer lived there. Reunited with her, Cecil was absorbed by her beauty and how she had changed. Her face was 'peakier', her mouth a vivid red, her nose sharper and more pointed. She was wearing a black peaked hat and a dark coat, inside of which her body seemed unduly thin, with scarcely an ounce of flesh on her. He could not understand her compulsive fear of invaded privacy, although he accepted that she regarded the film world as a 'jail'. Most of all, he was baffled by what seemed to be her determination to drop him from her life, something that would cut him to the quick since he was 'deeply in love with Greta as if I had been a man half my age smitten for the first time'.[6] He struggled with the pain of never knowing where he was with her: it was almost unendurable, hence his decision to back off and feign indifference. For a time it teased her into suggesting that she 'make an honest man' of him. 'No, it's too late,' he responded, 'you're not the marrying type.'[7] He left without telling her where he was going and consoled himself by imagining the telephone ringing unanswered in an empty room.

By early December, Beaton's studied cool seemed to be working. Now that he was 'busy', he found that 'Greta is no longer as busy as she was while I was not busy!' Moreover, she now intimated that she adored him. There was talk of sharing their lives and he felt able to tell her that city life was wrong for her. 'You are so out of your element here with the pavements under your feet and smuts in your eyes.'[8] That Christmas, the city was deep in snow, not white any longer but stained and pitted, while throughout Boxing Day, fresh snow fell on New York from a threatening 'soup-brown sky'.

* * *

A pleasant day lying in and by the pool. Graham and I drove to Oyster Bay, where there was a dinner party: Maggie Case, Christopher Isherwood and a friend, both of whom I liked, and Garbo. A really cosy evening.[9]

Noël Coward's diary, New York, 3 August 1947

1947 was a difficult year for Noël Coward. He was unsettled professionally, *Pacific 1860* having closed, and the reaction to *Peace in Our Time* was lukewarm. If it was to be a flop, he declared that he would 'be forced to the reluctant and pompous conclusion that England does not deserve my work.'[10] The poor notices troubled him ('I fear we are a flop'); he was sickened by the atmosphere of Hollywood; disturbed by the venom of the press, who, when he arrived at Southampton on returning from the States, badgered him with questions about whether it was true that he was sick of England. He was worried about his health. The only glimmers of hope on the horizon were his deepening relationship with his lover Graham Payn and the discovery of Jamaica, which he had loved at first sight. Even then his preoccupations with health were evident: he rented (at a cost of £50 a week) Ian Fleming's house 'Goldeneye' on the island and waspishly dubbed it 'Golden Eye, Nose and Throat'. It was not the most comfortable of houses: the showers were cold, the beds hard and the cooking unspectacular, the whole experience reminding him of hospital. But the island seemed like paradise with its clean white sand, blue skies and warm seas, and by the end of the year he had located a site for his own property, some 5 miles along the coast. It was secluded, protected by a coral reef and uplifting in its beauty.[11]

It had been a year of mixed fortune and it ended with Coward suffering from gout and rheumatic fever. He had woken on New Year's Eve in agony and was obliged to reach the bathroom on his bottom and only with great difficulty. Desperate to return to America, and Graham, Noël consulted two specialists that morning who examined him thoroughly; gave the illness a name; blamed 'streptococci'; and dished out penicillin. He was able to drink in the New Year; a week later, he was in New York; and by the 13th, with Graham in San Francisco.

Chapter 24

Another Year Nearer the Grave

I am your devoted swain.[1]

Cecil Beaton to Greta Garbo, Broad Chalke, 3 April 1948

The stars are enormous and very bright and infinity is going on all round and I don't really mind about the notices of *Tonight at 8.30*.[2]

Noël Coward's diary, Jamaica, 5 April 1948

I am not at all well ... and can hardly make myself do anything at all. By hook or by crook, I hope to get three weeks' walking in the Dolomites to restore the inward balance.[3]

Freya Stark to Jock Murray, Bridgetown, 3 April 1948

For both Cecil Beaton and Freya Stark, 1948 was an emotionally charged year. Cecil was tormented by his unresolved love affair with Greta Garbo, while Freya, soon after joining Stewart in Barbados, realised that her marriage was in difficulties. He had, for example, written her a 'melancholy little finance note' sufficiently pernickety that it prompted her to insist her writing money should not be used for the expenses of everyday living. If they had to economise, they could let the chauffeur go: who needs one on an island after all? Moreover, she loathed the very idea of someone else driving since she loved being at the wheel, although she confessed to preferring 'a Commando scooter to a car'. Noël also needed to economise after purchasing the land in Jamaica where he would build a house: the Rolls Royce at Goldenhurst was sold and he was frequently seeking to raid his London bank for cash, usually through instructions to Lorn Loraine. 'On one occasion her reward was the following telegram:

Dear, Kindly, Generous and Loving Lorn
So grateful am I that cannot speak
That you should yield so much from plenty's horn
I shan't need any more till Tuesday week.'[4]

Money aside, the combination of his relationship with Graham and the revelation that was Jamaica, made Noël broadly content. The same was not true for Cecil, whose relationship with Greta Garbo was anything but placid or straightforward. She could be charmingly domestic, for example, when he had installed a 'Frigidaire', she advised him to fill it with 'avocados and radishes and cheese and biscuits and fruit', but her behaviour was frequently quirky, inconsistent and often manifesting her chilling obsession with privacy. He invited her to England, but that prospect she found unsettling: 'Was there still rationing?' Was it possible to get fresh butter? Or newly-baked fresh bread? Then there was the perpetual spectre of someone else – the 'little man', the Russian financier, George Schlee. Once Cecil lingered outside a telephone kiosk, desperate to speak to Greta, seething with impatient anger as he waited for the occupant to vacate the booth. He contemplated hammering on the door, only to find when the man finally emerged it was his rival. The stalemate was resolved in February when Greta left New York for the West Coast. Beaton was greatly relieved. Then, a month later, he elected to fly to California to see her, beset by his 'old fears at the prospect of taking flight' generated by his wartime air crash. Despite everything, he remained obsessed by her: walking with her in the Californian mountains, he could not take his eyes off her. 'Her beauty was at its zenith. Her fine skin had the sheen of a magnolia, her hair fell in smooth, lank bosses, her figure lithe and thin, flat haunches, flat stomach.' He knew by then that he 'had made her love me,' but it was not enough to ensure a shared happiness. Early in March, after a tearful farewell, he took the train back east.

* * *

In Beaton's archive at St John's College, Cambridge, there is a faded menu from a New York restaurant. On the back is a sketch of Greta drawn by Cecil, while on the other side is a picture of 'Mercedes' sister' by Garbo. It is dated March 1950. I see Cecil and Greta, in candlelight facing each other across the table, him sketching and her staring at him as his hand travels across the table; every so often he looks up to check a detail of her face. There is wine left in his glass, ruby red in the light, and the wreck of Long Island scallops and Florentine au Gratin ($2.25) has yet to be cleared. They are both, in different ways, wary of the future and where it might take them.

* * *

Freya Stark left for the West Indies in early January, her luggage including five big straw hats and four parasols, but in the event, she would only stay with Stewart for three months. The journey out proved 'beastly' from first to last: stranded at the outset by Yugoslav railway sabotage in a clammy, cold Milan station for a whole day while the rain fell without stint; and then enduring a sustained hurricane aboard the SS *Ariquain* crossing the Atlantic. She arrived in Barbados on 9 February. She found it neat and very English, soporific, as if it was 'always afternoon'; it also had 'a sadness of old slavery'. Perowne was happy enough, enjoying his role as the archetypal civil servant, but Freya felt caged, writing to Jock Murray in evident distress: 'Don't repeat this, Jock, but I did look down into an abyss and am still very wobbly.'[5] She felt, she wrote, 'as if I were imprisoned in a dewdrop.'[6] In May she left him, travelling in a troopship via Trinidad and Jamaica, the ship notable for its bleak efficiency and its blaring megaphone. The SS *Empire Windrush* reached Gravesend on 21 June, a cold, unwelcoming day with bitter winds, a green-brown sea, and fog on the Goodwin Sands. There was a dock strike and she felt 'a sad feeling of England and her river slipping away into the silence of the past'.[7]

She was back in Asolo by July, cheered by the state of the garden and uplifted by walking in the hills, where the high pastures made her think of the Garden of Eden. Three years after the war ended she realised that, for the first time since then, she could just potter, with the sole aim of just seeing the world. She wrote fondly and regularly to her husband, assuring him that she did not love him any less – but was very reluctant to return to him. Finally, she travelled there again, flying this time at a cost of £180 each way.[8] She liked Barbados no better: the 'Euphrates pulls at my heartstrings,' she thought, and she disliked the climate. Life on the island seemed mundane:

'I give away cups. I see my frightful pictures in the paper and long for Asolo and London.' Asked if she liked a 'life of grandeur', she replied that she thought she was 'born for the gutter'.

By the end of April 1948, Freya was back in London. She visited Sissinghurst and Cliveden, Leonard Woolley's house in Bradford on Avon – 'the Mendips swelling like breasts' – the Chelsea Flower Show, the Duff Coopers at Chantilly, where, in June 1949, she sat next to Cecil Beaton at dinner whom she thought 'agreeable to talk to'. He had 'a <u>medieval</u> face … with a velvet cap on one side he would make a Dürer or Clouet with those sad eyes and frustrated mouth and small artistic impotent hands.'[9] He told her he would love to visit Asolo. Freya was not to know that, when they had met during the war, he had later described her in his diary as 'just the sort of bumptious woman whom I detest'.

Back in Italy, on a train to Verona, she told Stewart that she would have faith and wait for his heart 'to find its way'. She insisted that 'If we can be happy, I don't much care about other things.'[10] She acquired a Vespa, from which she frequently tumbled: she described how she would see a ditch, know she was going in and then be overtaken by a kind of paralysis. She became terrified of the pesky scooter ('the little brute just <u>pranced</u>'). Walking in the Dolomites, to her surprise, she decided that the high mountains now frightened her. She suffered from insomnia, which could only cured by walking, embroidery or weeding the garden. Working on a volume of autobiography, she had begun reading old letters, which she found uplifting and warming, and she recognised that both she and Stewart were very lucky in being able to reveal their true selves in letters; she was, she wrote, bewitched by the 'panorama of one's life all tucked away in yearly envelopes'. Reading the letters from the war, she remarked on the urgency, the pace, the variety of lives they were living all at once. Perowne came to Asolo for leave at Christmas 1949; he 'descended from a blue sky, all the Alps without a cloud behind him.' Freya still hoped that the marriage could be saved: 'Oh, dearest, do you think we can make a success of it after all?' Aged fifty-six, she wrote that she had chosen 'seventy-seven as a nice age to die'.

* * *

Never forget that I shall always love you as I always have done, and if you come to me with your troubles, and listen to my advice, I will do all I can to help you and stand by you.

Captain Tommy Davies to Dorrie, RMS *Pilcomayo*, at sea, 4 January 1948

Just before Christmas 1947, Tommy Davies assumed command of *Pilcomayo*, setting sail for South America at three o'clock on the morning of Christmas Eve. Tom thought her a 'lovely little ship … very fast … [with] a lively movement', features that he evidently savoured more than the passengers, who were, without exception, very seasick. He was beginning a series of sailings on the UK–South America route, carrying maize, linseed, passengers and once, a complete electric train from Birkenhead to Brazil for the Central Brazilian Railway, as well as sixteen Austin motor cars. Life at sea had its comforting routine: 'up at six-forty-five, pint and a half of tea, crap, shave and breakfast. Take a sight, and come down and write to you.' In the ship's quiet moments he read – Nigel Balchin's *The Borgia Testament*, for example, or *The Life of Captain Cook* – hunkered down, half aware of the dull, healthy throb of *Pilcomayo's* engines, occasionally glancing up to see spray flung on to the bridge windows, and beyond, the distant blue sky and trailing wisps of cloud, while he clutched a mug of tea and a good book, and thought of home, as the hours passed.

With censorship over, and perhaps with the advent of grumpy middle age, Tommy's letters became more cantankerous. For example, he was scathing about the clothes of a fellow captain, 'Piggy' Hooper: that oatmeal tweed suit; the red, white and blue bow tie and his 'ruddy old hat. You can understand eccentricity in poets and musicians and authors etc., but it doesn't go well with a ship's master.' He was equally sniffy about the Czechs, a nation that he believed shared – along with Neville Chamberlain – responsibility for the war. 'They … generally … are never sure which side they are fighting on.' Like many men and women at the time, he was pessimistic about the way the world was turning: 'all this Russian business, it certainly looks like another war before very long.' He was sure that this would mean 'the end of civilisation'.

The post-war years were to prove stormy for many, a bleak time of austerity, hardship, uncertainty and all with the ever-increasing prospect of a third and cataclysmic world war. The conflict that had recently burned itself out had left many people vulnerable, undernourished and emotionally drained. As the years passed, Tommy Davies, for example, became increasingly preoccupied with both his health and the precarious nature of the peace. On one occasion, he wrote gloomily to Dorrie, 'It really wouldn't much matter whether I died at sea, or from the effects of an atom bomb ashore,' before pointing out, in an endearing change of tone, that he was 'afraid I shall miss the Golf Club Dance this year darling.' He was worried about the Russians, writing to his daughter Angela, suggesting that she learn Spanish, 'unless of course she likes to learn Russian and thus be prepared for the invasion.' His stomach troubled him frequently, complaining in one letter about the 'damned leeks' that gave him wind: 'I farted the *Blue Bells of Scotland* and *Alice, where art thou* before I got to Retiro station (Buenos Aires) and felt much better.'

* * *

We've just received your letter of the 21st in which you speak of (at last!) getting in electricity.

Major Donald Macdonald to his parents, Port Said, 26 December 1947

By March 1948, Donald Macdonald was pressing GHQ to approve his leaving the Middle East for good and heading home to Scotland. Egypt's appeal had long since faded: in a letter written on Boxing Day 1947 he had described the two corpses he had seen the previous day – 'both had died violently.' The 3rd Officer of the *Empire Rival* 'had been stabbed to death by a Somali steward after lunch yesterday,' while a young Cypriot soldier had blown his head off in the evening. A bomb had exploded under a Jewish vessel in the harbour, but with no fatalities. In the midst of this un-festive mayhem, he had eaten a large Christmas lunch with the 2nd Officer of the *Empire Rest* – a thick buttery soup; boiled ham with fresh peas and flaky pastry patties; 'a mountain of turkey with all the fixings'; plum pudding and sweet white sauce (no Bird's custard); nuts, white wine and fruit. It was the third anniversary of his arrival in Port Said. His Christmas card from May that year was for her 'dear, dear husband' and the pen and ink drawing inside was of a cosy front door, an English garden with a white picket fence, and a tiled roof – as far from Port Said as could be imagined. In pale-blue fountain pen ink, she had written, 'Our Dream Cottage', and as she slipped the card into its envelope, she imagined the three of them – for she was pregnant with her firstborn – at home, enacting a life far from Egypt. She smiled at the way her Donald, in his usual irrepressible fashion, had broken the news to his parents: 'Did I hear someone doing some mental arithmetic?'

* * *

> My Darling
> This voyage I feel rather lost at sea and cannot settle down as I usually do.
> It has been foggy and misty since Saturday midnight, and it was only at noon today (Tuesday) that I was able to get the first observation since leaving England, otherwise dear, within 25 miles I didn't know where the hell we were!
> We should now be in Las Palmas at 05.00 on Thursday.

Captain Thomas Davies to Dorrie, at sea,
on board *Pilcomayo*, 24 May 1949

On Thursday, 13 January 1949, Tom Davies was fifty-one (my mother Greta was thirty-six on the same day). His birthday over, he wrote to Dorrie: 'Today is the first day of another year nearer the grave.' It must have struck a chill in Dorrie's heart. He went on to report that he didn't 'feel my fifty-one years too badly,' although, he added, 'the bloom of youth isn't blinding me, so to speak.' He hoped he would be spared 'many more years' to spend with her, reflecting on how he would not wish to survive without her by his side. He had sailed from Swansea for South America in *Pilcomayo* earlier in the month, with a cargo that included seven racehorses, weighing anchor in pouring rain at 10.00 pm on the 6th – gingerly easing past the port's reefs and sandbanks – and going without sleep until well past the Scilly Islands at nine the following morning. It was February before they reached South America.

Once in Buenos Aires he fell ill, writing on 28 February that he was 'scared when my chest goes wrong.' Typically, he left it until page seven of the letter before he told her. He had taken to his bed with a hot water bottle, only getting up when he got bored. 'The pain isn't so bad today dear,' he told

Pilcomayo, Tom's Final Command. *(Angela Awbery White)*

her, 'but, as it stabs me when I breathe deeply, it reminds me very much of pleurisy pains.'

A savage gale en route to Montevideo 'almost blew the ship adrift', and by the time *Pilcomayo* reached Rio, Tom was again clearly exercised about his health; Dorrie's too, pleading with her not to play tennis, citing 'pals dying with wonky hearts.' Soon after he began fretting about the absence of letters from her – 'only two letters from you this voyage' – and reminiscing about the happy time they had spent, the three of them, at Robin Hood's Bay on Yorkshire's east coast. He was momentarily cheered by the prospect of docking in Liverpool in mid-August, but the hope proved false. Instead he was in Dakar in September, then Buenos Aires in October; before tentatively suggesting that he might be back for Christmas. Writing on 21 November, he was downcast, depressed at the way of the world; the dullness of the voyage; the slow cargo loadings that seemed to conspire against ever getting home again; the dreary prospect of rain in Belfast ('even in the summer it's always raining there!'); and a photograph that 'makes me look quite old'. Laurence Olivier's *Henry V* ('which I saw in Vancouver') sent him to sleep; he complained at the changeable weather; bouts of catarrh; and a swollen ankle, which he attributed to gout. Stubbornly determined to avoid going

CAPT. T. DAVIES

All Royal Mail Line ships in port on Monday flew their flags at half mast as a mark of respect for Capt. Thomas Davies, Master of the R.M.M.V. Pilcomayo, who was interred at Forest Town Cemetery on that day. A service at St. Alban's Church, Forest Town, conducted by the Vicar (Rev. R. J. Spencer), preceded the interment. Capt. Davies passed away suddenly at his home, 285, Eakring Road, Mansfield, on Friday. He was fifty-two. He leaves a widow and one daughter. Born at Folkstone (Kent), he was educated at Marylebone Grammar

School, and was for the greater part of his life at sea. During the first World War he served as a lieutenant in the R.N.V.R. with the famous Dover Patrol. In the 1939-45 World War he was on active service, and was awarded the Atlantic Ribbon and Star and the Africa Star. Mourners were :—Mrs. D. I. Davies (widow) ; Commander and Mrs. J. B. Mein (brother-in-law and sister-in-law) ; Peter Mein (nephew, also representing Dr. and Mrs. K. G. Gallagher, niece and husband) ; Mr. and Mrs. A. Mein ; Mrs. D. Vincent (also representing Mr. Vincent) ; Mr. and Mrs. J. Taylor ; Mr. and Mrs. J. C. Wardle ; Mr. D. Wardle ; Mr. and Mrs. H. Potter (Burton Joyce) ; Lieut. (E) A. W. Fairhead, R.N., M.B.E. (representing Mrs. Fairhead and Lieut. (E) G. Fairhead, R.N.) ; Captain S. J. Hill (representative of the Sea Staff of the Royal Mail Line) ; Mr. C. V. Fry (representative of the directors, management and staff of the Royal Mail Line) ; Mr. and Mrs. Morrison ; Mrs. P. A. Foster (representing Mr. P. A. Foster) ; Mr. G. Lane ; Mrs. J. Foster ; Mrs. E. Jackson (representing Mr. Jackson); Mrs. S. E. Clegg (Sutton-in-Ashfield) ; Mrs. Beacroft, Mr. Featherstone, Mrs. Mills and Mrs. F. Pearson. A Royal Mail flag, especially sent from headquarters, draped the coffin.

Captain Thomas Davies, passed away 1950. (*Angela Awbery White*)

to 'the quack [since] he's too darned fond of whipping you off to hospital,' he suffered alone, if not in silence. He must have feared the prospect of dying at sea, far from Dorrie and Angela, but the end came when he was at home, on leave.

Tommy died early in 1950, at the age of just fifty-two, of bronchial pneumonia. The *Mansfield and North Notts Advertiser* noted that his death happened 'suddenly at his home. All Royal Mail Line ships in port on Monday flew their flags at half-mast as a mark of respect.' More than sixty years later, his daughter Angela observed that, 'The stress of two wars was more than his poor body could take.'

There was a final, cruel twist, which Angela recalls: 'Mother went to a tribunal a bit after the war to try to claim a war pension; however, she was never granted one. This was possibly,' Angela surmised, 'because Father did not die at sea, but at home on leave – or, perish the thought, because he was Merchant, not Royal Navy.'

* * *

The Under-Secretary of State for Defence (Armed Forces) presents his compliments and by Command of the Defence Council has the honour to transmit the enclosed Awards granted for service during the war of 1939–45.

I claimed the medals that Jack never did soon after he died, sixty years after the war was over.

The ribbons were fresh and the medals themselves new-minted. I wondered if Jack was not alone in spurning the nation's grateful thanks for his three wasted years. I suspected he would not have approved me sending off for them, but it seemed right to me, and after all, it was almost the last clue left before he faded even further into obscurity. I have kept them in their original box, labelled so that whoever follows me knows what they are before they are put in a cupboard, or a skip.

From 1946, the trail goes cold, the evidence for Jack's post-war life limited to hearsay and fading memory. He managed the tailor's shop in Old Market Street, Bristol for many years, grimly dismissive of the changes that consigned his kind of tailoring to the margins. He probably blamed the Beatles and would complain about the length of my hair until I was married with children. He did not approve of jeans (flared or otherwise), collars without ties, sloppy sweaters or the cult of the 'smart-casual'. By the end, the shop – Russell Brothers – was overrun with mice and customers were a novelty. He worked six days a week; gardened on the seventh; had no hobbies or time for such frivolous behaviour; voted Tory; took Greta to Conservative dinner dances, both of them in their finery, he togged up like the toff he would have liked to have been.

At much the same time as Tom Davies died, my mother, Greta, was diagnosed with tuberculosis, and in a moment, was spirited away to a sanatorium, presumably with the expectation that she would die. She was not yet forty and had caught the disease from me. My contraction of the illness was limited to glands in my neck and a week in hospital as a four-year-old. She was confined for two years, while I was despatched for the duration to her sister's, back almost to where I had been born. My brother remembers visiting our mother in Cairns Cross Sanatorium in Stroud with Jack, catching the bus at the end of the road every Sunday for the one-hour journey through south Gloucestershire.

Greta survived and I came back to the family home in Bristol. I did not see Jack's exhaustion then, but he must have been desperately tired after two years of looking after his elder son, continuing to work long hours, and visiting our mother, those weekly reminders of her fragile health, wrapped in blankets on the sanatorium lawns, other patients slumped in wheelchairs, skin pale and bloodless in the sunlight. Greta convalesced at home, taking to her bed in the afternoons, and listening to me read to her when I got home from school.

In the years that followed, you would not have known that she had been so close to death. The family preoccupation was with the decline of Jack's work. They bought the house we had rented for many years and then, perversely, they began a cycle of moving from house to house, briefly settling in Leicestershire, Somerset, Gloucestershire again, and Devon. It was there where Greta died of cancer aged sixty-nine. Jack married again (at the age of seventy-three); moved house several times; became a widower again and with equal distress, and then lived alone almost to the very end. He never once offered more than a glimpse of his own past: it was as if he could not bear to think about his childhood, his work, or his wartime service.

* * *

It is as if he never was. In Jack's garden shed, in clearing the confusion of tools, ancient paint tins and ghastly weed killers, I found almost the only physical memento of his time overseas: it was a spirit level, marked with an Air Ministry stamp and the date 1943. Why would he keep that of all things? Did it mean something? Had he kept it because it reminded him of something? Now I would never know. People often complain after a death that they wished they had asked more questions. I do of him. I had the questions – I was just not brave enough to ask them, and get him to talk.

I was struck by a phrase I read in the last throes of writing this book: 'Men who are nothing, who allow themselves to become nothing, have no place in it.' So many of us are 'nothing' – we don't matter when politicians or generals dictate orders and make plans. Life for us is something you just get on with – either with determined optimism, or untamed anxiety, like Jack. He spurned his medals; lost touch with his RAF mates almost as soon as hostilities ended; showed no pride in the war he had fought; and kept his secrets about where he had been and what he had seen and done, taking them to his grave.

If he had died during the war he would have been better served in terms of the paperwork recording his service and contribution than he was as a survivor. My father passed through the war years and the places he was sent almost unnoticed and certainly unrecorded, blown away in the wind. Even the letter someone had promised me, which he had planned to pass to the archives at the Imperial War Museum, proved to be illusory, lost in a burglary six decades after he wrote it – if indeed he did … In such a highly documented war, finding the details of men like Jack is looking for the proverbial needle. He would have smiled at that – after all, he never wanted to leave any trace. That was why, perhaps, the medals were uncollected and his memories left unspoken.

* * *

My six exiles were chosen – inevitably – by chance; well, five of them anyway, since I had always wanted to write about my father's silence from the day he died. Apart from Jack, I knew only one of them – Donald Macdonald – but the writing of this book drew me close to each one. That is one of the things that writing does, after all, the revealing of the half-hidden or the deeply buried, something that Donald, the author-manqué, would have recognised and which passed Jack by. There were things about each to which I warmed, perhaps most of all, the shared willingness to outface difficulty, true even of 'Binder' Knott! I would so have liked to sit beside Freya or Tommy as their respective trains steamed across America; to drink with Cecil and Noël in some officers' mess in India or Egypt; to step down from an aircraft into the blistering heat of Habbaniya and walk past my father sweating in a line of disgruntled policemen; to swim in the Mediterranean from the shore of Cyprus with Donald after a long day on the wards …

I began my writing unsure of the legitimacy of drawing these six seemingly random characters into a single story. But as I wrote, I became encouraged by the connections and parallels; the differences too. There were the shared journeys – convoys around the Cape; the streets of Cairo; the dust of Iraq; the imperial splendour of India; the skein of railways (Nottingham to Swansea Docks, perhaps, or Toulon to Calais, or through the Alps to Italy); the mutual love of the written word (with the exception of taciturn Jack); the longing for home (Asolo or Ashcombe); the growing weariness that they all felt as the war years drifted on; and the uncertainties surrounding life after 1945. The differences are intriguing too: their political persuasions, for example; the comparison between three long marriages (Jack's, Tom's and Donald's), with the complexities of the others' affairs of the heart; and the six children fathered by those married men, and their complete absence in the lives of Cecil, Noël and Freya. It is, though, the similarities that are most striking – how for each of them the war rolled like the tide over their plans and hopes; how home became more treasured and less secure, and exile inflicted pain and heartache; and how each of them – apart from poor Jack, of course – sought solace in the written word.

Chapter 25

A Post-War Postscript

Donald Macdonald, in one of his many letters to me, written in his early nineties, chided himself for failing to ask the right questions of his parents: in his case he wished he had asked his father, 'Daddy, why did you get married?' Evidently I was not alone in neglecting to get a parent to tell their story. It occurs to me in writing that sentence that thus far I have not been encouraged to tell my own … But first of all in this postscript, what happened to those who have shared the book with Jack?

* * *

Three of the six protagonists of this story lived long lives: Jack was ninety-two when he died; Freya Stark was 100; and Donald Macdonald was ninety-six, dying on 18 July 2015. The comparison with Tom Davies's brief life is painfully sharp. Cecil Beaton died in 1979, aged seventy-six; Noël Coward preceded him, dying in March 1973. Tommy's wife, Dorrie, never married again and died in 1985 aged eighty-seven.

After his experience in Cyprus and the Middle East, Donald worked as a GP in Scotland through the 1950s and 1960s, before becoming a lecturer in Health Education at Jordanhill College. He was a committed member of the Campaign for Nuclear Disarmament and the United Nations Association; a crooner with a good line in Sinatra impressions; and a theatre lover and newspaper critic (as 'Sebastian' for *The East Fife Mail* and *The Scotsman*) – he would write a review of the previous night's show before he took morning surgery. He often admonished himself about his failure to become the writer he yearned to be, but he was a committed and dedicated correspondent until the very end, his flowery black-inked handwriting on the envelope invariably lifting my spirits. His dear wife May pre-deceased him, dying on 19 March

1996. My last contact with Donald before he died was a telephone call, which finished with a song, a crooner till the end.

Freya Stark separated from Stewart Perowne in 1952, although she did not divorce him. Thereafter she divided her time between travelling and writing, based throughout in Asolo, where she died in April 1993. Her travels in the last decades of her life included exploration of Persia, India, Turkey and Afghanistan, the latter 'into a nearly inaccessible area' at the age of eighty. The resulting book from that journey prompted the gift from an admirer of a camper van, which 'with, Freya at the wheel, was dangerously "inclined to wander" through fences and into cow-filled meadows.'[1] Eventually, at the age of eighty-five, she gave up driving and 'contented herself with horseback riding instead.'

By the 1960s, Noël Coward, despite his concerns immediately after the war about the uncertain direction of his future career, had become the Grand Old Man of British Theatre and was knighted for his services to the stage in 1970. He starred in cabaret in Las Vegas in 1955, wrote a successful comic novel, continued to write both plays and film, as well as acting, including, for example, in *The Bridge on the River Kwai*. He was asked to play the lead in Ian Fleming's *Dr No*, but was reported to have turned it down in characteristic fashion: 'No, no, no, a thousand times no!' His last acting role he approached with the words, 'I'd like to act once more before I fold my wings.' Towards the end he began to struggle with a fading memory, a harsh fate for any actor.

Cecil Beaton was knighted two years after Coward, and in 1975 suffered a stroke, which paralysed him down his right side. He continued to work but became frustrated by his limited mobility. His portfolio of sitters photographed through the post-war period is extensive: Elizabeth Taylor, Grace Kelly and Maria Callas in the 1950s, for example; Andy Warhol and Albert Finney in the 1960s; and David Hockney and Jane Birkin in the 1970s. His theatre work was predominantly concerned with art and costume design, ending with the musical *Coco* in 1970, some ten years before his death.

* * *

While there were no extant letters from my exiled father to my mother during the war, there is nothing to stop me writing one for him, to be posted perhaps from Port Said just before he stepped on board the *Cameronia* …

I am longing to be home and hope that you feel as I do. There is so much to tell you and I am only sorry that the censor and my lousy letter writing has, to a degree, left you in the dark – for years, I realise. I know that others have been more wordy than me and have had 'better' wars. Perhaps that's why they managed to find a voice.

I have learned a lot in the time we have been apart: for example, this is not a part of the world to which I ever want to return (too hot, too dangerous) and I no longer wish to take orders from anyone (except you, perhaps!); I have had enough of other people stupider than me telling me what I must do. I need to be as near my own boss as it is possible to be. I can't say I'll miss many of the lads. And I have hated how we have been obliged to live out here, the unnatural surroundings wherever we have been, from the ship out, all the way to Cairo. How I envy those who have had an eventful war – I don't mean one where I might have been cut off in my prime (!), but how I've longed for something other than routine. That's partly why my letters home have been somewhat irregular – there's been so little to tell you, and to be honest, I have sometimes had to push all thoughts of home to one side because I could not bear to think of you both.

Oh, it will be so nice to be settled! And in our own house, don't you think, away from your beloved sister? Yes, and my sisters too.

I hope we can be happy together. I am all too aware that separation like ours has broken other marriages and I pray that you have kept faith. I am older, balder (!) but no less fond, dear.

We will be boarding soon – I cannot wait for the cool breeze off the sea and that moment when I can look back at Port Said disappearing in the distance, never to be seen again.

Give Peter a hug from me and love me when I get home.

Your Jack

Acknowledgements

This book began life as the story of my father's mysterious war: it was to have been called – with due apologies to T.E. Lawrence – *Jack of Arabia*. Its transformation into *Posted in Wartime* was prompted by a growing interest in, and empathy with, other men and women who spent long periods of time abroad during the war. The focus on letter writing emerged from my comparing the complete absence of any correspondence from my father with the examples of others who were infinitely more diligent as writers, particularly Thomas Davies and Donald Macdonald, whose letters are the bedrock of this book. I should like to thank Tom's daughter, Angela Awbery White, and Donald's daughter, Anne Marie Saine, for their interest and willingness to help throughout this project. During the writing of *Posted in Wartime*, Jeannette Croft loaned me the extensive archive of her father John's fascinating war, and I am grateful to her for that and her interest overall. I am also very grateful to my editor, Linne Matthews, who has been immensely supportive at every stage.

When I first began work on the book I received a number of letters from veterans of the Middle Eastern campaign, many of them describing their experiences at RAF Habbaniya and elsewhere. I am grateful to all of them, and in particular, I should like to thank Les Gillard, Jim Heslop, Jim McKnight and Don Mason. It would also be remiss of me not to note the contribution of my three 'celebrities' – Cecil, Noël and Freya – whose lives and letters provide the backdrop for this wartime story. I owe a debt to three of their biographers: Hugo Vickers, Philip Hoare and Jane Fletcher Geniesse, who, in each case, drew me into the lives of their remarkable subjects.

I should also like to thank my brother Peter for his interest in the book and his willingness to dig deep into his memories of wartime childhood. I am also grateful to Max Buckmaster, David Gowland, Stephen R. Davies, David Croft, Joseph FitzGerald, Caroline Moorehead, and my wife, Vanessa, whose eye for structure and coherence is unequalled and whose patience with a troubled writer is similarly remarkable.

The following organisations have been particularly helpful: The National Archives; the Imperial War Museum (and the copyright holders of the following papers held at the Museum: G.R. Bantock, W.R. Bleach, E.R. Leggett, S. Carson); Gloucestershire Archives; Bristol University Theatre Archive; St John's College Library, Cambridge University; Mrs Kathryn McKee, Special Collections Librarian at St John's College; the British Library; the RAF Habbaniya Association; the Cecil Beaton Studio Archive at Sotheby's; Getty Images; and the Royal Geographical Society. I also acknowledge the following: extracts from *The Letters of Noël Coward* © NC Aventales AG & Barry Day; extracts from *The Noël Coward Diaries* © NC Aventales AG by permission of Alan Brodie Representation Ltd. I am grateful to John Murray Press (now part of the Hodder Group) for permission to quote from Freya Stark's letters. I am indebted to both Lucy and Caroline Moorehead, who edited those letters so capably.

Finally, I should apologise for any errors of fact that I may have made and for any omission of gratitude: I am very conscious of the way my reading and conversations have helped this book emerge into the world.

Above all, my thanks are due to Donald Macdonald (whose correspondence I much miss); to Thomas Davies, whom I never met, but I feel I know so well; and to my parents, Jack and Greta, without whom this writer would not be here.

Notes

Chapter 1

1. P.G. Wodehouse, *A Life in Letters*, ed. Sophie Ratcliffe, p. 283.
2. Charles Hannam died in 2015, aged 89. See an obituary by Sonia Jackson in *The Guardian*, 26 September 2015.
3. *Freya Stark Letters*, ed. Lucy Moorehead, Vol. 3, pp. 271-2.
4. *Freya Stark: Passionate Nomad*, by Jane Fletcher Geniesse, p. xvi.
5. Ibid, p. 3.
6. *To War with Whitaker*, by The Countess of Ranfurly, p. 111.
7. Fletcher Geniesse, p. 29.
8. Ibid, p. xvii.
9. Ranfurly, p. 161.
10. *Selected Letters of Martha Gellhorn*, ed. Caroline Moorehead, p. 374. The letter is to Lucy Moorehead and dated 14 October 1971.
11. *The Harold Nicholson Diaries 1907–1964*, ed. Nigel Nicholson, p. 205.
12. The National Archives, CO 732/85/7.
13. Lucy Moorehead, op. cit., (Vol. 3), p. 253, letter to Venetia Buddicom, 9 May 1939.
14. The National Archives, CO 732/85/7.
15. Lucy Moorehead, op. cit., (Vol. 3), p. 272. The letter was to Herbert Young.
16. Tom's daughter Angela vividly remembers being taken down to Southampton Docks to see the ship being stripped of its luxury fittings.
17. *The Letters of Noël Coward*, ed. Barry Day, p. 376.
18. Imperial War Museum, file 95/25/1, papers of Captain G.R. Bantock, the orphaned son of Leedham Bantock, former manager of London's Lyceum Theatre.
19. *Harold Nicholson*, by Norman Rose, p. 157. This was Nicholson's view in 1927; by 1930, he thought Coward 'a nice eager man'. See Nicholson, p. 86.
20. *A Talent to Amuse*, by Sheridan Morley, p. 167.
21. Day, p. 369. Noël Coward in a letter (1938) to Alec Woollcott.
22. *Future Indefinite*, by Noël Coward, p. 35.
23. Morley, p. 244.
24. *Future Indefinite*, op. cit., p. 18.
25. *Cecil Beaton*, by Hugo Vickers, p. 235.
26. This is James Lees-Milne's description, written in 1942. Of the photographer's skills of observation, Lees-Milne wrote: 'He sees everything – the speck of potato on one's chin; the veins on one's nose, the unplucked hair sprouting from the ear.' See *Ancestral Voices*, by James Lees-Milne, p. 17.

27. St John's College Library, Papers of Sir Cecil Beaton. Undated letter to John Hill.

28. *Self-Portrait with Friends: The Selected Diaries of Cecil Beaton*, ed. Richard Buckle, p. 11.

29. *Did You Really Shoot the Television?*, by Max Hastings, pp. 84–5.

30. See *The Years Between, Diaries 1939–44*, by Cecil Beaton, p. 11, and *Ashcombe*, by Cecil Beaton, p. 78.

31. Letter to the author, dated 13 October 2011.

Chapter 2

1. Day, p. 377.

2. *Noël Coward – A Biography*, by Philip Hoare, p. 298.

3. The spy Guy Burgess was already in that department; Kim Philby was about to join it. See Hoare, p. 299.

4. *Australia Visited 1940*, by Noël Coward, p. 2.

5. Hoare, p. 303.

6. *Future Indefinite*, op. cit., pp. 86–7.

7. Lucy Moorehead, op. cit., (Vol. 3), p. 272.

8. Ibid, p. 277: letter to Sir Sydney Cockerell from the Metropolitan Hotel, Cairo, dated 2 November 1939.

9. Lucy Moorehead, op. cit., (Vol. 4), p. 6.

10. The National Archives, CO 725/74/15.

11. Lucy Moorehead, op. cit. (Vol. 4), p. 35.

12. *The Years Between*, op. cit., p. 14.

13. *Greasepaint and Cordite*, by Andy Merriman, p. 38.

14. *The Years Between, Diaries 1939–44*, op. cit., p. 17.

15. St John's College Library, Papers of Sir Cecil Beaton.

16. Lucy Moorehead, op. cit., (Vol. 4), p. 47.

17. Ibid, letter to Flora Stark, dated 1 April 1940, p. 43.

18. Ibid, pp. 63–4.

19. *An Italian Diary*, by Flora Stark, p. 3.

20. Lucy Moorehead, op. cit., (Vol. 4), p. 73.

21. *The Zodiac Arch*, by Freya Stark, p. 65.

22. *Brittany* was torpedoed by a German U-boat off Madeira in October 1942; fourteen members of the crew died out of a ship's complement of fifty-seven.

23. Day, p. 407.

24. *Future Indefinite*, op. cit., p. 88.

25. See *Ruling Passions*, by Tom Driberg, p. 98. Other names on the list, according to Driberg, were Douglas Fairbanks Jnr, Charlie Chaplin and Paul Robeson.

26. *Future Indefinite*, op. cit., p. 139.

27. Hoare, p. 309.

28. Day, p. 397.

29. *Australia Visited 1940*, op. cit., pp. 2–3.

30. *Future Indefinite*, op. cit., p. 122.

31. Hoare, p. 309.

32. *The Irregulars*, by Jennet Conant, p. 83.

33. Day, p. 403.
34. *Middle East Diary*, by Noël Coward, p. 26.
35. Day, p. 410.
36. The National Archives, INF 1/543; letter to Duff Cooper, dated 3 December 1940.
37. *Diana Cooper*, by Philip Ziegler, p. 211.
38. *Chips: The Diaries of Sir Henry Channon*, ed. Robert Rhodes James, p. 262; diary entry for 24 July 1940.
39. St John's College Library, Papers of Sir Cecil Beaton.

Chapter 3

1. Stephen Davies, RAF Police historian, pointed out to me in a letter that would-be policemen faced an interview and a relevant test. 'Of course, when they completed their training they left into the big wide RAF world as acting corporals with two stripes on their arm and a lot of authority.'
2. See *Nobody's Hero*, by Bernard Hart-Hallam, pp. 22–31, for his description of RAF Police training.

Chapter 4

1. Lucy Moorehead, op. cit., (Vol. 4), pp. 130–1.
2. A decision taken by the First Lord of the Admiralty, Winston Churchill, and the First Sea Lord, Admiral 'Jackie' Fisher.
3. The dangers were noted at the time: in 1904, the Member of Parliament heading the Oil Committee, E.G. Pretyman, commented that 'whereas we possessed in the British Isles the best supply of the best steam coal in the world, a very small fraction of the oilfields of the world lay within the British Dominions, and even these were within very remote and distant regions.'
4. *Power Play*, by Leonard Mosley, p. 29.
5. *Dust in the Lion's Paw*, by Freya Stark, p. 12.
6. *The Grand Alliance*, by Winston Churchill, p. 227.
7. Piers Brendon in his review of *No More Champagne*, by David Lough in the *Literary Review*, December 2015/January 2016.
8. *Over the Rim of the World, Selected Letters of Freya Stark*, ed. Caroline Moorehead, p. 47; letter to Viva Jeyes, November 1929.
9. Mosley, p. 96.
10. The National Archives, AIR 20/6026.
11. *Dust in the Lion's Paw*, op. cit., p. 91.
12. *Keith Douglas: the Letters*, ed. Desmond Graham, p. 179.
13. Hoare, p. 316.
14. *Future Indefinite*, op. cit., p. 165.
15. Two days later, Coward was in Sussex visiting Diana Cooper, and despite his own problems, bringing a gift from America: 'Noël Coward too came down, fresh from America and lecturing for the Red Cross in Australia. He brought us some lovely nylon stockings.' See *Darling Monster*, by Diana Cooper, p. 116.
16. *Winged Squadrons*, by Cecil Beaton, p. 6.

17. *The Years Between, Diaries 1939–44*, op. cit., p. 86.
18. Ibid, p. 107.
19. Ibid, op. cit., pp. 117–19; Day, p. 463.
20. Lucy Moorehead, op. cit., (Vol. 4), p. 129.
21. *East is West*, by Freya Stark, p. 152.
22. *Dust in the Lion's Paw*, op. cit., p. 96.
23. This was the view of T.E. Lawrence and quoted in *Memories of Eden*, by Violette Shamash, p. 259.
24. *The Golden Carpet*, by Somerset De Chair, p. 105.
25. The National Archives, FO 954/12B.
26. Shamash, p. 291. Fifteen months later, in October 1942, Cornwallis was fortunate to survive a would-be assassin's bomb.
27. *Dust in the Lion's Paw*, op. cit., p. 127.
28. Lucy Moorehead, op. cit., (Vol. 4), p. 143.
29. *Dust in the Lion's Paw*, op. cit., p. 129; 29 March 1942.

Chapter 5
1. Vickers, p. 255.
2. *Near East*, by Cecil Beaton, p. 7.
3. Ibid, p. 10.
4. Ibid, p. 12.
5. The first WS convoy had sailed on 29 June 1940, heading to Suez via South Africa. From 1940 to 1943, 458 ships made the long journey around the Cape of Good Hope. On average, they took just under fifty-one days to reach Suez.
6. The National Archives, AIR 19/309.
7. Gunner Croft sailed in SS *Oropesa*. His nickname 'Syd' came from his perceived likeness to the distance runner Sydney Wooderson.
8. Graham, p. 189.
9. *The Fringes of Power*, by John Colville, p. 399.
10. *The Letters of Evelyn Waugh*, ed. Mark Amory, p. 174.
11. The National Archives, AIR 19/309.
12. Ibid.
13. From the papers of 'Syd' Croft.
14. *The Winston Specials*, by Archie Munro, pp. 285–6.
15. Amory, p. 163.
16. *The Desert War*, by Alan Moorehead, p. 204.
17. *Dust in the Lion's Paw*, op. cit., p. 131.

Chapter 6
1. *The Years Between*, op. cit., p. 183.
2. *His Father's Son*, by Winston S. Churchill, p. 133.
3. St John's College Library, Papers of Sir Cecil Beaton; postcard from Beaton to Lady Juliet Duff, 17 May 1942.
4. *The Years Between*, op. cit., p. 135.

5. *Near East*, op. cit., pp. 30–1.
6. St John's College Library, papers of Sir Cecil Beaton.
7. Ibid.
8. St John's College Library, papers of Sir Cecil Beaton.
9. *The Years Between*, op. cit., p. 158.
10. *Near East*, op. cit., p. 75.
11. The National Archives, AIR 28/711.
12. Correspondence with Flight Lieutenant L.G. Gillard, who commanded RAF Sharjah in the 1950s.
13. Probably on the SS *Tinombo*, which arrived from Basra on 20 June 1942.
14. RAF medical officers spent much time on the issue of effective latrines in the desert: 'a perfect deep trench latrine is satisfactory. The unavoidable fact remains, however … that they have been found in practice to have been fly breeding, fly feeding or fly attracting … [and] should be strictly avoided.' The National Archives, AIR 49/43.
15. Details from the 244 Squadron newsletter, edition number 42. I am grateful to Jim Heslop and Jim McKnight.
16. The National Archives, AIR 28/711.
17. Five airmen died during the war as a result of swimming accidents. See *RAF Sharjah – the Early Days*, by L.G. Gillard, first published in *Air Britain*. See also, The National Archives, AIR 28/711.
18. *Beyond the Blue Horizon*, by Alexander Frater, p. 123.
19. Letter to the author from Don Mason.
20. *The Years Between*, op. cit., p. 187.
21. Ibid, p. 172.
22. Ibid, p. 180.
23. Vickers, p. 267.
24. Ibid, p. 205.

Chapter 7
1. Lucy Moorehead, op. cit., (Vol. 4), p. 220.
2. *A Cloud of Forgetting*, by Pamela Cooper, p. 147.
3. *Dust in the Lion's Paw*, op. cit., p. 137.
4. Lucy Moorehead, op. cit., p. 241; letter dated 1 September 1942.
5. Ibid, p. 253; letter from Baghdad dated 4 November 1942.
6. *The Years Between*, op. cit., p. 218.
7. *The Noël Coward Diaries*, ed. Graham Payn and Sheridan Morley, diary entry for 31 December 1942.
8. *Mountbatten*, by Philip Ziegler, p. 171; he is quoting a letter from Coward to Mountbatten dated 19 September 1941 (see Broadlands Archive, A48).
9. Ibid, p. 172.
10. Caroline Moorehead, op. cit., p. 145; the letter is to Ernest Hemingway from Cuba and dated 26 June 1943.
11. *Sing When the Guns are Firing*, by Richard Hughes; see *History Today*, Vol. 62, issue 3, March 2012.

12. *Five Came Back*, by Mark Harris, p. 296.

13. *Future Indefinite*, op. cit., p. 195.

14. The book *Near East* was published in the spring of 1943.

15. Vickers, op. cit., p. 269. For his part, Coward thought Cecil's photographs 'far and away the finest' he had seen of any stage production.

Chapter 8

1. Lucy Moorehead, op. cit., (Vol. 4), p. 3.

2. *Demobbed*, by Alan Allport, p. 59.

3. Lucy Moorehead, op. cit., (Vol. 4), p. 47.

4. From the papers of John 'Syd' Croft.

5. Ibid, letter dated 5 March 1941.

6. Amory, p. 161.

7. See *My Dear Bessie*, by Chris Barker and Bessie Moore, p. 14.

8. From the papers of John 'Syd' Croft.

9. Amory, p. 164.

10. *Graham Greene: A Life in Letters*, ed. Richard Greene, p. 111, letter to Marion Greene from Freetown, 2 April 1942.

11. From the papers of John 'Syd' Croft.

12. Amory, p. 176.

13. Cooper, p. 174. Captain (later Major) Hore-Ruthven was a soldier with the SAS. He died in Libya on Christmas Eve, 1942.

14. From the papers of John 'Syd' Croft.

15. Lucy Moorehead, op. cit., (Vol. 4), p. 170.

16. Barker and Moore, p. 73.

17. Ibid, p. 32.

18. From the papers of John 'Syd' Croft.

19. *Masters of the Post: the Authorized History of the Royal Mail*, by Duncan Campbell-Smith, p. 349.

20. From the papers of John 'Syd' Croft.

21. Lucy Moorehead, op. cit., (Vol. 4), pp. 80 and 67; letters to Sir Sydney Cockerell, 24 July and 7 June 1940.

22. *The Barbed-Wire University*, by Midge Gillies, p. 22.

23. Gloucestershire Archives, papers of Lascelles Abercrombie, D10828 1/1/7.

24. Cooper, p. 104.

25. From the papers of John 'Syd' Croft; letter dated 4 November 1940.

26. *Petting Cafés*, by E.S. Turner in *The London Review of Books*, Vol. 25, No. 23, 4 December 2003.

27. Graham, p. 203.

28. Lucy Moorehead, op. cit., (Vol. 4), p. 147.

29. Imperial War Museums, papers of W.R. Bleach, 11/13/1.

30. Letter of 6 September 1942.

31. Gillies, p. 22.

32. Amory, p. 154.

33. Imperial War Museums, papers of Mrs E.R. Leggett, 96/4/1.
34. Ibid, file K 95/225, *Instructions to the Postal Censorship Staff*.
35. Allport, p. 99.
36. From the papers of John 'Syd' Croft.

Chapter 9
 1. *Guide for US Forces Serving in Iraq 1943*, p. 20.
 2. *James Boswell, Unofficial War Artist*, by William Feaver, p. 75.
 3. Leading Aircraftman Carson in a letter to his parents: Imperial War Museums, 86/5/1.
 4. *Middle East 1940–1942: A Study in Airpower*, by Philip Guedalla, p. 139.
 5. One hundred of LAC Carson's letters home are held by the Imperial War Museums (Ref. 86/5/1). Habbaniya became one of Saddam Hussein's fighter-bomber stations.
 6. *Under the Red Eagle*, by Frank Pearce, p. 34.
 7. *Going Solo*, by Roald Dahl, pp. 276–7.
 8. *The Habbite*, May 1998. This is the routine described by Flight Lieutenant Jim Bodman, an instructor at No. 4 Flying Training School, in February 1941.
 9. Establishment at Habbaniya in the late 1940s totalled some 27 men: see *The Habbite*, No. 6, April 1999, p. 11.
10. See *RAF Police Cape Town to Kabul 1918–2006*, by Stephen R. Davies, p. 31.
11. *East is West*, op. cit., p. 136.
12. The National Archives, FO/954/12B. AIR 28/330 has details of wartime station life at RAF Habbaniya.
13. The enthusiasm is LAC Carson's, not Jack's; see Imperial War Museums 86/5/1. Carson thought the *Hollywood Film Stars* was 'the best stage show I've ever seen'.

Chapter 10
 1. Day, pp. 488–9.
 2. Bristol University Theatre Archive, file MM/REF/PE/WR/CNO/36/1-20.
 3. Munro, p. 366.
 4. £3.50 (£3 and 10 shillings), evidently.
 5. Day, pp. 489–90. Coward met Eisenhower on 5 August 1943.
 6. Merriman, p. 176. An alternative title for ENSA was 'Every Night Something Atrocious'.
 7. Ibid, p. 171.
 8. *Middle East Diary*, op. cit., pp. 19–20.
 9. *My World of Theatre*, by Peter Daubeny, p. 29.
10. *Middle East Diary*, op. cit., p. 64.
11. *The Habbite*, edition No. 6, August 1999. Lady Astor clearly had a talent for causing offence. Denis Healey, in his autobiography, recalls that she labelled troops fighting in Italy as 'D-Day Dodgers'. See *The Time of My Life*, pp. 62–3.

Chapter 11
 1. Lucy Moorehead, op. cit., (Vol. 4), p. 270.
 2. Lucy Moorehead, op. cit., (Vol. 4), p. 274.
 3. The National Archives, MT 9/3882.

4. See *Liberty: The Ships that Won the War*, by Peter Elphick, p. 131.
5. Lucy Moorehead, op. cit., (Vol. 5), p. 6.
6. The party was held in honour of the Wavells and organized by Chips Channon: Rhodes James, p. 377.
7. *Dust in the Lion's Paw*, op. cit., p. 167.
8. *The Zodiac Arch*, op. cit., p. 58.
9. Lucy Moorehead, op. cit., (Vol. 5), p. 24; letter to Gerald de Gaury, 24 November 1943.
10. Ibid, p. 31.
11. *The Years Between*, op. cit., p. 233.
12. Ibid, p. 239.
13. Vickers, p. 273.
14. *Far East*, by Cecil Beaton, p. 4.
15. Lucy Moorehead, op. cit., (Vol. 5), p. 48; letter to Elizabeth Monroe, 21 January 1944.
16. Ibid, p. 24; letter to Elizabeth Monroe, 24 November 1943.
17. Day, p. 495.
18. Lucy Moorehead, op. cit., (Vol. 5), p. 43.
19. Ibid, p. 61.
20. *Freya Stark in America: Orientalism, Anti-Semitism and Political Propaganda*, by Efraim Karsh and Rory Miller, *Journal of Contemporary History*, 2004, p. 316.
21. Ibid, p. 318.
22. Lucy Moorehead, op. cit., (Vol. 5), p. 43; letter to Sir Sydney Cockerell, 6 January 1944.
23. Ibid, p. 66; letter dated 3 March 1944.
24. Ibid, p. 45; letter to Christopher Scaife from Chicago, 14 January 1944.

Chapter 12
1. The National Archives, AIR 28/249.
2. Ibid.
3. Ibid, AIR 28/250.
4. *Guide for US Forces Serving in Iraq 1943*, op. cit., p. 35.
5. The National Archives, AIR 40/1740.
6. *The Deed*, by Gerold Frank, p. 18.
7. There were no aircraft on station on 6 January: AIR 28/249.
8. David Raziel, a Russian-born Jew who became commander-in-chief of Irgun in 1937.
9. The National Archives, AIR 28/249.
10. *The Levant Trilogy*, by Olivia Manning, p. 507 (Vol. 3: *The Sum of Things*).
11. I am grateful to my grandson, Joseph FitzGerald, for this anecdote, taken from his project, *World War 2 in the Eyes of Different People*. He was told the anecdote in a letter from Max Buckmaster, the evacuee who pushed my brother into that ditch all those years ago.

Chapter 13
1. An EFM was an Expeditionary Forces Message telegram.
2. Lucy Moorehead, op. cit., (Vol. 5), p. 92; letter to Elizabeth Monroe, 12 May 1944.
3. Ibid, p. 98; letter to John Grey Murray, 22 May 1944.
4. Ibid, p. 100.

5. Ibid, p. 104; letter to Mrs Otto Kahn, 4 July 1944.
6. *The Years Between*, op. cit., p. 242; entry for 25 December 1943.
7. Vickers, p. 276.
8. *The Years Between*, op. cit., p. 245.
9. Vickers, p. 277; letter to Clarissa Churchill, 26 January 1944.
10. *The Years Between*, op. cit., p. 252.
11. Ibid, p. 253.
12. Ibid, p. 256.
13. *Far East*, op. cit., p. 111.
14. Vickers, p. 279.
15. *Far East*, op. cit., p. 44.
16. Vickers, p. 286; letters written on 26 and 27 April 1944.
17. Ibid, p. 289.
18. The National Archives, INF 1/543.
19. *Future Indefinite*, op. cit., p. 242.
20. *Tony Benn – Years of Hope: Diaries, Papers and Letters 1940–1962*, ed. Ruth Winstone, p. 42.
21. Gloucestershire Archives, file D6885 2/2.
22. Imperial War Museum, file 03/22/1.
23. Merriman, p. 247.
24. *Future Indefinite*, op. cit., p. 263.
25. Vickers, p. 290.
26. '… in Dorothy Parker's famous phrase …', from *Lucky for Some*, Macdonald's description of his early RAMC days.
27. Correspondence with the author, 6 February 2008.
28. Diary entry for 10 December 1944.
29. Vickers, p. 281; Day, p. 502; Lucy Moorehead, op. cit., (Vol. 5), p. 111.

Chapter 14

1. Rhodes James, p. 396.
2. J.H. Dunn, quoted in *Mandate Days*, by A.J. Sherman, p. 170.
3. The National Archives, FO 371/46109.
4. The National Archives, FO 371/46110.
5. Speaking in the House of Commons on 17 November 1944.
6. The National Archives, FO 371/46110.
7. The National Archives, FO 371/40128: Gort's telegram was to the Secretary of State for the Colonies.
8. Lucy Moorehead, op. cit., (Vol. 5), p. 126.
9. *Future Indefinite*, op. cit., p. 273. 'Altogether, 9,251 V-1s were unleashed … the death toll was 5,375, while 15, 258 were seriously injured.' A further 2,500 were killed by the V-2s. See *London 1945*, by Maureen Waller.
10. Lucy Moorehead, op. cit., (Vol. 5), p. 127.
11. *Future Indefinite*, op. cit., p. 272.
12. *The Happy Years: Diaries 1944–48*, by Cecil Beaton, p. 25.

13. Ibid, p. 36. Things had not improved a year later. 'It seems as if the nightmare is over,' he wrote to Billy Henderson. 'But Paris isn't gay – it is very drab and sad too.' Most houses were without heating, and while there were orchids for sale in the shops, the people were invariably hungry. See St John's College Library, Papers of Sir Cecil Beaton.
14. Letter to Donald Macdonald from Dr Patrick Woodcock, 16 July 1981.
15. Diary entry for 20 December 1944.
16. When I opened this letter many decades later, the flowers were still a vivid red.
17. Lucy Moorehead, op. cit., (Vol. 5), p. 130.
18. Lucy Moorehead, op. cit., (Vol. 5), p. 165; letter of 27 March 1945.
19. Ibid, p. 189.
20. Ibid, p. 190.
21. Letter of 12 February 1945.
22. Letter of 26 April 1945.

Chapter 15
1. Payn and Morley, p. 31; entry for 17 May 1945.
2. Day, p. 373; the poet Stephen Spender was also on the list: see *London Review of Books*, 17 December 2015.
3. Ibid, p. 37; entry for 8 August 1945.
4. Day, p. 509; letter dated 15 August 1945.
5. Morley, pp. 307–308.
6. *My Bolivian Aunt*, by Cecil Beaton, p. 89.
7. *Ashcombe*, op. cit., p. 110.
8. Rhodes James, pp. 407–408.
9. *Ashcombe*, op. cit., p. 123.
10. *The Happy Years*, op. cit., p. 114. Manny Shinwell was the Labour Minister of Fuel and Power.
11. Ibid, p. 131.
12. Lucy Moorehead, op. cit., (Vol. 5), p. 214.
13. Ibid, p. 237; letter to Lord Amherst, 6 November 1945.
14. Ibid, p. 218; letter to John Grey Murray, dated 18 August 1945.
15. Ibid, p. 231; letter to Hilda Besse, 21 October 1945.
16. Ibid, p. 236; letter to Nigel Clive, 5 November 1945.
17. Ibid, p. 249; letter to John Grey Murray, 23 December 1945.
18. The National Archives, AIR 8/790.
19. The National Archives, AIR 2/5292.
20. The National Archives, AIR 23/1163.
21. The National Archives, BT 26/1209.
22. Letter to Donald's parents, 30 August 1945.
23. *Never Again, Britain 1945–51*, by Peter Hennessy, p. 94.

Chapter 16
1. Donald Macdonald was in Haifa at much the same time.
2. Vickers, see pp. 208–13.

3. Lucy Moorehead, op. cit., (Vol. 4), p. 151; letter to Flora Stark, dated 9 September 1941.
4. Anwar Sadat, later President of Egypt, was arrested for this atrocity, but subsequently acquitted.
5. *My Dear Bessie*, op. cit., p. 325.
6. *Wartime Britain 1939–1945*, by Juliet Gardiner, p. 576.
7. Payn and Morley, p. 50; diary entry for 26 January 1946.
8. Ibid, p. 53.
9. Hoare, p. 367.
10. Day, p. 519.
11. *The Happy Years*, op. cit., p. 55.
12. *Loving Garbo*, by Hugo Vickers, p. 67.
13. Lucy Moorehead, op. cit., (Vol. 5), p. 255.
14. On one occasion, Freya noted that a letter had taken a month to arrive.
15. Lucy Moorehead, op. cit., (Vol. 5), p. 262; letter dated 5 March 1946.
16. Buckle, p. 176.
17. Hoare, p. 270.
18. *The Happy Years*, op. cit., p. 79.
19. St John's College Library, Papers of Sir Cecil Beaton.

Chapter 18
1. Winstone, p. 25.
2. The National Archives, BT 389/11/148.
3. The letter is postmarked Haiti, and Tom has written 'CLIPPER' on the envelope – presumably he had again entrusted a letter to a flying boat service.
4. Tom's daughter Angela remembers Tom talking about the experience: 'I used to sit behind the settee so as to get a clear idea of what was going on from adult conversation.'
5. Barker and Moore, p. 333.

Chapter 19
1. Sherman, p. 130.
2. Ibid, p. 145.
3. Ibid, p. 148.

Chapter 20
1. *The Children's Book*, by A.S. Byatt, p. 149.
2. Waller, p. 410.
3. Ibid.
4. *Middle East Diary*, op. cit., pp. 61–2.

Chapter 21
1. Fletcher Geniesse, p. 325.
2. Payn and Morley, p. 73.
3. Letter to the author, dated 18 July 2008.

Chapter 22
   1. St John's College Library, Papers of Sir Cecil Beaton.
   2. Ibid. Letter dated 24 March 1947.
   3. St John's College Library, Papers of Sir Cecil Beaton. Letter of 9 March 1947.
   4. Ibid, letter dated 24 March 1947.
   5. Lucy Moorehead, op. cit., (Vol. 6), p. 4.
   6. Ibid, p. 2.
   7. Ibid, p. 1. In the event, the Murray's board turned the deal down.
   8. Payn and Morley, p. 79.
   9. Ibid, p. 78.
  10. Hennessy, p. 283.
  11. Payn and Morley, p. 81.
  12. Typically, with tongue in cheek, he wrote to me long afterwards declaring that I was 'in the presence of greatness'!
  13. This was written on 12 May 1947.

Chapter 23
   1. Lucy Moorehead, op. cit., (Vol. 6), pp. 22–3.
   2. Ibid, p. 27.
   3. Ibid, p. 31.
   4. Fletcher Geniesse, p. 327.
   5. St John's College Library, Papers of Sir Cecil Beaton.
   6. *The Happy Years*, op. cit., p. 147.
   7. Ibid, p. 151.
   8. Ibid, p. 159.
   9. Payn and Morley, p. 89.
  10. Ibid, p. 92.
  11. Hoare, p. 377.

Chapter 24
   1. St John's College Library. Papers of Sir Cecil Beaton.
   2. Payn and Morley, p. 107.
   3. Lucy Moorehead, op. cit., (Vol. 6), p. 50.
   4. Payn and Morley, p. 99
   5. Lucy Moorehead, op. cit., (Vol. 6), p. 47.
   6. Ibid, p. 50.
   7. Ibid, p. 56.
   8. £9,000 in today's money.
   9. Lucy Moorehead, op. cit., (Vol. 6), p. 103.
  10. Ibid, p. 104.

Chapter 25
   1. Fletcher Geniesse, p. 360.

Appendix: The 'Postings'

Date	Jack Knott	Freya Stark
1940: 22 May	Reports to RAF Reception Centre, Cardington, Bedfordshire.	In Aden, working in propaganda to minimise Italian influence amongst the Arabs. A month later, on 24 June, her mother is arrested in Italy.
30 August	Returns to RAF Cardington.	Still in Aden but soon to be posted to Cairo.
4 October	To RAF Topcliffe, North Yorkshire.	In Cairo.
1941: 7 February	To RAF Cheadle.	At the Hotel Cecil, Alexandria on a five-day 'evangelist tour'.
1 April	RAF Leighton Buzzard, Bedfordshire.	In Baghdad, with a rebellion brewing.
1942: 14 April	Sails for the Middle East (Iraq). Arrives in Durban on 17 May.	In Baghdad, soon to leave on a tour of northern Iraq.
22 June	Arrives at RAF Sharjah, 244 Squadron, by boat from Basra.	In Baghdad and 122° in the shade; just returned from Habbaniya.
1943: 22 June	Arrives RAF Habbaniya.	In Baghdad.
1944: 6 January	Arrives RAF Ein Shemer, Palestine.	On a speaking tour in the USA; on a train to Chicago.
1945: 10 April	On board the *Cameronia*, bound for Liverpool.	In Delhi, India, after surviving a storm on a flight from Mysore.
19 April	54 Maintenance Unit, Newmarket.	In Rajputana, India.
1946: 4 February	Released from the RAF.	Back home in Asolo, having completed a six-week tour.
7 February	Second son, Richard, born.	In Asolo.

Date	Cecil Beaton	Tommy Davies
1940: 22 May	Lucky to avoid a trip to the Maginot Line since the invasion of France had begun. Approached to visit America.	Chief Officer, *Brittany*. Sails for France in the aftermath of Dunkirk.
30 August	Having just returned from the US, photographing bomb damage in London.	Chief Officer, *Brittany*.
4 October	Working on photographs for a book entitled *London Under Fire*, with James Pope Hennessy.	Chief Officer, *Brittany*.
1941: 7 February	Visiting RAF stations in Wales.	*Nela* sailed from Freetown for the UK on 30 January.
1 April	Continuing with visits to RAF stations in the UK, including Tangmere.	Set sail for Buenos Aires, heading down the Mersey.
1942: 14 April	In the Middle East, about to set out from Cairo for the desert.	Part of WS17 south of Freetown, arriving in Cape Town on 23 April; carrying troops for Bombay.
22 June	Photographing army demonstrations near Beirut. Passes through RAF Habbaniya.	On board *Almanzora* en route from Cape Town to Freetown.
1943: 22 June	In England working on a variety of assignments.	Avonmouth Docks, Bristol. The following month he sails for the US on board *Aquitania*.
1944: 6 January	In India, soon to leave Delhi for Calcutta.	Sailing to Aden from Bombay as skipper of *Samthar*.
1945: 10 April	Photographing stage productions.	Returning from Canada on board *Samzona*.
19 April	Photographing stage productions.	Sailing for Canada.
1946: 4 February	In February 1946, sails on a troopship via Canada to New York	On leave in the UK.
7 February	In the USA.	On leave in the UK

Date	Noël Coward	Donald Macdonald and the war in general
1940: 22 May	In the US. He returns early in June by flying boat to Lisbon.	Donald at Glasgow University. Battle of Boulogne under way in northern France.
30 August	Touring the US, having returned there in late July.	The Battle of Britain at its peak.
4 October	Will leave the US for Australia (on 16 October, arriving a month later).	The Battle of Britain continues.
1941: 7 February	Flew from New Zealand on 3 February and was delayed on Canton Island for over a fortnight by a cyclone.	130,000 Italian troops surrender south of Benghazi, Libya.
1 April	Back in the UK; two weeks later his house is damaged in an air raid.	The Blitz continues and British troops retreat in the desert.
1942: 14 April	Working on the film *In Which We Serve*. The week before, the King and the Royal Family had visited the set.	Concerns about the potential loss of Malta.
22 June	Working on the film *In Which We Serve*.	Tobruk fell yesterday.
1943: 22 June	Soon to be travelling on HMS *Charybdis* for Gibraltar and the Middle East.	The build-up to the invasion of Sicily continues.
1944: 6 January	In Jamaica.	The Red Army advances through Poland.
1945: 10 April	The film of *Blithe Spirit* opens this month.	The concentration camp at Buchenwald is liberated.
19 April	Various film and theatre engagements.	The Allied advance continues.
1946: 4 February	'Working like a dog.'	
7 February	'Working like a dog.'	

Bibliography

Allport, Alan, *Demobbed*, Yale University, 2009.

Amory, Mark, *The Letters of Evelyn Waugh*, Weidenfeld & Nicholson, 1980.

Barker, Chris & Moore, *Bessie, My Dear Bessie*, Canongate, 2015.

Beaton, Cecil, *Ashcombe*, Batsford, 1949.

—— *Far East*, Batsford, 1945.

—— *My Bolivian Aunt*, Weidenfeld & Nicholson, 1971.

—— *Near East*, Batsford, 1943

—— *The Happy Years, Diaries 1944–1948*, Weidenfeld & Nicholson, 1972.

—— *The Strenuous Years, Diaries 1948–1955*, Weidenfeld & Nicholson, 1973.

—— *The Years Between, Diaries 1939–1944*, Weidenfeld & Nicholson, 1965.

—— *Winged Squadrons*, Hutchinson, 1942.

Buckle, Richard, *Self-Portrait with Friends*, Weidenfeld & Nicholson, 1979.

Byatt, A.S., *The Children's Book*, Vintage, 2010.

Campbell-Smith, Duncan, *Masters of the Post: the Authorized History of the Royal Mail*, Allen Lane, 2011.

Churchill, Winston S., *His Father's Son*, Weidenfeld & Nicholson, 1996.

—— *The Grand Alliance*, Cassell, 1950.

—— *Their Finest Hour*, Cassell, 1949.

Colville, John, *The Fringes of Power*, Weidenfeld & Nicholson, 2004.

Conant, Jennet, *The Irregulars*, Simon & Schuster, 2008.

Cooper, Diana, *Darling Monster*, Vintage, 2014.

Cooper, Pamela, *A Cloud of Forgetting*, Quartet, 1993.

Coward, Noël, *Australia Visited, 1940*, Heinemann, 1941.

—— *Future Indefinite*, Methuen, 2004.

—— *Middle East Diary*, Heinemann, 1944.

Dahl, Roald, *Going Solo*, Jonathan Cape, 1986.

Daubeny, Peter, *My World of Theatre*, Jonathan Cape, 1971.

Davies, Stephen R., *RAF Police, Cape Town to Kabul, 1918–2006*, Woodfield, 2007.

Day, Barry, *The Letters of Noël Coward*, Methuen, 2007.

De Chair, Somerset, *The Golden Carpet*, Faber & Faber, 1944.

Driberg, Tom, *Ruling Passions*, Quartet, 1978.

Elphick, Peter, *Liberty: The Ships that Won the War*, Chatham, 2006.

Feaver, William, *James Boswell, Unofficial War Artist*, Muswell Press, 2006.

Frank, Gerold, *The Deed*, Simon & Schuster, 1963.

Frater, Alexander, *Beyond the Blue Horizon*, Heinemann, 1986.

Gardiner, Juliet, *Wartime Britain 1939–1945*, Headline, 2004.

Geniesse, Fletcher Jane, *Freya Stark: Passionate Nomad*, Pimlico, 2000.

Gillies, Midge, *The Barbed-Wire University*, Aurum, 2011.

Graham, Desmond (ed.), *Keith Douglas, The Letters*, Carcanet, 2000.

Greene, Richard (ed.), *Graham Greene, A Life in Letters*, Little, Brown, 2007.

Guedalla, Philip, *Middle East 1940–42*, Hodder & Stoughton, 1944.

Guide for US Forces Serving in Iraq 1943, Dark Horse, 2008.

Harris, Mark, *Five Came Back*, Canongate, 2014.

Hart-Hallam, Bernard, *Nobody's Hero*, Woodfield, 1999.

Healey, Denis, *The Time of My Life*, Michael Joseph, 1989.

Hennessey, Peter, *Never Again*, Jonathan Cape, 1992.

Hoare, Philip, *Noël Coward*, Sinclair-Stevenson, 1995.

James, Robert Rhodes (ed.), *Chips; The Diaries of Sir Henry Channon*, Weidenfeld & Nicholson, 1967.

Manning, Olivia, *The Sum of Things*, Weidenfeld & Nicholson, 1980.

Moorehead, Alan, *The Desert War*, Aurum, 2009.

Moorehead, Caroline, *Freya Stark*, Allison & Busby, 1985.

—— *Selected Letters of Martha Gellhorn*, Henry Holt, 2006.

—— *Over the Rim of the World: Selected Letters of Freya Stark*, John Murray, 1988.

Morley, Sheridan, *A Talent to Amuse*, Heinemann, 1969.

Mosley, Leonard, *Power Play*, Weidenfeld & Nicholson, 1973.

Munro, Archie, *The Winston Specials*, Maritime Books, 2006.

Nicholson, Nigel (ed.), *The Harold Nicholson Diaries 1907–64*, Weidenfeld & Nicholson, 1994.

Payn, Graham & Morley, Sheridan, *The Noël Coward Diaries*, Weidenfeld & Nicholson, 1982.

Pearce, Frank, *Under the Red Eagle*, Woodfield, 2004.

Ranfurly, Countess of, *To War with Whitaker*, Heinemann, 1994.

Ratcliffe, Sophie (ed.), *P.G. Wodehouse: A Life in Letters*, Arrow, 2013.

Rose, Norman, *Harold Nicholson*, Pimlico, 2006.

Shamash, Violette, *Memories of Eden*, Forum, 2008.

Sherman, A.J., *Mandate Days*, Thames & Hudson, 1997.

Stark, Flora, *An Italian Diary*, John Murray, 1945.

Stark, Freya, *Dust in the Lion's Paw*, John Murray, 1961.

—— *East is West*, John Murray, 1945.

—— *Letters (Volumes 1–6),* (ed. Lucy Moorehead), Michael Russell, 1974–81.

—— *The Zodiac Arch*, John Murray, 1968.

Vickers, Hugo, *Cecil Beaton*, Weidenfeld & Nicholson, 1985.

—— *Loving Garbo*, Jonathan Cape, 1994.

Waller, Maureen, *London 1945*, John Murray, 2004.

Winstone, Ruth (ed.), *Tony Benn – Years of Hope, Diaries, Papers and Letters, 1940–1962*, Arrow, 1995.

Ziegler, Philip, *Diana Cooper*, Hamish Hamilton, 1981.

—— *Mountbatten*, Guild Publishing, 1985.

Index